WHEN ONE DAY AT A TIME IS TOO LONG

Practical Answers to 42 of Life's Toughest Questions

Gerald

Riverbend
Press

Austin, Texas 78746

Riverbend Press
4214-B Capital of Texas Hwy., North
Austin, TX 78746

The passages from the Bible were taken from the *Good News Bible*
published by the American Bible Society.

First Riverbend Press paperback edition published 1998
Original hardback edition published by McCracken Press 1994

Library of Congress Cataloging-in-Publication Data

Mann, Gerald
        When one day at a time is too long / Gerald Mann
                p.   cm.
        Includes biographical references.
        ISBN 0-9647272-2-6
        1. Apologetics–20th century–Miscellanea. 2. Hope–
Religious aspect–Christianity–Miscellanea. I. Title.
BT1102.M295   1994   94-1589
        239-dc20   CIP

10 9 8 7 6 5 4 3 2 1

Printed in the United States of America

CONTENTS

INTRODUCTION   *3*

PART I: QUESTIONS OF GOD'S WORTH   *13*

1. CAN'T BUY NONSENSE
   The Origin of Evil   *15*

2. WHY DOES GOD LET BIG PEOPLE KILL KIDS?
   The Issue of Moral Evil   *23*

3. IS GENESIS A DINOSAUR?
   Science and the Bible   *30*

4. WHY DOES GOD LET DISEASES KILL KIDS?
   The Issue of Natural Evil   *36*

5. HEAVEN AND HELL AND WHO'S GOIN'
   The Afterlife for Unbelievers   *42*

6. THE DEVIL DIDN'T MAKE ME DO IT
   Picturing Satan in Modern Terms   *47*

7. HOW DO YOU PICTURE GOD?
   Reconciling the God of the Old Testament
   with the New   *56*

8. THE PUZZLEMENTS OF PRAYER
   When Prayers Don't Work   *66*

9. BIBLE 101
   The Trustworthiness of Scripture   *75*

10. ONE TIMES ONE IS ONE
    Understanding the Trinity   *85*

11. WHY DO THE WICKED PROSPER?
    The Issue of Divine Justice   *89*

12. WILL THERE BE ANY MOSLEMS IN HEAVEN?
    Comparative Religion   95

13. DOES THE CHURCH DISPROVE GOD?
    The Authenticity of Organized Religion   100

14. WHY DID JESUS HAVE TO DIE?
    Understanding the Atonement   107

PART II: QUESTIONS OF SELF-WORTH   113

15. THE TRAP
    Sexual Temptation in the Workplace   115

16. PANGS OF A PARIAH
    Guilt and Abortion   121

17. MY NAME IS LEGION
    Facing Sexual Peculiarities   127

18. FROM THE DARK
    The Handicapped and Faith Healing   133

19. DOESN'T NEED A SERMON
    Sexual Need and an Incapacitated Spouse   143

20. WILL GOD GIVE IT BACK?
    When a Loved One Commits Suicide   149

21. WIDOWHOOD AMERICAN STYLE
    Singles, Faith, and Sex   153

22. CONDONED OR CONDEMNED!
    An Honest Look at Homosexuality   160

23. CAN'T FIX IT
    Institutionalizing Someone You Love   166

CONTENTS

24. UNEQUALLY YOKED?
    Living with an Irreligious Spouse   172

25. DOES GOD HAVE A PRICE?
    Your Money and God   179

26. THE VICTIM
    When Your Loved One Is Murdered   184

27. THE ICEMAN COMETH
    Hope on Death Row   190

28. DAMNED IF YOU DO, DAMNED IF YOU DON'T
    Divorce and Remarriage   194

PART III: QUESTIONS OF LIFE'S WORTH   199

29. FREE OF THE SHAME
    Recovering from Child Abuse   201

30. THE 500-POUND PRISON
    Helpless Isn't Hopeless   206

31. THE RIGHTEST OF ALL WRONGS
    Making Ethical Decisions   211

32. APOCALYPSE NOW?
    Facing Discouragement About the World   216

33. MAKING LIFE COUNT
    Choosing How to Spend Your Life   223

34. OVER NATURE, UNDER GOD
    *A Sensible Approach to Humans and
    Their Environment*   230

35. TEENAGERS: PEOPLE GOD DIDN'T CREATE
    Guides in Parenting   237

CONTENTS

36. STAYING TOGETHER BUT COMING APART
    Recovering Intimacy   244

37. TOOLS FOR OLD FOOLS
    Divorce Recovery   251

38. GETTING RIGHT WITH GOD
    Understanding Religious Experience   258

39. WHEN YOU'RE CAUGHT RED-HANDED
    Recovering from Disgrace   265

40. KIDS WHO WEATHER THE STORM
    Equipping Children to Face Life   271

41. BURNING BUSHES FOR THE BURNED OUT AND BUSHED
    Recovering from Burnout   277

42. BACKUP SYSTEMS
    Handling Temptation   284

CONCLUSION
    THE SEEPING POWER OF GRACE   289

NOTES   294

ABOUT THE AUTHOR

WHEN ONE DAY AT A TIME IS TOO LONG

OTHER BOOKS BY GERALD MANN:

– *The Book of Wisecracks*
– *When the Bad Times Are Over for Good*
– *Common Sense Religion*

INTRODUCTION

On the way to the retreat where I'm writing this, Lois and I stopped for hamburgers. While we waited for our order I happened to notice that the calendar on the wall said June 12.

"Do you know where you were thirty-three years ago today?" I said.

"No. What day is it?"

"June the twelfth."

"Oh," she let out a sad sigh. "It's June the twelfth."

We were moving to the seminary after college graduation to continue preparing for the ministry. Everything we owned was piled into Dad's pickup and the U-Haul which trailed behind.

A carload of Army reservists—summer soldiers enroute home to their families—ran the stop sign at an open-country intersection. The world went black.

When I awoke I was sitting in the truck in the middle of the highway. Gasoline dripped steadily from the ceiling where it had been splashed when the fuel tank ruptured.

Lois was halfway out of the front window lying facedown on the hood. I pulled her inside. She was unconscious. Blood was everywhere.

I tried the doors. They were jammed. We were trapped. A man with a cigarette dangling from his lips came running up to the truck. I rammed the door, breaking my shoulder. The door popped open.

Miraculously we emerged with relatively minor injuries... to our bodies that is.

The summer soldiers were another story. One died an hour later while holding my hand and calling for his wife who was eight months pregnant. Two of the others were crippled for life.

I knew the accident was not my fault. But I couldn't shake the awesome reality that I had steered a machine that had altered life, love and history.

June 12 was not over. There was more to come that day. It would be the commencement of three decades of a tragedy which still goes on.

Our baby girl was eighteen months old and had never spoken an intelligible word...only screams and babbles. A neurologist, a close family friend, had tested her the week before. He was to relay his findings to us through my brother whom I would call when I arrived at the Seminary.

I called my brother from the hospital where they took us after the collision. When he heard my voice, he began to cry. He already knew about the accident. He couldn't bear adding to the tragedy the day had already brought.

After a while he was able to relay the doctor's diagnosis: severe mental retardation.

All this in one day! In less that 24 hours, while I was enroute to prepare myself to tell the world that God is great and God is good...Well, you get the picture.

You can also understand why the mere mention of June 12 would set us to remembering. We talked for hours. We replowed old fields of pain. We spoke of the rat-infested parsonages, of the rigid littleness of rule-bound church folk, of the preachers and elders who had intimated that our Cindy's problems were God's punishment.

We waded back through the muck of our struggle to raise and train a handicapped child whom we later discovered to be profoundly deaf, *not* mentally retarded. The sum total of our three decades of trying to give her the best appears, at least for now, to have resulted in little more than a destructive self-hatred on her part. We spared ourselves most of the details, so I'll spare you as well.

The real point of all of this is what happened next. Our conversation came around to where it always does: to THE question, *How did we ever make it from there to here?*

Here, Lois and I are still in love and "in like" with each other. The hounds of hurt and depression have ripped at the heart of our togetherness without success.

Here, I still believe in God after bouncing from naive trust to cold nihilism and back.

Here, I lead a one-of-a-kind church which began with 60 brave souls and now numbers into the thousands.

Here, thousands of people cram the phone lines on Sunday nights as I sit before live television cameras to hear their hurts.

"How did we make it from there to here?" Lois said it all for both of us. "If I had known ahead of time what I'd have to go through, I'd have trusted God's mercy and committed suicide. But since I didn't know I guess we made it by taking one day at a time."

"Bull!" I said. "One day at a time was too damned long!"

I just blurted it out. I'd never heard it or said it before. It was one of those phrases that "thought me up."

I have spent my life connecting with those for whom one day at a time is too long...people who are hurting so much that they need hope to make it from moment to moment.

This in no way discredits or demeans the one-day-at-a-time method of recovery practiced in the Twelve-Step programs originated by the founders of Alcoholics Anonymous. I read and practice the Twelve-Steps myself. They have liberated millions. There are hundreds of Twelve-Steppers in my church. I'll take all of them I can get. The title would never have grabbed me if I hadn't read the *One Day at a Time* book of Al-Anon. But for some, one day at a time *is* too much.

  Hope is the operative word of this book. I believe it is the scarcest commodity in the American psyche today. Our entire culture is enshrouded in a kind of melancholia. We are emotionally depressed.

The seventy-fifth anniversary issue of *Forbes* magazine agreed with this diagnosis. It was devoted to addressing the question: "Why do we feel so bad, when we have it so good?" It noted that Americans today live in the lap of unprecedented luxury. Compared to the rest of the world today and to Americans of 75 years ago, we have it better materially than any society in history. Our poor are rich by Third-World standards. Our middle class is "upper," and our upper class rivals King Midas!

Yet we are in the throes of a national funk. Why so? *Forbes* sought the opinions of eleven scholars and expert analysts. Political speechwriters, novelists, sports commentators, professors, historians, and poets waxed eloquent on the subject.

They were all long on description and short on prescription. They extensively described the problem but sparsely prescribed a remedy. And although there wasn't a theologian, ethicist, or clergyman in the bunch, they all sounded like moralizing preachers, except for a couple who were trying to be "artistic."

The general consensus was that something is missing at the spiritual core of the American psyche. No one ventured very far into this void or suggested how it might be filled.

My opinion is that the elusive element they were hinting at was hope. However, I must quickly define the word *hope* as I am using it. I'm not talking about hope for more manufactured stuff—toys and nerve-tingling stimulations.

I'm referring to what our Puritan forefathers called "eternal hope." Eternal hope was not synonymous with heaven, in their thinking; although it did include the promise that there was both more to come and an ultimate justice in the next life. For the most part, eternal hope meant that the Eternal was always *present* in the *present*. It meant, we're not alone. Our condition is never hopeless because we can be addressed by a Timeless Presence in the midst of our time and space.

Puritans have been caricatured as "other worldly" and as haters of "this world." That's untrue. The "pursuit of happiness" which is held up as the inalienable (God-given) right of every human, meant the pursuit of this world's property, bounty, and prosperity.

The much maligned "Puritan ethic" was centered in the notion that because the Eternal is present in our midst we can reap nature's bounty to the benefit of the whole. And our forefathers set about doing just that on a grand scale.

They also succeeded in giving people what I'm calling "Lifelines of Hope." We can debate whether these lifelines were seen as the promise of material prosperity or blissful union with God. They were *both*, in my opinion; but they were also practical approaches that energized life and gave people meaning.

Many Americans are in a state of depression because they've lost their lifelines of hope. They have no way of grabbing onto the eternal in the midst of the present.

This is not merely my opinion. I have been conducting my own research poll via television and the mail for five years.

I realize that Americans at large have stopped "buying" the God packaged by traditional religious institutions. Most still believe in God, they just can't connect with Him through their churches. Most still claim affiliation with a particular brand of religious expression, that is, they "belong" to some church or synagogue. But many don't attend; and of those who do, some attend by rote: They come, sit, and leave.

I also realize that religious television and radio reaches only a small segment of the audience. We have the technological means of reaching every square inch of the planet in a split second with a TV signal, yet many care not to listen.

Talk radio and television eventually *have* to talk about faith and values. From Donahue to Geraldo to the sleaziest radio talk-show host, they can't avoid "spiritual" subjects.

And so I launched my own little boat into the sea of talk-programs, unashamedly telling the audience, "This show's about connecting a real God with real people in real life."

Our first show was on a talk station in the worst time slot imaginable: Sunday afternoons from 5:00 to 7:00. Management said to expect five calls an hour...no one wants to talk on NFL Sundays.

We proved them wrong. The first Sunday, I "filled" for three minutes and every line in the studio stayed lit for two hours. It never stopped.

I've been doing this on television now for three years. Corporate America hasn't caught on yet. They won't sponsor "religious" anything. But people indeed do want to talk about spiritual matters, especially if the host is there to help and not to moralize and preach to them.

I am now in 20 million homes on a small religious network one night a week. For the past three years I have carefully logged every question. I have received thousands of questions by mail and on the air.

What people need are lifelines of hope—they need practical answers to life's toughest questions. Every day they are bombarded with "bad news": the ozone layer, deforestation, homelessness, AIDS, or congressional gridlock. The litany of woes never ends.

And conventional churches are of little help. What are people getting when they do venture into the sacred halls? Well, it depends.

If they go to a "traditional mainline Protestant church," they're apt to hear that they should be doing something about the ozone layer, deforestation, the homeless, and congressional gridlock. Or gaybashing, re-distribution of wealth, sexism, and civil rights.

All of the above are legitimate concerns to be sure. The problem is that they are not "practical." They do not energize people to make it through the night—let alone a full week! Would you believe that clerics from these groups are wondering why their churches are in decline? People do not join churches in order to be reminded every week that they are not Mother Teresa, or that they are wicked consumers, or that they should feel ashamed for having a roof over their heads while others don't, or that they are in one way or another a rotten lot.

I have a bit of news for you: *They already know their faults when they come!* In fact that's precisely why they are there! They're hoping for a morsel of forgiveness or a brush with eternity which lets them feel hope.

Some go to apocalyptic churches. No sermons about social reform here. The world's too far gone for that. It's us against them. Keep your bags packed. The chariot is about to sweep down and carry the righteous to the skybox seat where they can view the doing-in of this hopeless world.

Many of these churches are filled up and growing. And I'm not surprised. You see, there is a lifeline of hope being thrown out at these churches. It's a lifeline from "out of this world," but at least it *is* a lifeline. Polarization, a siege mentality, and isolation from the world are required to sustain its vigor, but its devotees are still "hope-full." The explosion of apocalyptic churches is a phenomenon that reinforces my opinion that what people want most are lifelines of hope.

And then there are the megachurches. In 1972, there were only twenty-four churches in America which averaged 2000 or more in attendance on Sunday morning. Today there are ten times that number and it is increasing annually.

Megachurches are not peculiar to one denomination or belief system. You'll find them in every faith group. But they all have one thing in common. They offer the lifelines of hope I've been talking about.

The church I serve is a megachurch, yet it is neither apocalyptic, fundamentalist, mainline, nor charismatic. Many think it is a pure anomaly, an exception. It is not. It is simply a congregation which offers practical answers to people for whom one day at a time is too long. It translates all of its rhetoric, ritual, rules, and regulations into a helping hand for the hopeless and mishandled. It finds practical ways to create an intersection between the hopeless and hope.

The pages which follow illustrate how this happens. The subjects I will address weren't chosen by me. They are from real people in the real world who hunger for a lifeline of hope thrown out by a real and living God. I have changed the names and circumstances to preserve anonymity. I have also edited and condensed the letters, but the questions are authentic.

In my experience almost all of the questions of these hurting people are "fronts" for three basic questions. In other words, there are three fundamental questions being asked of God. These three form the headings for the three major parts of this book. They are: The question of God's Worth, the question of Self-Worth, and the question of Life's Worth.

Questions about why the innocent suffer, or why prayers don't work, or why the Bible is difficult to understand are questions about *God's worth*. Is God worth our allegiance in the face of the mysteries and the apparent contradictions we experience in life?

The many questions which begin with the phrase, "I'm a believer, but..." are questions of *self-worth* before God. For example, when someone says, "I'm a believer but I don't go to church," they are about to ask if they are still *worthy* of God's acceptance. They're saying, "Is there any hope for a flawed person like me? Am I still of value to God?"

The third group of religious questions are about the question of *life's worth*. Questions about chronic physical or psychic or intellectual pain are asking whether life is worth the trouble and how to make sense out of it.

At first I refused to respond to academic questions like, "If God is predetermining everything, why pray?" Then I realized that such a question was not always an idle mental gymnastic. Faith always causes pain for our reason. Faith must make some rational sense in the midst of the mysteries or we are left without any rational lifelines of hope.

One thing more before we go to the real questions of real hope-seekers. I am very hopeful about our society and the world in general. The pollsters and seers are telling us that one of the megatrends of the dawning century is the respiritualization of society. Along with the change from the manufacturing age to the information age, the globalization of all of life, and the increase in the rate of change, there is an openness of mind toward spiritual sources for life's meaning.

This doesn't mean that Americans will be flocking back to church. This won't happen unless the church starts serving up something different.

We in the church must make a fundamental choice. We must choose to admit that we are no longer established fortresses in a friendly environment from which missions are launched into foreign territory. We *are* missions in the midst of foreign territory. If we do not choose to recognize this reality then we are historical shrines which future tourists will visit in order to admire the architecture.

I believe the former will be our choice. I believe it because Americans are still a religiously hungry people. The questions they ask on the following pages confirm this. But I believe it mostly because God does not leave people without lifelines of hope. There's always something Eternal to grab onto in the present.

PART I

QUESTIONS OF GOD'S WORTH

1

CAN'T BUY NONSENSE
The Origin of Evil

Dear Dr. Mann:

Where did Evil come from? I mean, in the first place? I know a lot of it dwells within me. I don't like it. Well, sometimes I actually do like it, or I wouldn't let it come out of me. But I don't "like to like it."

But who/what put these evil desires inside me in the first place?

I've heard the classic lines about "Satan the fallen angel" and "Adam the fallen man." They don't make sense to me. For example, if Adam and Eve were created in perfect fellowship with God, why would they want to rebel?

How could God create them with the potential flaw to rebel and then blame them for rebelling? If that's what happened, it seems to me that God is ultimately responsible for creating evil.

If you remove the origin of evil one step and place it on Satan the fallen angel, you still have the same problem. How can an Angel created by God and living in union with God, try to take over Heaven, unless God had created him with that evil potential?

Also, what about God's foreknowledge? If He could foresee that His creatures were going to become so evil, why did He go ahead with creation?

Dr. Mann, I suppose I'm really struggling with the fairness of God. How could He blame me for having a sinful condition

I didn't create and can't cure?

I want to believe but I cannot live with an irrational faith. Whenever I ask ministers and theologians these questions, they either yawn or launch into double-talk. They don't seem to recognize that I'm in pain intellectually.

I want to believe, but I can't buy nonsense.

Dear Karl:

I know what you mean by intellectual pain. A religion which can't withstand the application of human reason is painful. It must be embraced in a state of constant uncertainty. For an honest person to live with lies, or possible lies, hurts.

So your question about the origin of evil is more than a eggheaded dalliance. We all know that evil exists within ourselves and others. Just read the daily paper or watch the nightly news. And those who choose to deny the evil within themselves never fully become persons.

I share the same objections you hold to the traditional explanations of the Origin of Evil. In fact, you have stated them so well that I won't add to them here. I will come straight to the point. We must rethink and restate the biblical message concerning the origin of evil and its cure. The traditional interpretations of Genesis 1–3, simply won't wash given the advances in human knowledge—a knowledge which I believe is God-given and therefore not to be feared.

Karl, I hope to show in responding to your letter and to those which follow in this section, that I see no conflict between the biblical account of the world's origins and the findings of human reason and science. Our enemy is not the truth. It is the distortion and fear of the truth.

The classic explanations of creation and evil were sufficient for the past but they will no longer work.

The explanations I will share are not all that new for the most part. They have been well discussed by Church leaders and thinkers before me. However, most of the discussion has taken place in academia and far from the earshot of laypersons.

It is time to share these discussions on a popular level and in terms which common folk can understand.

Let me begin by "throwing a grenade over the wall." *God is ultimately responsible for the origin of evil.* I didn't say God is evil, or that He made evil. I said that evil's existence is God's responsibility. Karl, your instincts are correct on that score.

But before I explain how God is responsible, I want to define evil. What is evil? How we answer is crucial. There are two kinds: *Natural evil* (earthquakes, disease, natural disasters) and *human evil* or *moral evil.*

I want to focus on moral evil for now. The best way to define moral evil is to define its counterpart, moral goodness. Biblically speaking, what does it mean to be and to do *good?* From the Bible's viewpoint, moral goodness depends entirely upon a person's relationship with God. To be good is to be aware of God as goodness and love and to entrust Him with your will...to accept gladly your own status as a finite creature, yet one who is loved by a gracious God. To be good is to know and trust and love God on an intimate basis.

Doing good comes from being good. When you are in personal union with God, you have no need to be the center of the world, or to protect your self and your concerns, or to fight others for property, i.e., to be defensive, grasping, and fearful.

A vivid personal awareness of God as loving and caring would exclude greed, cruelty, and the need for power over others.

Karl, moral evil is the opposite of what I've just described. Evil is defined in terms of our relationship to God. Evil actions are the results of a broken relationship with our maker.

Now I can return to my statement that God is ultimately responsible for evil's origin. You are correct, Karl, the traditional concept that the first humans lived in a state of innocent bliss and in perfect harmony with God, and then rebelled doesn't make sense.

For beings (angelic or human) to be in paradise and then choose not to be is illogical unless God created them with the potential flaw to rebel, that is, to break fellowship with Him. So God is responsible for creating a being who could *do evil*—that is, violate the personal relationship with Him.

Karl, I will throw another grenade here. The traditional explanation of the first human living in Eden's bliss is not only illogical, it also doesn't square with what we now know of human origins via the findings of geology or paleontology. But I will get to this later. Just stay with me. Believe me, I am a Bible believer. I know God on a personal basis. This is not an attack on the foundations of faith.

To summarize: (1) Evil in human terms (moral evil) is relational. To be evil is to be out of fellowship with God. To do evil is to violate the love of God, self, others. (2) God created humans with the potential to break relationships with him. (3) So, God is ultimately responsible for moral evil.

The next question is whether God knew what humans would do before He created them. Did He foreknow what would happen to his world? Not if humans were created truly free to choose whether to love or not love Him.

Okay, I'll explain. As I say in Chapter 14, there are some things God can't/won't do. He won't contradict Himself, for example. God can't do anything, if "anything" means self-contradiction.

Therefore, if He were going to make a truly free being, how could He know what the being would do before the being existed? If God chose to know the being's actions beforehand, He would be contradicting His intention to create a free being.

To create a free creature, God would have to take the risk that the creature would reject Him. God could not know what the creature would do until after the creature came into being. God chose to limit Himself for a purpose He deemed higher—namely, love.

Karl, I believe that God thought it better to create a world where evil was a realistic possibility so that the higher possibility of uncompelled love between God and humans could occur. It was better to create the world as it is than to create one where real love couldn't happen.

There can be no love without free choice. *God risked the evolution of evil for the sake of love.*

Karl, we do this constantly in everyday life. Love is a risk. To love another is to give them the power to hurt you. To love is to limit ourselves to the choices, good or bad, of those we love. They can enrich us or crush us. There can be no love without the potential of evil, if you define evil as betraying relationships.

Your first question was about the origin of evil. I have said that moral or human evil came from God's choice to make beings who had the freedom to reject His love. This is what happened and still happens. Humans choose to worship the created order instead of the Creator. This is Paul's definition of evil in Romans 1.

In getting to this conclusion, I have raised many questions and no doubt some eyebrows. I have tipped you off that I do not agree with the most popular traditional beliefs about evil and the creation of perfect humans. All I can say is, "Read on!"

I want to turn to the second part of your question now. If God is ultimately responsible for evil, how can He hold us accountable for having a condition we didn't create?

My answer is, I don't think He holds us accountable for having the condition. I think He holds us accountable for what we do with it.

Karl, I will show in Chapter 3, how I believe that the Genesis stories of the Creation and the Fall (Gen. 1–3) are vehicles for telling timeless truths. They are not historical narratives. In others words, I believe they are describing the human condition *not as it was prehistorically* but as it is for all rational humans. "Adam and Eve" are every man and every woman.

But for now I simply want to say that all of us are born in the world as innocent babes. When it comes time to choose whether to depend on our awareness of God or the world we are in, we choose the world. The deck is stacked against us. For we are born into an environment where love is used to gain and keep power over others, and self-interest and protection are necessary for survival.

This is our condition. We are not responsible for inheriting it. We are only responsible for what we do with it once we discover that there is an alternative: to trust and depend upon God. Do we cultivate our world worship or do we subjugate it to our trust in a loving God? In other words, do we proliferate evil in ourselves and our environment, or do we allow God to enter into the core of our being and begin the lifelong work of turning our love into a positive force?

Do we allow evil to be reversed and transformed? *This* is our responsibility, Karl.

Which brings me to the question of what God has done to take responsibility for having created a world where evil could originate. If God hasn't and doesn't do something about His actions, then He is not all-loving.

Karl, I am a Christian by choice not inheritance. I had an

encounter with God before I met Jesus. I studied other world religions before I read the New Testament. When I did, I found that the God I had encountered has "a face and a name"—Jesus.

The New Testament claims that God became a human being and the human, Jesus, was the embodiment of goodness which I described earlier in this letter. Jesus was "the opposite" of evil. He lived wholly in a right relationship with God. He trusted the Father completely with direct vivid awareness of God as gracious and loving, therefore He was totally obedient, free from greed, fear, grasping. He saw His status as utterly insignificant...no protective self-concern.

Living this way in a world-worshipping environment He elicited the worst in human nature's responses and was killed. But His death proved the best of God's nature. For God raised Him up! The Resurrection is our proof that God will ultimately make all of the *wrongs* He risked creating turn into *rights*.

Karl, I will speak more of this later, but I believe that Jesus' crucifixion has to be understood as God's taking upon Himself the responsibility for making the kind of world He did. God will eventually turn all evil into good.

When I answer questions about heaven and hell later, I will look more completely at God's correcting evil in some future time. I hope you will wait until after you read that part before judging what I've said here.

Also, Karl, I haven't dealt with natural evil in this letter, i.e., How God could be good and sovereign and permit natural disaster and disease. Please wait for my discussion of that topic in Chapter 4.

What I've tried to do here is give you some thought-starters for your specific questions. I haven't reviewed the time-honored theories and systems of thought concerning evil and suffering. I have merely tried to answer one man's probing questions.

In summary, I believe that evil is the result of God's decision to make a world where authentic love could exist between Him and His people. Satan didn't invent evil. If so, then evil was invented by a creature who was created by God with the tools to create evil.

God took responsibility for His risk-gone-wrong by continuing to try to reestablish relationship with His people. That's what the Bible's about. It is record of God's attempts to redeem His creation. His efforts culminated in the advent of Jesus. God became one of us. Evil is no longer our only choice. We can now use love as a power to reverse evil in ourselves and in the world.

Of course, we can continue to use love as a tool for exploitation as well. There's a sucker for love born every minute.

Our choice to use love either to grow or to control others depends upon our relationship with God. Karl, I do not think we are capable of loving others and ourselves into existence without the power of God's love within.

I enjoy those pop-psychology books which urge us to tap the power of love within but never call it "God." They are better than nothing, and they do appeal to folks who don't want God involved in the equation of curing the world's ills. But they urge us to do something we cannot do alone. To try, is to continue within the grasp of evil.

2

WHY DOES GOD LET BIG PEOPLE KILL KIDS?
The Issue of Moral Evil

Dear Dr. Mann:

Hi, my name is Susan. I am ten years old. I want to know why God lets big people kill kids. Some kids were being killed in my town. I was scared and my friends were scared. At Sunday School they told us to pray and God would take care of us. Then one of my friends who prayed was murdered. God didn't stop it. Can you tell me why? If He could, why didn't He?

Author's Note: I didn't receive this question by mail. It came to me on television...live! Susan from Florida asked it. I am using the way she framed the question because out of the thousands of letters I receive which ask why God—if He is both all-powerful and all-good—allows the innocent to suffer, hers hit me hardest.

A ten-year-old child cuts through to the quick of the issue. In all of her innocence, she raises the question behind the question of physical, intellectual, and spiritual hurt. It is the question of God's worth to us.

Can we depend on the God who has been presented to us via tradition and the Bible? Is He really with us, or did we invent Him because we couldn't face up to the stark truth that we are alone to fend for ourselves on this tiny blue orb?

I will try to repeat what I said to Susan live and unrehearsed. Then I will relate what I hope to have the privilege of telling Susan when she is older.

Live Response:

Susan, I simply do not know why God allows big people to kill kids. It bothers me as much as it bothers you. If I ever have the opportunity to stand before God face-to-face, that's the first question I'm going to ask Him.

The only thing I can tell you is that God allows people to be bad if they choose to be. Maybe He could stop them but He doesn't. I think He leaves it up to good people to stop this kind of thing and we are not able to stop it all of the time. I also believe that God will turn all evil into something good. Maybe not now, but in the next life.

Tell me, Susan, are you alone tonight? (She tells me her parents are in the next room...that her mom and dad have taken her to a counselor several times since her friend's death...and that she has visited with her pastor.)

Susan, God is taking care of you through your parents and others who love you. I know you're confused about God's care right now.

You will never be able to answer your questions completely, nor can anyone else. You will have to choose whether there is enough evidence of God's care and goodness in the world to offset the bad. And you will have to make the choice throughout your life. You will never be free from making this choice.

Susan, I believe that God can be trusted, even though there are always reasons for me to question. In my own life I have experienced too much goodness for me not to believe in God. If the bad stuff proves God doesn't care, what am I going to do with the good stuff? Susan, your sweetness and kindness make me believe in God. No one but God could make someone like you.

Susan, will you do me a couple of favors? ("Yes," she says, before she knows what I'm going to ask of her. Talk about goodness!) First, write to me. I want to stay in touch. Six

24

thousand calls come into six lines here in the studio every hour. Yours got through. Susan, I don't believe this was an accident. I believe God wants us to be friends.

The second thing I want you to do is stay close to some adult in addition to your parents—someone you really trust and can tell secrets to that will be kept. Do you have someone like that? (A grandmother! Great!) Tell her everything you're feeling inside.

Finally, Susan, keep your mind open about God. I mean, don't give up on Him. He's there. Keep asking Him the question you asked me. He doesn't mind. I think you're a little angry at God for allowing your friend to die. That's okay, I am angry too.

By the way, I want to say something about your friend. She is not dead. She went on to the next life ahead of us. We're sad and angry and frightened. But, Susan, from God's viewpoint there is only life: What we call life is a small part of total life.

The real proof that God cares and protects us is that we live on after this life. If we don't, then I would have to agree that it's hard to believe that God cares.

Susan, do you have someone to hug tonight? (Thank God, she does.)

What I Hope to Say to Susan When She's Older:

Susan, when you were ten years old and called me on television, I was under great pressure. I only had a few moments to treat the biggest issue of all religion and more importantly, to calm a frightened child so that she could make it through the night.

I have replayed our conversation many times. I wish I had said a lot more a lot better. However, I think I said the three things that must always be said in response to the question of

25

why the innocent suffer.

First, *it's a fair question.* There is nothing wrong, sinful, or dumb about asking why God allows suffering if He can stop it. Several writers of the Bible asked it. While the authorities were coming up the hill to arrest Jesus and put Him on the cross, He Himself questioned whether God might consider some alternative to the suffering of the cross.

To hide behind the position that we are not to question God is just that—hiding. Our faith is centered in the beliefs that (1) God is personal, (2) we are individual personal entities of worth to God, and that (3) our personal identities are not erased by death. We live on and continue to be addressed by God in the next life.

In other words, the Christian way is the way of personal relationship between people and God.

If we were of the Buddhist faith, then we would not be concerned about personal survival. We would see suffering as the result of being caught in this world, separated from the World Soul. Our goal would be to cease to exist as individuals and be reunited with the world soul.

Buddhists do not want to be "saved" in the Western sense of the word. They do not desire to remain detached individuals. Suffering itself is an illusion which belongs to the false world of individuality. To be saved is to vanish as a separate being.

However, our hope is that we as persons will continue beyond the present. My point is that questions are altogether appropriate in our faith. If we cannot question and doubt and attempt to pierce the armor of God's mystery, then our religion is not personal. So, your question is a fair question.

The second response I gave you, Susan, is still valid as well. *I do not know the answer to your question.* God is great...God is good...the innocent suffer. Of these three you can only keep two and keep logic as well. If God can't stop suffering then He's not great. If He can, then He's not good... that is, according to our understanding the concepts of "great" and "good."

Some say we need to take a new look at what the terms *great* and *good* mean. To say "God is great," does not mean that God can contradict *His* own logic. For example, He cannot make a four-sided triangle. Having created the reality of triangularity (meaning three-sided), God cannot change that reality. I suppose it's better to say God *will* not.

The point regarding suffering is that having set the world to operate a certain way, especially with the freedom of humans to choose to do evil, God doesn't alter His own created reality.

In fact to alter the reality which applies to the whole would be unfaithful on God's part. So, in order to be "good" God does not prevent the innocent from suffering.

Susan, there is a measure of truth to this viewpoint. But it raises a more serious question for me: Why did God create such a world in the first place? I will deal with this question later. All I'm trying to do here is show that no matter how we reason the issue: God is great... God is good... the innocent suffer, we only succeed in opening the door to further questions.

In the Book of Job, there is an attempt to "corner" God with this issue. Job is a righteous man who has suffered multiple calamities through no fault of his own.

Job finally demands to know "Why?" God's answer is a series of "who-are-you's?" and "where-were-you's." "Who are you to question me, Job?" says God. "Where were you when I made the world?... You cannot even ask, let alone understand!"

Job ends up admitting that he cannot understand as God *understands*. He says, "Up to now I had only heard of Thee. But now I have seen Thee with my own eyes" (Job 42:5).

Susan, I do not know more than Job discovered. I know that I don't know why the innocent suffer and probably, I never will know. But Job's experience has been mine as well, which brings me to the third response I gave you on that night you called.

I know that God is good. Sandwiched up against the impenetrable mystery of suffering is the extraordinary goodness and love of God. I have "seen Him with my own eyes," to quote Job.

Susan, many before me have pointed to the *problem of goodness*. I agree with them. If you're going to let evil erase God, how are you going to explain extraordinary goodness? Where did it come from?

Look at the world. Look at human nature. There is no reason to be good except to protect our own self-interest. Granted there is much goodness that is no more than that.

But what about the countless acts of goodness which have no self-serving motive? As Harry Emerson Fosdick used to say, "Goodness is a far greater problem for the atheist than evil is for the believer."

If God is great and God is good, why do the innocent suffer? Three responses: (1) It's a fair question. Keep asking it. Your search is more apt to lead you to God than to despair. (2) I do not know. The question cannot be answered to our logical satisfaction. If we could answer it we would be God. Suffering lets us know we're not God. (3) I do know that there is an extraordinary goodness in this world which cannot have originated from the natural order including us humans. It can only come from a Transcendent Reality. I know in fact that it does; for "I have seen Him with my own eyes."

Susan, I have studied your question more than any other (religious question) throughout my life. In the following chapters, I will summarize my conclusions in a formal way. My purpose here has been to encourage you to keep seeking. Don't give up because there are mysteries which you cannot yet comprehend. If God were completely "unveiled," you would have no say in whether you chose to love Him. *You would not be free to love.*

3

IS GENESIS A DINOSAUR?
Science and the Bible

Dear Dr. Mann:

My grandson is only twelve, but he already knows that what he's learning about the natural order at public school is different from what he's being taught at Sunday School. Recently he has begun to ask me questions which reveal that he is suspicious of the creation accounts in Genesis.

He is a sweet Christian kid and a joy to our lives. He loves church and has already been baptized at his own request. The current popularity of the "dinosaur thing" has made him bolder. He wonders how he can trust the Bible's claim that God made the world in six days, when it is obvious that science has disproved it.

I told him that it didn't matter how or how long it took God to make the world. The important thing is that God did it and why He did it. I suggested that perhaps the six days of creation meant six long periods of time.

He came back on that one and wanted to know how to reconcile the evolution of humans from Homo erectus *to* Neanderthal *to* Cro-Magnon, *with the Genesis claim that original man was created perfect and in a garden setting.*

I told him what I heard a preacher say on TV. Dinosaurs and monsters and underdeveloped humans were the result of Adam and Eve's fall from God. Originally, there was no harsh environment. Earthquakes and disease and man's evil toward man came after the Fall.

The preacher also said evolution was a pure guess and could be explained another way. He said that God could have created graduating species one after another.

Dr. Mann, I don't think I convinced my grandson. I'm afraid that he will come to distrust all of the Scriptures. I need some help from a minister who won't get defensive and attack me for doubting. I also need to know how to retain my respect for the Scriptures. I'm beginning to think that maybe the Book of Genesis is the real dinosaur. If I can't believe it, how can I believe any of the Bible?

Dear Earl:

I continue to be surprised that people want to know how to reconcile Genesis 1–3, with the findings of modern research. I thought that was all settled about seventy years ago. Many great minds have explained—thoroughly, I thought—that the Genesis accounts are not threatened at all by scientific discoveries.

Yet your question crops up almost every week in the mail and on television. I am coming to realize, Earl, that you and many other people of faith are really concerned about the Bible's reliability when you ask such questions.

If the Bible is God's word and it gives an erroneous account of the created order, how can we believe any of it? I think that is a question we must continue to answer. I will deal with the Bible and how to understand it in a later chapter.

Right now I'm going to respond specifically to your question. It is a good sequel to the two previous questions I have just answered.

I will start by telling you where I'm going to end up, and then fill in the details.

I accept the Genesis accounts of Creation and human nature as accurate. *And* I accept the findings of modern geology and paleontology as well. I think they are not in conflict. Both can be embraced without threat to the other.

I am a "creationist" to be sure. This means that I believe God is the Creator of all things. Modern computer science confirms that the chances of life—as it is on this planet—occurring without a creative designer are nil... mathematically impossible. The concept of a self-creating universe is no longer a serious consideration.

I also believe that humankind originated just as modern science claims. The first Homo sapiens were primitive creatures who had to survive in a harsh world. Over the eons these creatures became aware of a reality higher than that of nature. They became aware of God.

At this point they became human and had to decide whether to cultivate this awareness into a personal relationship with God, or to depend on nature for their fulfillment.

Earl, you have probably already figured out the implications of what I am saying. The first humans were not created perfect and in a paradise. They were created at a "distance" from God.

God had to create them at a "distance" in order to preserve their freedom to choose to love Him. Had He created them in a state of paradise they would never have chosen to love Him freely and the divine human relationship would have been "rigged" (as I explained in Chapter 1).

In this sense, humans were created "fallen." God deemed it better to create us at a distance but with freedom, than to create us in a "have-to-love" state.

I believe that the Genesis stories are not historical narratives. They are myths. The word *myth* doesn't mean *lie*. A myth is a form of storytelling which conveys truths which

31

can't be told any other way. These truths apply to all of us at all times in history.

Most of the world's major religions use myths to convey truth. Let me show you what I mean by taking a new look at the Genesis stories.

God summoned man out of the dust of the evolutionary process. ("God took some dust from the ground and made man out of it" (Gen. 2:7 [Good News Bible]). The man now had God's breath or spirit in him (Gen. 2:7). That is, the man was now aware of his creator. He was no longer Neanderthal or *Homo erectus*. He was capable of a relationship with his Maker.

He was also now "in Eden," in the sense that nature no longer completely ruled him. He was now the master of the world, more than an animal, and the ruler of animals. He could now make nature serve him. He was no longer a help-less pawn.

However, he was still bound to die and he knew it. He now knew that he was part of earth as well as part of Heaven. He could depend on nature for his life or he could depend on his relationship with this creator.

This awareness of the choice between the creation and the creator is called "the tree that gives the knowledge of good and evil" (Gen. 2:9).

The knowledge of good and evil simply means distinctive human *knowledge*. Humans evolved to a point where they had awareness of the world of nature and the world beyond nature. They were aware of death. They could observe themselves objectively.

The serpent who tempts man to eat of the tree was not iden-tified with the full-blown tempter, Satan, until the end of the Old Testament era. I'll deal with this later. All I want to do here is point out that in the Genesis 3 account, the serpent is not portrayed as evil.

I agree with many scholars that the serpent is a symbol of humankind's curious experimental nature. Tasting the forbidden fruit is "the first scientific experiment," in which humans lost their fear of nature as God's creation and chose to be their own masters. By turning their vision upon nature in order to fulfill themselves, they lose their vision of God. By immersing themselves in conquering and robbing nature's bounty, they become alienated from God and subsequently from each other—as well as from their own selves.

Earlier I mentioned that I see Adam and Eve as every man and every woman. My meaning should be clear by now. I believe that the stories of the Creation and Fall are intended to explain what happens to all of us. They are not historical accounts of what happened in the past.

We are all born powerless. When we become aware of our power, we must choose how we will use it. We can worship nature and seek meaning only there. We can use love to gain advantage. We can become self-centered or God-centered. Because we are already powerless and immersed in nature, we choose to fulfill ourselves through nature. This is the meaning of *original sin*.

Earl, that is my story and yours, isn't it? We are born "fallen." Without redemption from beyond ourselves, we are helpless. The biblical record beginning with Genesis 12 is the story of what God has done in history to accomplish precisely that— our redemption from self-centeredness to reunion with God.

To summarize, I think the Genesis accounts of the Creation and the Fall are intended to tell us who created the world and why. God created it. The same God who called Abraham and Israel. The same God who came in Jesus Christ.

Why did He create? The world is the result of God's desire to share His aliveness. He wants other things to live as He lives. That's why He looked at what He made and called it "good."

He created humans because He wanted creatures to love as He loves—freely and without being forced to. This required that God remain obscure, hidden, veiled—that humankind be at a distance, immersed in nature, but with the choice of relating to God.

Okay, that covers the Who and the Why. Your grandson's problem—as well as mine and many others—is the How. The problem goes away when we stop trying to make Genesis 1–3 a manual of modern cosmology.

Genesis is not a science book. Nor is the rest of the Bible. It is a collection of stories designed to describe what went wrong between humans and God, between humans and each other, and between humans and themselves. And it is story of what God has been doing to heal the breach ever since.

I have tried to show briefly how the ancient stories fit with the knowledge which God has allowed us to gain through the scientific method.

Tell your grandson that Genesis is no dinosaur. Its truths are only verified by the advances of human knowledge.

4

WHY DOES GOD LET DISEASES KILL KIDS?

The Issue of Natural Evil

Dear Dr. Mann:

When the doctor said "leukemia," my insides felt as if they had left me. Lanie was our "grace" child: adorable, bright, cheerful . . . pure sunshine. At only eight years of age she was precocious spiritually. She spoke often of Jesus and how she loved Him.

She also seemed to know at the beginning of her illness that she was dying. Just after we received the doctor's diagnosis, she said, "Mom, I believe that God wants me to come and live with Him."

I suppose it was her *faith that kept me in one piece through the three-year roller coaster of her being in and out of remission. She was a brave trooper. Through the pain and the awful treatments she never lost her fighting spirit.*

The day she slipped into a coma with a raging fever, she patted my hand and told me not to worry, Jesus would take care of her.

Thousands came to the funeral. We were resolved to make it a celebration. We sang upbeat songs and the ministers concentrated on the theme of hope. I didn't even cry. My husband did. He still is, these three years later. He's not crying tears now. He's drinking and golfing and neglecting his business. We hardly talk.

Dr. Mann, I'm so bitter. I want to know why God could

*make something so beautiful and alive, and then allow some-
thing as hideous as leukemia to destroy His handiwork. When
Lanie would cry out in pain and ask God to take it away, I had
to bite my tongue. Under my breath I was saying, "Don't ask
that so-and-so! He's deaf and blind!"*

*My little girl had the faith and kept it to the end. I have lost
mine. I think I could recover it if I could only find an answer
to my question. I know that most of the world's evil is caused
by humans hurting each other. And I understand how that
could be. We are free to hurt ourselves and others.*

*But, Dr. Mann, my child was not the victim of human evil.
Oh, I've read the theory that says things like leukemia come
about because angels and the first humans betrayed God.
I don't buy that. How could God punish an innocent child for
something she didn't do. If He did that, He wouldn't be God!*

*Dr. Mann, I'm dying a little more each day. I would've
taken my life already except for my son and my lack of courage.
Soon my son will go to college. After that, who knows?*

*I don't know why I'm writing to you. You can't help me. No
one can. Don't give me mush. I'm choking on it already. But
I guess I want something or I wouldn't have taken the time to
write.*

Dear Althea:

I cannot give you what I think you want—peace with God
and life; no more hurt; your child's return; justification for God.

All I can do is share with you how I have managed to live
and love for thirty-five years with a child who was deformed
by a disease while in her mother's womb. I won't give you
philosophical theories, although some of them have helped me
and will show up in the words which follow. Instead, I will
simply give you my testimony and hope there is something in

it which will become cool water for your thirsty soul.

First, I want to tell you about my search to satisfy the question of how a good and sovereign God could allow natural evil (disease, earthquakes, storms, etc.) to kill and deform innocent people. Then I will share my search to satisfy my "heart."

Obviously, I agree that the traditional explanation that nature has been perverted by fallen angels and primeval humans is unacceptable. That should be clear from what I have said in other parts of this book. To find a God who is fair and cares, we must take another path.

As I began to search for that path, I realized that there's a difference between pain and suffering. Pain is a physical sensation. It has some value. It warns us away from things that threaten us.

Also, there is some pain which we welcome. Athletes endure pain in order to increase performance. The pain which comes with curative surgery doesn't "bother" us to the extent that we decide not to have it.

Suffering on the other hand is our reaction to pain. We can remember the past. In your case, you remember the beauty and joy of your child. We can also anticipate the future. We can look at a child and dream of what she can be or could have been. We can also anticipate death and all of the emotional hurt which lies ahead for us.

Althea, I began to ask myself what the world would be like without any suffering. What if we lived in a pain-free, suffering-free environment? One answer was clear. We would be as fully evolved as we were ever going to be. There would be no more development and growth in our nature. So, I concluded that one reason God must allow suffering is so that we can grow in our relationship with Him.

I immediately saw the fallacy of this reasoning. I thought to myself: *You mean God lets kids die of disease so that the rest of us can become one with Him?!!? Well, if so, then why not give us the disease? Why take it out on the children? And here's another question: Why such severe pain? Wouldn't a little bit be enough to remind us that we are dying creatures who need to get right with God? And, if suffering is required to produce fully evolved humans, why didn't God create us fully evolved in the first place?*

Althea, I kept on thinking and reading. I concluded that there are two kinds of suffering: self-centered and other-centered. Self-centered suffering is the result of our thinking that the world and God should accommodate themselves to what we want.

In my case, I was angry at God for allowing *my* world to be altered by a Rubella virus which attacked my child in her mother's womb. This tragedy caused me to alter my hopes and dreams for my child and my life.

Other-centered suffering is our choosing to endure hurt for another. Again, in my case it meant making sacrifices which would help my child live as best she could with her limitations.

Over a period of time I came to realize that my real anger at God was because of the self-centered suffering. God had not and would not change reality to suit my wishes. If I were going to survive emotionally—*and with faith*—I would have to use my suffering as the means by which to do it. My only other choice was to allow my suffering to destroy me, to live out my life in bitterness. Althea, I call this, moving from the "why-stage" of suffering to the "how-stage" of suffering. I realized that I would never fully know *why* God allows suffering. I had gone as far as I could go with the *why*. Now I had to decide *how* to get on with my life, given the two facts that: (1) I had a child with a birth defect and (2) no fully satisfactory explanations for why God allowed it. I decided to get on with my life and try to bring some good out of my suffering.

One of the most effective ways I've found to do this is through other-centered suffering. By giving my time and help to my child and to others, I have developed a toughness to persevere which I would not have had otherwise. I have understood life and love in a different way.

Althea, I have come to understand what Jesus meant when He said, "He who clutches his own life (i.e., tries to alter reality to fit his self-centeredness) will lose it. But he who pours out his life for my sake and for others (i.e., becomes other-centered) will gain eternal life (i.e., the kind of life which God has)" (Matt. 16:25).

In short, the only explanation of suffering which comes close to satisfying my reason is the one I've been referring to here and in the previous chapters. Suffering is necessary if we humans are going to continue to grow into oneness with God. It is the tragic by-product of God's desire to have an "uncompelled" relationship with us.

But, Althea, this rational explanation has not satisfied my heart. I still hurt like hell. I know you do too! My words have probably only made you angrier because reason can only go so far and it will never answer all of the questions. As I said, the hard fact is that we will never know why God allows the innocent to suffer. If we continue to believe in God, we will have to do so without all of the answers.

So let me share something of how I have satisfied my heart—my feelings, the emotional side of suffering. First, I've had to ask myself whether I would rather have never had my child as she is. To be honest, I've had moments when I would have answered "Yes!" But on the whole, I'm glad to have been touched and graced by this struggling child who has never heard my voice, or a song, or a baby cry, yet refuses to give up and curse the darkness.

Althea, is it better to have had Lanie for eleven years and

lost her than never to have had her at all? Can you be grateful that her joy and sunshine graced you? My heart has been buoyed by this question.

But now I'm going to give you the only ultimate comfort I have found for both my head and my heart. It is the only real answer to the question: "If God is good and God is great why do the innocent suffer?"

God will have to fix the broken things "which are too broke to mend" in some future time, or else He is not both good and sovereign. In the Western world we are so deep into naturalism that we have difficulty believing in life after death. Many modern theologians re-interpret resurrection to mean "rising above our evil circumstances." They say it means nothing more than "victorious living."

Well, here is where I must part company with them. Unless there's a day coming when you will be reunited with your Lanie and I will sing along with my Cindy, then God is not sovereign or He is not good.

Althea, my entire faith and hope rests on God's redeeming the future...on His bringing good out of evil. The only answer to your question that makes sense to me is that God allows suffering for two reasons: (1) to constantly remind us that this world is not our home; and (2) to constantly remind us that our place is at home with Him. "In my Father's home there are many rooms," said Jesus. "I'm going there to get them ready for you" (John 14: 1–2).

5

HEAVEN AND HELL AND WHO'S GOIN'
The Afterlife for Unbelievers

Dear Dr. Mann:

I know that the Bible says that every person will die and then face God's judgment. It is clear that we have our chance to get right with God in this life and that if we don't we will have to face the consequences.

I have a problem with this because of my husband. He died relatively young of a heart attack. He was an excellent student and a brilliant man. He was also a good father, a good lover, and a good friend. I've never known a more decent human being.

However, he had an intellectual problem with believing in God. He studied many religious thinkers. Books by St. Augustine, Thomas Aquinas, Luther, Calvin, and C. S. Lewis filled his library.

My husband said he wanted to believe. He was not anti-God. He called himself an Agnostic. He said that if there was a God, we couldn't know Him.

I was faithful to my church all of our married life. He never objected. In fact, he encouraged me to enjoy my faith. He told me that he wished he could believe like I did.

Dr. Mann, you can guess my problem. Is my husband in Hell? Will God leave him in that state forever? My husband told me once that Hell as an eternal dimension of existence was contradictory to the God of the New Testament. Jesus taught that He was God with us. He also taught that we should

41

not use evil to combat evil. My husband used to say, "How could God use evil to get rid of evil, when He forbids us to?"

Dr. Mann, it's hard for me to believe that God would have anything to gain by punishing my husband eternally. I'm a lonely old woman. I was loved and cared for by this dear man for over twenty years. If he's not in Heaven, I don't want to go. Would you comment? Do you think God will punish my husband forever?

Dear Helen:

I must tell you up front that the question of Heaven and Hell and Who's Goin' is the most frequent topic on my talk program. I have continued to be surprised by this. I have tried to figure out why it's the number-one question. I think it's due in part to the fact that we are into big-time denial regarding death. Our society is so filled with "goodies" that we hardly "long for the next life" the way our forefathers did.

Death is not a frequent topic in America's pulpits. Yet, lurking beneath the surface of our consciousness is the constant nagging anxiety which tells us that we are beings unto death. Is there more to come? How do I qualify for the "final cut" on God's Heavenly Team? If we're going to deal with religion at all, we'll have to deal with your question, Helen.

If you've read my responses to the other letters in this book, you can probably anticipate my reply. If we start with the belief that evil is the result of God's choosing to create humans at a "distance" from and without full knowledge of Him, it is obvious where we will end up.

I believe that Hell is a reality, but it does not have to be permanent. In fact, I don't believe that God will ever be content for one of His creatures to remain unredeemed. Logically it seems possible that some could continue to reject God beyond the grave. But, practically, from what we know of God in Jesus Christ, it is probable that God will continue to try to bring good out of evil.

If He keeps trying, He will probably succeed. But He will have to succeed without compelling us to love Him. The choice will always be ours.

William James in *The Will to Believe* (Dover, 1956) used the illustration of a chess match to explain what I've just said. The game is between a master and a novice. The novice is free to make whatever moves he wishes and delay the outcome. But the outcome is certain. Eventually the master will win.

The problem with what I'm saying is the several statements of Jesus about Hell which appear in the New Testament. He spoke of the wicked being cast into outer darkness where there would be weeping and gnashing of teeth (Matt. 25:30). He also said that they would suffer in a place where the "worm dieth not and the fire is not quenched" (Mark 9:48). In the story of the Rich Man and Lazarus, He has the rich man begging "Father Abraham" to return to this life and warn his brother not to be as calloused toward the poor. Abraham refuses (Luke 16:19 ff).

What are we to do with these? First, we take them seriously. No doubt there will be a time and place for all of us to reap what we have sown. It is undeniable that Jesus taught that divine judgment will result from humankind's selfish and cruel deeds done in this life. God loves his people too much to allow them to go away from Him without feeling the sting of that separation.

And, Helen, this is the key to understanding God's judgment. It is not gleeful vengeance. It is correction. It is a positive force designed to redeem, not to pay back.

I believe that we can accept everything Jesus taught about

Hell without making it a state of eternal torment. Your husband's instinct was correct. How can God use evil to destroy evil when He taught us not to? The idea of perpetual torture is simply not compatible with the God of the New Testament.

Helen, I might add that scholars have long questioned the meaning of the word translated *eternal* in the New Testament. Jesus spoke Aramaic. The earliest New Testament documents are in Greek. Some scholars claim that the Aramaic had no concept of eternity as being a fixed state.

My point is simply this: Hell does not have to be a perpetual or a final state. On the contrary, the notion of God perpetually tormenting his wayward children without relief or redemption seems blasphemous to me.

I believe that God will continue to seek a relationship with us beyond the grave...even the most heinous and evil of us. Look at it this way. None of us dies "perfect and ready" for heaven. We will all have to be perfected when we die. Further development is mandatory. Whether God perfects us instantly or by a process, I believe He will continue trying to win our love beyond the grave.

Two other objections to what I've said come to mind. First, if God's going to redeem everyone anyway, why should we try to reach people with the Good News? Why not shut down our mission efforts! Second, if we have another chance beyond the grave, why be good?

My reply to the first objection is to ask, what's the motive for telling people the Good News? Is it to save them from eternal Hell? If that's the only reason, then my belief is definitely a threat. However, if I believe that the only way to live a meaningful life is to be in union with God; and if I believe that Hell is a realistic experience of reaping what I've sown (although temporarily) then my zeal to share the Gospel will not be diminished.

I want to add that religion which is based entirely upon escaping the wrath of an angry God, is a kind of Hell in itself. How can you love a God you're afraid of? You can obey Him but you cannot love and enjoy Him.

This kind of religion is also unbiblical in my opinion. I'm going to say something here that may seem radical to you and many others. If you read the teachings of Jesus carefully you will find that the primary purpose of Christian conversion is not to escape punishment but to receive the power to love in a way which is otherwise impossible.

In other words, we do not need to be converted primarily to gain Heaven; we need to be converted in order to love as God loves. This is the point of Jesus' teaching in Matthew 5:43-48. In essence He says to His disciples, "If you love only friends, family and cohorts you're not doing anything extraordinary. That's natural. Even criminals and pagans do that. But I tell you, love strangers, enemies, and even persecutors. Why? So that you will be loving the way God loves!"

The primary purpose of accepting Christ is to become empowered to love "unnaturally," or "against" your natural inclinations to love only those who love you.

I think we've missed the main point of what distinguishes a Christian from the rest of humanity. It is the radical, "unnatural," power to love—not eternal safety! Our primary motivation is to be saved—made whole, empowered to love the unloveable, not to be safe in Heaven.

I'm not trying to demean Heaven. It's a wonderful expectation and hope for me. But it is not the primary reason for embracing Christ. The biblical phrase, "Eternal life," most often refers to the kind of life God has and not to life after death.

Near-death experiences are enjoying a great appeal nowadays. Many people are saying that they have died, gone to the other side, experienced Jesus, angels, and bliss, and then returned to this life.

Orthodox Christians are threatened by these claims. They feel that if Hell is removed from the Christian scenario, Christianity has no point. How ridiculous! I would not care if we developed the medical technology to "kill" people, send them to the other side, let them see Heaven and bring them back.

With the fear of eternal damnation removed from the equation, we could finally get down to the primary need for Christian conversion—namely, to change the hearts of people so that they can love someone not their own kind.

Without this kind of Christian conversion our planet has no hope. Until we are converted to love strangers, enemies, persecutors, and the unloveable, we have no way out of racism, nationalism, and tyranny.

As to the second objection: Why be good if God's not going to make me pay? I say two things. First, morality based on fear is false morality. Second, it is clear that we *will* reap what we've sown, either in this life or the next. I'm simply saying it does not have to be perpetual torment.

Helen, I digressed from addressing you and your problem directly. I wanted others who will read this to hear me out. But I felt it was okay to do so, because you told me that your husband was a thinker. I hope what I have said has been of comfort to you and others who need to apply reason to their religion.

Whether I'm right or wrong in my viewpoint, I know that God is fair and loving. Your husband may have been closer to Him than you think. There are two kinds of doubt: Dishonest doubt which refuses to believe because it would require commitment; and honest doubt which wants to believe, but won't settle for easy answers.

It sounds to me like your husband was an honest doubter. I believe God fulfills the hunger of doubting souls, if not in this life, then in the next.

6

THE DEVIL DIDN'T MAKE ME DO IT
Picturing Satan in Modern Terms

Dear Dr. Mann:

I'm a fifteen-year-old sophomore in a Christian high school which meets on the campus of a large church. My parents enrolled me here because they felt I would be safer and receive a better education. The public school district where we live is filled with drug users and gangs, so I was happy to have an alternative.

There are no drugs and violence here, but I am terrified by another thing—the Devil and his demons. Every day we are taught that Satan is in control of the world today and that the end of time is near. Most of the kids in my class don't think they will finish high school before the end comes.

The church just completed a new building. As part of the dedication ceremonies, the pastor and leaders marched around the perimeter of the church property stationing angels at various points to ward off Satan. Then they went into every room of the church facilities and exorcised Satan and his demons.

However, we are reminded every day that we can be "carriers" of Satan. They tell us that if we don't repent we can re-infect the church and school with the Devil.

Dr. Mann, I'm having nightmares. I have never been afraid of Satan until now. I certainly never thought of myself as a "carrier" for evil. I love Jesus and pray every day, but I'm still terrified.

To make things worse, I told one of my friends about a visit with my pastor (we go to a different church). My pastor said that Satan was real but not regal. He couldn't control me without my permission. My pastor said that they were practicing "voodoo religion" in the name of Christ at the church where I go to school, and for me to get out of there as fast as I could.

My friend told the "Devil-Chaser" (that's what a few of us call the pastor at my school) and he made an example of me. He demanded that I submit myself for exorcism or leave school. I submitted. I didn't want to change schools in mid-semester.

To my surprise, I felt much better after the ceremony. I don't know why. I'm really confused now. I don't want to belong to Satan. The nightmares are getting worse. I dream that Satan is after me and I have nowhere to run.

Dr. Mann, I don't understand how God could allow Satan to continue to do evil. I thought Jesus died and rose again in order to defeat Satan. Are there two Gods—a good one and a bad one? How can God love us yet allow us to be overcome by an evil force?

Dear Debbie:

My first word to you is: Listen to your pastor! Go to another school. After you're enrolled in the new school and have your transcript from the church-school, write the Devil-Chaser a note. Ask him if they're going to have school at his church next year. If he says yes, ask him why?

Then ask him why they built a new church building. They could've used the money to warn more people about the End. They're not going to need that church building if he's correct. You might also ask him if he carries any life insurance. If he does, ask him to make you (or me) the beneficiary. He's not going to need it.

Debbie, I'm being tacky. I'm doing it on purpose. I choose to be tacky because I am incensed at the way the Devil-Chasers are trafficking in the tender spirits of youngsters like you. Satan has always been a convenient tool for gaining power over others and getting them to do one's bidding.

Your feeling that God's love would be suspect if He allowed His children to be the helpless pawns of Satan is right on target. I want to reinforce that feeling, Debbie. There's no need for you to live in terror. The nightmares are signs that you are healthy and that the Devil-Chaser is not. Nightmares are relief valves for the fears which we push down into our subconscious.

But they need to go away. They will, once the fears go away.

How can I best help you? That's the question. I've thought on it a great deal, and I've decided to do two things. First, I want to give you a brief summary of what the Bible says about Satan. It will be no more than a sketch. I encourage you to study the subject more extensively. Second, I want to replace your fear with a deep-down awareness of God's love and care for you. The first part will be easier than the second. That is because you will have to play a key role in coming to spiritual bravery.

Your pastor was correct. In fact, the two things he said about Satan make a good outline of the Bible's teachings: (1) Satan is real; (2) But he's not regal.

What do we mean when we say, "Satan is real"? Well, I can tell you what *I* mean. I feel an evil power in the world at large and in me personally which I cannot handle by myself. I need God within me and God's people around me or I am helpless.

And the mysterious thing about this power is that it seems to have a life of its own. It seems to be larger than the sum of its parts. It's superhuman!

Paul felt the same thing. He says in his letter to the Romans 7 that he doesn't understand himself. The very thing he promises not to do, he ends up doing. The thing he promises he will do, he never gets around to doing. He ends up crying out in despair, "Oh wretched person that I am! Who will deliver me from this body which is taking me to death" (v. 24).

Debbie, I have the same experience. There's something sick and wrong inside me. I have a shadow side of my nature. There are urges and power plays which astonish me. I believe everybody who is more or less healthy psychologically experiences the same thing.

I believe the writers of the Bible gave this superhuman darkness within us a name—Satan. Other religions have given it other names. It is *real*. It exists. But before I go further let me give you a short course in the development of the concept of Satan in the Bible.

In the Old Testament the word *Satan* is not a proper name until very near the end of the Old Testament era. Before that time he is called "a satan" which means "questioner" or "prosecutor." After the Jews returned from slavery where they were introduced to the religion of the Persians who believed in two Gods (one good and one bad), they began to see Satan as a full-blown evil reality who was at odds with God.

The serpent who tempted Adam and Eve in the garden was not identified with Satan until the period between the two Testaments. At this time the Babylonian king which Isaiah 14:12 predicts will fall from heaven, began to be identified with Satan or Lucifer the fallen angel. "King of Babylon bright morning star, you have fallen from heaven. In the past you ruled nations but now you have been thrown down." Morning Star was now translated *Lucifer.*

At the dawn of the New Testament era, Satan was viewed as

an archdevil inhabiting the earth. He had lieutenants (demons) who attempted to infiltrate everything and everybody to distort God's purpose. What we now call mental disorders were called "possessions." All illness and natural disaster and national calamity was now connected to Satan. He was the Liar and Deceiver. He lured and compromised and killed.

These were the common views of Satan when Jesus began his ministry. He did not refute them. But before I get to that let me point out, Debbie, that many scholars believe that Satan was elevated to a higher stature in the Jewish mind after the return from captivity in Persia for an obvious reason.

The Old Testament prophets had predicted the return and re-establishment of Israel as a world power. They did return and rebuild their temple and land. Then the Greeks under Alexander the Great conquered them. They revolted and over-threw the Greeks. Then, here came the Romans and conquered them again.

Here was the national problem: *How to keep the Old Testament prophecies of world domination and explain these multiple defeats?* Satan was a convenient target! Blame it on him! This way we keep the integrity of the Prophets on the one hand and we don't have to blame ourselves on the other. Satan had already been mentally elevated to the status of arch-enemy due to the Persian influence.

Debbie, please follow me for a little while longer. I'm not denying that Satan is real. I'm just trying to show you how he emerged in the ancient mind.

As I said, Jesus never discredited Satan as a fabrication of the human mind. He saw Satan as a real enemy.

The question is, what did He see when He saw Satan? Is Satan a thing? Does he have a body? Well, Debbie, this is where medieval literature, art, and Hollywood movies come into play. They describe Satan more than the Bible does.

Nowhere does the Bible give Satan physical characteristics. There are no horns, cloven hooves, or spinning heads. These are the creations of artists who are trying to depict their images of evil and its source.

Debbie, I have been accused of not believing in a literal Satan. Actually, I do believe in Satan, but not the one depicted by Dante, Milton, and Hollywood. Their Satan is too "small" and too "ugly." Who could be deceived by him?

To me Satan is the personification of all of the forces which stop God's efforts to reunite with people. He is all of the lies rolled into one, yet mysteriously greater.

I'll tell you where I see Satan, Debbie. I see him in slanted news reporting. I see him in all of us who demand that the government do more for less. I see him in all of our myths of superiority—that is, our feelings that we are better than others because of our color, rank, education, wealth, rationality, *and religion!*

I see Satan alive and well in the manipulation and brutalization of sophomore girls in the name of defeating Satan! Satan is indeed real. However, we must find new ways to describe him and his work which can connect with the modern mind.

We now know that disease is not caused by little demonic critters floating around in the air. Much disease is caused by our own pollution of the air and our bodies. That is definitely "demonic."

We now know that what the Bible calls "demon possession" is our subconsciousness taking control of our consciousness because of factors whose origin we could definitely call evil. I know a woman with multiple personalities. Most of her "persons" are destructive. They are thieves, prostitutes, and substance abusers.

She was raped by her father and brothers from the age of 8 through 18. She had four abortions and came to enjoy her incest. She didn't know there was another way to live.

The Bible would call her "demon possessed." I would too, as long as you let me define my terms. By "demon possessed" I mean that she has been victimized by evil actions and influences to the point that in order to survive she must switch roles.

How can she be cured? By the grace of God which can come to her in many forms—psychotherapy, a loving community, or perhaps a direct spiritual encounter with Jesus Christ.

Debbie, I hope I have explained what I mean when I say, Satan is real. Evil is ever present. It would be foolish to deny its existence and power.

However, I do not believe he was once a fallen angel. I have explained this in former chapters. God didn't create a perfect being who chose to become imperfect. Nor do I believe that the medieval and Hollywood images do him justice.

Now I must get to what I hinted at a moment ago. I do not believe that we have to be bound to the images of Satan which were prevalent in Jesus' day. Jesus simply took the popular images of evil and used them to communicate His message. For example, the Bible says that Jesus was tempted by the Devil for forty days in the wilderness (Matt. 4).

If you study this encounter carefully, you will see that Jesus' temptation was over whether to become the kind of Messiah which the Jews expected or to do it God's way. So "the Devil" in this instance would be the inward powerful urge to give in to the prevailing popular notion of what the Messiah had to be like. Would Jesus give into this popular notion or would He go to the cross and save the world another way?

Debbie, Satan is alive and well in many popular distortions today. Let me mention a couple. How about the lie which says, "Government can create a social utopia in which everyone will be happy, wealthy, and wise"? How about the lie

which says, "If you're pretty or smart, you're somebody"?
Watch for these lies on your newsstand and TV. They're ever-present.

Satan is real—your pastor was right. But he is not regal.
Right again! Someone said, "Satan is always the perfect gen-
tleman. He never goes where he ain't welcome."

Debbie, you do not have to be afraid that Satan will dominate you against your will. He won't come into your bedroom
some night and inhabit you. He can't. The only thing you
have to fear is your own tendency to do evil. If evil controls
you, it will be from within, not from without.

That's what Paul was talking about in the passage from
Romans 7, which I mentioned earlier. He could not control the
evil within himself. So he cried out in despair (Rom. 7:24),
"Who will deliver me from myself?" In the next verse, he
answers his own question: "Thanks be to God, who does this
through the Lord Jesus Christ."

Debbie, evil has already had it! Satan is not in control of
this world. All evil converged into one and killed Christ. God
raised Him up. Although evil is a present and powerful force,
the outcome of the struggle between good and evil has already
been decided.

Okay, I've given you a sketch of the biblical concept of
Satan: Real but not regal. Now I want to introduce you to
something more. I sense that you already have it. It's the
awareness deep within that you are inhabited by God's spirit of
love and protection. I don't think you would have written me
or gone to see your pastor, if God were not already guiding
you. As I said earlier, even your awful nightmares could be
God's way of helping you survive your fears until you can get
something better. Dreams are like painkillers. They're good in
a pinch, but not good in the long run.

Debbie, I would suggest you get someplace quiet and tell

God you love Him and want to be loved by Him. Ask Him to come into your heart. Then I would stick with loving people who do not dwell on fear-centered religion. Someday you will be able to see the fearful folks as disturbed and frightened souls who have yet to discover God as grace and love. Maybe you can help them. They are not bad. They are afraid, and because they are afraid, they feel the need to scare others.

7

HOW DO YOU PICTURE GOD?

Reconciling the God of the Old Testament with the New

Dear Dr. Mann:

I grew up as a sort of secondhand believer. My parents went to church, so I went to church. We prayed at mealtime and bedtime. Our church was a pleasant experience for a young boy growing up. Our pastor was there for thirty years and didn't get mentally lazy.

It was because of his encouragement that I began an in-depth study of the Bible and dared ask some questions I haven't asked before.

For example, I've read your book Common Sense Christianity *in which you say God is a God of Grace. He intends to win us all with His love. Well, that seems to be the picture of God presented in most of the New Testament. But it certainly doesn't represent the God of the Old Testament!*

Take some of the major events of the Old Testament and then explain how God can be a God of Grace. Like Passover, for instance. I know that it is one of the most sacred events of Judaism. It should be. The firstborn sons of the Israelites were all spared (Exodus 12). But the Egyptian babies weren't.

God claimed credit for killing all of the firstborn males as a way of punishing the Egyptians for heeding their false gods instead of Him (Ex. 12:12 ff). Then he ordered the Jewish people to commemorate their deliverance for all time to come (Ex. 12:14).

Dr. Mann, how could God commit infanticide? Need I go on? He played a cruel game with Abraham telling him to kill his only son, to see if Abraham's faith was strong. He ordered the Israelites to slaughter entire tribes.

How do you square your God of Grace with such a bloodthirsty God?

Also I have a problem picturing God in my mind. Does He have a body? Is He an invisible force of some kind? Is He an organizing principle? Is He a male? How can He have a personality without a "body" or corpus of some kind? I can connect with the notion that God came to show us Himself in human form, i.e., in Jesus. But that causes problems for me as well. If Jesus was God in the flesh, was heaven vacant while Jesus was on earth? Who was Jesus praying to?

I suppose I want to hear how you deal with these questions in your own experience. How do you picture God in your mind's eye?

Dear Alfred:

To treat your questions adequately would take an entire library. Then after we were finished, your mind would not be completely satisfied. I have wrestled with the same questions all of my life. I have read numerous explanations. All come up short.

As in the case of explaining why God permits suffering, we will always have to choose whether to worship and love a partially hidden God. He won't make Himself so undeniably clear that we have no choice but to commit to Him. Nor will He allow us to capture Him within our human reason.

Alfred, you and I are the children of Western thought. I won't go into this except to say that in the Western world, to know is *to have power over.* Knowledge is power. Once you understand something, you rule over it. With the advent of computer and satellite technology, we have been made clearly aware that to control information is to rule the world.

Therefore, it is very difficult for us to commit our lives to anything or anyone we cannot fully comprehend. However, once we do fully know something or someone, we are in the place of superiority.

Obviously, you know where I'm leading. If we were to know God as we want to know Him, we would be God and He wouldn't.

So, Alfred, I tell you up front that I cannot answer your questions in a way that will satisfy the Western criteria of knowledge. Knowing God is a different kind of knowing than knowing the principles of mathematics or physics, etc.

Next I want to say to you that we have only space-time language to speak of God who is beyond space and time. This means that when we talk about Him, we are using symbols and analogies.

In other words, we can say what God is *not*, and we can say what God is *like*, but we cannot say what God *is*. All of our words have to be "stretched."

You have had the same experience if you've ever been "in love," Alfred. How do you put a first-love experience into words? My first love at age 12 was Ruby Queen. To this day, there are no adequate words for what Ruby was to me. I could write for quite a spell about what it was *like*, but I could never tell you what it *was*.

Okay, with that bit of housekeeping out of the way, let's get to your questions. You have asked three whoppers: (1) How to square the bloodthirsty God of the Old Testament with the Grace God of the New Testament? (2) How to picture God in our mind's eye? and (3) How to understand Jesus both as God, and separate from God at the same time?

I will save most of the third question for a later chapter concerning the Trinity, and I will start with your second question: How do I picture God?

In a word, I don't picture God! To me God cannot be given a form or physical properties. All of the terms used to describe God throughout history are failures. *Force*, *Wholly Other*, *Ground of Being*, *Organizing Principle*, etc., come up short.

I know that this is a matter of personal taste, so I'm not belittling these attempts. You spoke of the Jews. I agree with their refusal to give God a name. He is un-nameable. He transcends all of our picturing devices.

I don't picture God, I *feel* God. I use the word *feel* because it's the best one I have. In the very few times in my life that I have been certain of God's presence, I have felt one or more of five sensations. These five "feelings of presence" represent what I mean when I speak of God as being a God of Grace.

For me, Alfred, God *is* Grace. I won't give you a word study here. You can look up the word *Grace* in any biblical dictionary. There are dozens of excellent books on the subject. I use the word, *G.R.A.C.E.* as an acronym to describe what I have felt when I have been visited up close by God.

But before I describe these five sensations (G.R.A.C.E.), let me tell you that I am not given to mystical religion. As a matter of fact, I have always been suspicious of those with "direct lines" to the Almighty. I am guarded about mentioning my few experiences of God's Unmistakable Presence, because they carry great potential for abuse. Many people have never had such an experience and are caused to feel guilty. To make things worse, some give an unhealthy allegiance and authority to those charismatic leaders who claim firsthand knowledge of God. That's how the Jonestowns and Koresh compounds get started. By the way, the word *charismatic* comes from the root word which is translated "Grace" from the New Testament Greek text.

So, Alfred, I'm not claiming that my encounters with God are the only ways God can be encountered. Nor am I saying that everyone must have a mystical experience. On the contrary, I believe that maybe these dramatic encounters are more frequent among the spiritually immature, i.e., direct lines to God may be necessary because we have so little faith!

This has been true in my pilgrimage. God has not "visited" me except in those half-dozen moments (in thirty-five years) when I was totally bankrupt and bewildered spiritually. In short, He doesn't come when my faith is strong...He comes when faith is gone.

Now I will describe what I feel when I feel God. As I said, I use the acronym G.R.A.C.E. Each letter represents God on the "felt-level" to me.

G is for *gladness*. When God has come to me on the feeling level, I have been overcome with the feeling that He's glad to see me. I feel cheer and laughter. At the age of twenty when I first encountered God I knew only three things but I knew them for certain: He was there, He'd always been there, and He was glad to see me.

Jesus showed this kind of welcoming spirit. He came to people unarmed. They felt easy in his presence. In fact, it was his genuine gladness in the company of sinners that got him in trouble with the religious establishment.

Alfred, because of Jesus' approach to people and because of my own experience, I have the same problem as you do with the Old Testament accounts of a slaughter-minded deity. I'll get to that in a moment.

R is for *reprieve*. Forgiveness might be a better word, but reprieve begins with *R* and helps me remember. But more than that, I must say that whenever I have felt God I have felt like

I've been "let-off" because punishment would be unjust. You read it right.

Most theologians have traditionally defined *Grace* as "unmerited favor." That has *not* been my experience. When I say I have felt reprieve, I don't mean that I have felt snatched from the flames in the nick of time. Actually, I have felt the opposite. I have felt that God has chosen not to punish me because I belong to Him.

Grace is actually "merited favor." I don't mean I've earned God's favor because of the good I've done. I mean I don't *have* to earn God's favor and can't. I merit God's favor because of who I am... His child.

I'm simply saying that I have felt like the Prodigal Son when I've been close to God (Luke 15). He puts a ring and a robe on me and throws a party (Gladness). Then He makes me a son again, even though I would settle for being a slave. He makes me a son because I *deserve* it. I deserve it because of who He has declared I am, not because of what I've done.

A stands for *acceptance*. I agree with Lewis Smedes in his book, *Shame and Grace*, that unconditional acceptance is the most frequently described sensation people feel when they are met by God. We live in a world where we are constantly judged and shamed according to how we measure up. When God breaks in, He comes without conditions, shame or judgment.

C is for *chosen*. I have never felt God without feeling that he has chosen me for His own. I had a childhood friend who was adopted. In those days there was a stigma attached. Adopted children were referred to as "step-children." To have to adopt cast a shadow on the parents. They could not extend their "natural lineage."

My friend and his parents seemed unaffected by such notions. I asked him why. He said, "Let me tell you how I was adopted. My parents came to the agency and examined twelve children, cuddled and loved each one. But they chose *me!* When you were born, your parents had to take what they got. I was chosen!"

Whenever I have met God I have known that I was His by choice not by necessity. I may not have been born with royal blood in my veins, but I am royalty by God's decision.

E stands for *energy* . . . the power to stand up and take it, the nerve to believe without full proof, the power not to despair.

I have long believed that human tenacity is a sign of God's grace. I was glad to see an eminent psychiatrist like Scott Peck say as much in his book *The Road Less Travelled.*

Alfred, most people should go crazy and/or commit suicide. But most people don't. Most of us don't quit. We use our stumbling blocks as stepping-stones. Instead of breaking, we break records. That is grace.

I told you that I have had no more than a half-dozen encounters with God's unmistakable presence, and that each one came only after I had exhausted all of my strength. Well, after each encounter I have been re-energized.

So, Alfred, I do not picture God. He is unportrayable to me. I feel Him, and what I feel is G.R.A.C.E. God is Grace on the feeling level.

Jesus as God in the flesh has reconfirmed the God of my own experience. He was G.R.A.C.E. to others. John begins his gospel by saying in essence, "We finally saw God (the Word became flesh). He dwelt among us. And what we beheld (felt) was Grace and Truth" (John 1:1–14).

Jesus was sent to clear up the confusions we hold about God, confusions such as those you mention in your letter, Alfred. It is easy to conform God to our values and agendas. In fact, it's impossible not to. We are all guilty of that.

Also, as I have said so many times, God will not reveal

Himself so plainly that we are forced to believe without choice. This means that God always enters our perception at the level of its maturity. If we are primitive and savage people, God accommodates Himself to our mentality and begins to work with us from there. As we learn more about ourselves and the world around us, we learn more about God.

In an earlier chapter I shared my belief that God created original humans at a distance from Himself. They were immersed in a harsh environment and had to be "savages" in order to survive. Their civility had to evolve. As they opened themselves more and more to God, they learned more and more of His true nature.

Alfred, this "Principle of Accommodation," as scholars call it, explains why God's civility is increasingly revealed as the biblical history progresses. Fosdick used to tell a story about a little girl who read of God's commanding the Israelites to kill innocents. She went to her Dad with the problem. He read to her from the prophets who spoke much later in Israel's experience: "What does the Lord require of thee but to do justice, and to love kindness, and to walk humbly with thy God?" (Micah 6:8). Then he turned to the New Testament and read, "Beloved let us love one another, for love is of God, and he who loves is born of God and loves God." The little girl said, "Daddy, God grew better as He got older, didn't He?"

Alfred, you're probably already asking some troubling questions. Did God really kill those Egyptian babies? Did He tell Abraham to kill Isaac?, etc. Or, did the primitive writers simply *believe* that was the case.

There are two usual ways of responding to these questions and both leave us with problems. If you say, God told them to kill innocents, God's character is in question. If you say, they erroneously thought He told them to kill innocents, then you have to wonder if all of the Bible is simply the erroneous opinions of people and therefore not dependable as God's word.

There is another way, Alfred. I will say a little about it here and more later when I deal with the question of the trustworthiness of the Bible. If we see the Bible as the record of what God did in history to reconcile Himself with humans, then the problem is mostly resolved.

Remember what we said in earlier chapters. Humans developed to a point where they were aware of a Reality beyond nature, i.e., God. God was the creative force behind this development. When divine awareness emerged, God began to "court" humans into a relationship with Himself.

He had to work with what He had, Alfred. The Bible is a wonderful testimony as to how God worked with a primitive people, not enlightening them by force so that they would be compelled to believe in Him.

The closer to God they chose to be, the more of Himself He revealed. That, Alfred, is a description of the "March of Civilization," as far as I am concerned! That is why we no longer have slavery or condone male domination or execute people for adultery.

So, Alfred, my answer is that God did not kill Egyptian babies in order to punish the power brokers of Egypt. I believe there was an epidemic which killed them. I believe God warned his people on how to avoid epidemics. And I have no doubt that the Israelites were preserved because they were obedient. They also saw the survival of their children as a sign of God's deliverance.

It was a redemptive event in which God carried on His mission to eventually save the whole of humankind. Alfred, you and I would not be believers today if the Passover had not occurred.

Did God tell Abraham to kill Isaac? I don't know. But I think it could have happened this way: Abraham was a foreigner in a land where the people worshipped the god, Moloch. The most dedicated of Moloch's followers sacrificed their first-born sons to him. No doubt they constantly mocked Abraham for not loving his god equally. If his God were the only true God, then why not put Him to the test and see if Isaac would be delivered?

In a word, Abraham could've easily *thought* God was directing him to kill Isaac. Or Abraham could've been testing God! The point of the story, however, remains the same: *God intervenes to keep His redemptive plan intact.* Again, you and I are the heirs to Abraham's great act of trust in God's power.

Alfred, I hope I have helped you a little farther along in your search. I want to finish with one final thought. If I picture God at all, I think of Him as a Father. That's why I use the male pronoun when referring to God. I have no particular father in mind, and certainly not my own biological father whom I loved dearly.

I use the analogy "Father" because Jesus used it. My favorite New Testament story is the misnamed "Story of the Prodigal Son" (Luke 15). It is actually Jesus' portrayal of what God is really like. He told it in response to the criticism that He was hanging out with a bad crowd. Alfred, had you asked Jesus what God was like, He would have told you this story.

Go and read it. I don't know of a better one.

8

THE PUZZLEMENTS OF PRAYER
When Prayers Don't Work

Dear Dr. Mann:

I have several questions about prayer. First, why don't mine work? I have had a tragic life. My father sexually molested me. My mom knew it was going on and did nothing. I married at fifteen to get away. I've never been with a man who didn't use me and throw me away.

I've been married four times, but no one wants me now. My face was horribly disfigured by a fire. I am alone with no family. I could never have children which is a blessing, I suppose. But I'm so lonely.

All I'm asking of God is that He give me some inner peace and someone to love me. I pray more than twenty times a day. It does no good.

One day the question hit me: If God controls everything and knows everything that's going to happen, why pray? Someone told me that the purpose of prayer was to "commune with God." Well, I'm not getting through! And God certainly doesn't need to hear from me!

Also what good does it do to pray for other people? We're always being told to pray for so-and-so. Why? Does prayer change God's mind?

And why pray in public? Jesus told us not to (Matt. 6:6). He also said, "Ask and you will receive, seek and you will find, knock and the door will be opened unto you" (Luke 11:9). Well, I've asked, sought, and knocked and nothing happens.

Can you tell me how to get something out of my prayers?

Dear Peggy:

First, I want to praise you. Not many people have the raw honesty to ask these questions. I know your candor is due in part to your deep hurt, but there's more. You could not be this angry with God unless you cared deeply and yearned for His presence.

I have thought long and hard about how to respond. You are not a whining, self-centered person who wants to "carp" at God.

I have decided not to give you theories. Instead, I will share my own struggles with prayer and how I have come to an "approximate peace." I say "approximate" because there are still some things about prayer which I find puzzling.

I started my prayer life many years ago, in the same way most people do. We recited "canned prayers" at meals and bedtime. I learned the Lord's Prayer at Sunday School or somewhere. I would attempt to get God on my side before football games, exams at school and a fistfight or two. I also tried to solicit God's help in changing those who didn't agree with me.

When I became a minister, I figured God would heed my prayers more readily. Not so. I prayed more often than before and I learned all of the prayer lingo. I prepared good sermons on prayer and scolded the people for their lack of it.

Then something remarkable happened to me one spring. I was on the staff as a Junior Minister of a large church and our pastor suggested that we have an around-the-clock prayer meeting for three days prior to our Annual Revival Meeting.

Having the least tenure, I drew Saturday from 2:00-5:00 A.M. Three faithful church members showed up and we began praying in succession. Each round got longer and more emotional. We confessed all of the sins we dared and begged God repeatedly to rain down the Holy Spirit on us and all of the other worms in our community.

I was the last to pray in the fifth round and it was 4:30. I had thirty minutes to try to think of something to say that hadn't been said. My mind raced. I drew a blank. A few seconds passed. They seemed like hours. I began to weep.

I told God in front of my comrades that I couldn't think of anything more to say to Him, that I didn't even want to be there, that I'd rather be home asleep and that I hoped He and my friends wouldn't hold it against me. I said, "Amen." I rose to leave. It was 4:32.

Before a week had passed each of the three faithful church members confided separately that he had felt as I did—and for years. They detested all-night prayer vigils, thought them unnecessary, felt that revivals took on a life of their own, and that God didn't need to be begged in order to be present.

I knew that my entire approach to prayer was an exercise in magic. It was based upon the notion that with proper fervor and technique we can change God's mind.

The success of prayer, which meant having your requests granted, was thought to rest upon the sincerity of the one praying. If your requests weren't granted, then you weren't good enough and pure enough to turn God's head.

My initial response to this realization was to stop praying almost altogether. I knew that my old approach was wrong but I didn't know where to turn. I became a rebel. I wouldn't partake in the "prayer meetings" of others. I gave one-liners at worship and mouthed the same old "Bless our hearts and minds." Have you ever noticed how many times the phrase "hearts and minds" appears in public prayers?

Peggy, it was the unending pain and stress of my child's handicap which kept driving me back to prayer. I started studying the writings of the Saints for whom prayer was a crucial part of life. I counseled with people of prayer.

Immediately I discovered that they all had at least two things in common. First, prayer was not a ritual for them. They didn't "get all dressed up and prepared" to pray. It was a way of doing daily life. They seemed almost unaware that they were shifting their attention from the outward world to the world of God.

In fact, I was to learn later that they were not! For God is in this world all around us. To turn and have a word with God is as natural as turning to speak to one friend or the other.

The second thing they had in common was that prayer was not a grasping exercise, it was a receiving exercise. Henri Nouwen, the Catholic mystic, describes prayer as opening your hands with palms down, then turning your open hands upward to receive whatever God gives you.

All of the people of prayer whom I studied shared that non-desperate "unclenching" spirit.

My prayer life began to change. I didn't run to God helter-skelter. I simply "opened my hands" and did more listening than talking. I didn't see any visions or hear voices. Life and the universe were simply more manageable and friendly.

Soon I discovered, Peggy, that prayer is not designed to change God but to change us. Prayer does indeed "change things," but one of the things is not God. It is us and how we see and feel God all around us that gets changed.

Prayer is not changing God to fit my reality—what I want. It is changing me to fit the reality in which God put me! My typical prayer changed from "God, fix my deaf daughter!" to "God, fix me enough to give my very best to my deaf daughter. I ask for the power to help her as best she can be helped by a human father."

Peggy, you are alone, hurting, and disfigured in the autumn of your life. That is reality. Prayer is asking God to adjust you to fit that reality. That kind of prayer has "changed things" for me. I hope it will for you.

As I said in an earlier chapter, we only have two choices in circumstances such as yours. We can ask for magic and curse the darkness. Or we can ask for the power to use our circumstances and light candles.

I'm wondering at this moment how many disfigured people there are in your community. You know, Peggy, in our society overweight and underweight people are regarded as "disfigured." You could change things through prayer. God could make you an instrument of light to shine in the darkness of other people's disfigurements.

I want to tell you about my prayer life today, then I want to speak of Jesus' prayer life and teachings. Finally, I want to respond to your question about praying for others.

I awake early in the morning and very quickly. I'm asleep then *bang!* I'm alert. In fact, it's the most lucid part of my day. I lie in bed for at least thirty minutes, with my eyes closed and mind blank. I do not think about the responsibilities of the coming day. I just listen for God to speak through my thoughts. At the end, I say a simple sentence. "Father, let what's best for me happen to me." Then I think of each person I know who's hurting or tempted and say their name in my mind. Then I ask God to bring names into my mind.

It's amazing! I find out that some of the names who appear are in the midst of great trials. Others have just reaped great blessings.

Throughout the rest of the day I have little ongoing conversations with God, on the freeway, when I see something extraordinary, when I'm angry with Him. Well, Peggy, that is prayer as I *live* it each day.

Now I want to talk about Jesus and prayer. The New Testament portrays His prayer life as unforced and natural. As

I mentioned earlier, He detested prayer as magic ritual. When He faced the "unfixables" of life, He asked God to change Him to fit reality and not vice versa.

He used prayer to help Him face the "good stuff" as well. Whenever the crowds got too big and His "celebrity" began to rise, He left the crowds and went into seclusion for His "think" with God.

Once when He had returned from such a retreat, His disciples began to complain. (The Luke 11 passage which you mentioned.) "Teach us to pray like John taught his disciples," they said. The inference was that they weren't getting much out of their prayer-lives, at least as much as John the Baptist's followers claimed they were getting.

Jesus began by giving them the Lord's Prayer which should be called the Model Prayer. In essence, Jesus was saying, "If you want words, here's the only words you need: 'Father, may your name be honored and kingdom come here as in heaven. Give us what we need one day at a time—enough food, grace to forgive, power to withstand temptation.'"

These are all of the words we'll ever need to pray! Now Jesus defines prayer by telling a story (Luke 11:5–8). Suppose, He says, that you are tucked in for the night and an unexpected guest shows up asking for bread. You don't have any so you go next door to your neighbor to ask him. He's tucked in too. He doesn't want to be bothered.

If you keep banging on the door, says Jesus, your neighbor will finally give in and give you bread just to get rid of the nuisance.

Now, Peggy, here's where most readers miss Jesus' point— Verse 9. It begins with a word translated *But*. The word is always used to show contrast. "But" says Jesus, which means "on the other hand," or "contrarily."

So follow this: "On the other hand, I say, ask...

seek...knock, etc." Jesus is saying, "God is *not* like that neighbor! You don't have to beat and beg to get His attention."

Later Jesus says, "Would any of you who are fathers give your son a snake if he asked for a fish?...No! As imperfect as you humans are, you know how to give good things to your children." (Luke 11:10–11).

Now get this: "How much more, then, will your heavenly Father give the Holy Spirit to those who ask him!" (v. 13).

Peggy, God is a Father, but a perfect one. He gives to His children—not everything they ask for, but the Holy Spirit— that is, His inward presence, power, and care to live their lives in whatever circumstances they find themselves.

Jesus did not say we would get whatever we wanted, but whatever we needed to make life make sense. God never promised to exempt us from the trials of living. He promised to be with us in the midst of our trials. The Holy Spirit is the form of God's presence in the world today. He's available for you.

Now I want to respond to your most difficult question. If prayer is primarily designed to change the one who prays, and not God or circumstances, then why pray for others? What good does it do for us to intercede with God on another's behalf?

There's no doubt that we are urged in the Bible to pray for others. Jesus prayed for His disciples on the night He died (John 17). What's intercessory prayer all about?

I don't have an answer without holes in it. I don't under-stand *how* intercessory prayer works, but I know it *does* work! It works like the power of love works. One person's intense love for another changes the other. How? I don't know. That it does, is a fact.

One thought I have is that perhaps the persons we pray for are so immersed in their good or bad fortune that they cannot see their situation clearly enough to know that they should pray or how they should pray.

Maybe intercessory prayer is exactly that—we take their place before God and pray as they would, if they could.

Let me illustrate. Peggy, when I received your letter and let your frustration soak in, I began to feel what you were feeling. You were completely exhausted from praying. You are alone, no family, disfigured. You felt that asking for God's help was a complete waste of time.

I immediately prayed, "Father, Peggy's too beaten and bruised to know what to say to You. She doesn't even believe You care. But I know You do. So I'm standing in her place, asking You to meet her daily needs."

Peggy, I don't know how my saying your prayers for you makes a difference, but I know it does.

When I was eighteen years old I made the finals in the 100-yard dash in the biggest track meet of my life. My mom sent me a telegram which said, "Praying for you to win."

I lost. Came in fifth behind four guys I had beaten several times. I was bitter toward God. After the race, the coach yelled at me. My loss had cost us the overall championship. I tried to pray and couldn't.

I went to the bus. But I didn't sulk and lick my wounds. For some strange reason I rethought the race. I had broad-jumped, run the 220-yard dash, and anchored the relay before the race. Because of a foul-up with the clock, they scheduled the 100-yard dash as the last event of the day.

I realized that I had done the best I could *on that day*. I also realized that throughout my life I would lose contests I should win and win some I should lose. Life was like that race, but all of my life didn't depend on that race. If I couldn't handle this loss, I was in big trouble for the rest of my life.

When the coach came on the bus, he apologized and said I

had been one of the great joys of his career. He was recommending me for the state all-star football game.

Months later I learned that my grandmother had ridden a bus hundreds of miles to watch me run. She was in the stands. She said that just before the race, she prayed, "Father, don't let Jerry's performance in this race ruin his life."

When I lost so miserably, she prayed, "Lord, I know Jerry won't be able to pray after this. I also know that You can lead him to use this loss as a gain in his life. But since he can't pray, I'm doing it for him."

Now, Peggy, you tell me how my grandmother's prayer worked? I don't know the answer, but I know the result. I learned an invaluable lesson that day: how to lose and live through it.

Many times I have wondered what would have become of me had I won. Maybe nothing different. Maybe.

9

BIBLE 101

The Trustworthiness of Scripture

Dear Dr. Mann:

I am a longtime believer, but a short-time student of the Bible. At forty-four I have come to the realization that all of the things I trusted in when I was young just haven't worked.

I'm one of those disillusioned baby-boomers, I guess. I rebelled against organized religion and everything else my elders held dear. I believed that love and social reform could create utopia. I studied Zen and EST and smoked marijuana.

Now I'm married with small children and I'm the Establishment. I know that the answers to life's search lie in the spiritual realm. So I'm in a church and I'm advised weekly to study the Bible. It's supposed to be "God's Word," whatever that means. It's supposed to be inspired, a guidebook for living, and life's big answer book.

I can't make heads or tails of it. I know that Christians fight over it all the time. I'm not interested in their arguments. I want some help from the Bible.

Would you be willing to give me some suggestions on how to approach the Bible, understand it, and get some "food" from it? I'm not sure I believe everything in it. How can I be expected to trust something as obscure as a collection of sixty-six different kinds of stories? Some contain fanciful tales and myths. Some are made up of poems. Some are supposed to be historical narratives.

I need a condensed course in Bible 101.

Dear Alex:

You have asked an honest question which sends tremors through the religious community every time it is asked. All Christian denominations claim the Bible as their ultimate authority for faith and practice. This is especially true for Protestant groups. So, to question the authenticity of the Bible in any way is to strike at the heart of established religion.

However, your question about the reliability of the Bible and how to understand it must be answered. I receive numerous questions on the subject every week. We church leaders would prefer that people in general accept the authority of Scripture without question—especially *our interpretation* of Scripture. One of the reasons there are so many different denominations is because there are so many different "biblical authorities" who claim to hold *the key* to understanding the Bible.

I want to say up front, Alex, that I am not the holder of some new key. In fact, I don't believe there is one true method of interpreting the Bible. People will always come to the Bible with different needs. Because it is "God's Word" (I will explain what I mean by that term) it is a living thing which is there to meet different people on different need levels.

This means that we will never have one universally held method of understanding the Bible. God is alive and still working in our midst. Therefore, our understanding will continue to grow. There can be no *final understanding* of Scripture. The more we learn about ourselves and God and the world, the more we will have to alter our former views.

Alex, I think the best place to begin in responding to your questions about the Bible is to address the simple question: *What is the Bible?* How we answer this will determine how we study the Bible, what we mean when we call it the "Word of God," and how we depend upon it as our standard for doing and believing.

It would be easy to assume that we all know what the Bible is. Not so. It is seldom called anything but "God's Word," and that term is rarely defined. Some people think it's a rule book for living. Or it is a book of timeless laws—do's and don't's.

For me the Bible is a record of God's actions in history to redeem humankind—to lure people into a relationship with Him. It is the history of the acts of God. All sixty-six books are arranged around these *redemptive events*. They either describe the events and the people involved, or they interpret the meaning of the events, or they deal with questions which these events raise, or they speculate about the future results of these events.

Alex, the Bible is of one piece. Every book speaks to this redemptive effort of God to reach people. With this in mind, let me show you how the Bible can be seen as a whole.

The first eleven chapters of Genesis use mythical images to tell us that (1) God created everything, (2) He crowned His creation with beings who had a choice to accept or reject His love, and that (3) His plans went awry.

Then the long process of God's efforts to restore and right the ship of Creation begins to unfold. God decides to reach all people by making a covenant—a contract of love—with one man, Abraham, and his descendants.

In other words, God decides to reach people through other people (Israel). God's people are the ones who have a relationship (covenant) with Him. Their task is to trust God and obey only Him. His part of the bargain is to "bless" them, i.e., to be with them and care for them and all whom they bring to Him.

Almost immediately God's chosen people break their part of the bargain. The entire Old Testament after Genesis 12 is a repetition of God renewing the covenant and His people breaking it.

The redemptive events I spoke of begin with the call of

Abraham (Gen. 12). After a series of breakdowns and renewals between God and Abraham's offspring, the descendants end up as slaves in Egypt.

Then comes the second major act of God to carry on His plan to redeem the world: the Exodus—the deliverance from bondage and the formation of twelve tribes into one nation under the Laws of Moses given at Mt. Sinai.

But God's people break the covenant when they refuse to go into the Promised Land because they are afraid.

They wander for years as nomads until God raises up Joshua, renews the covenant, and they conquer other people.

The people break the covenant again and worship the foreign gods of the lands they've conquered. Enter the Dark Ages (Judges) where the nation is held together by heroic warlord types.

I won't go further here with biblical history. It's not my purpose. The point is that the Bible is rich and understandable when you see its rhythm. God makes a deal with a certain people who are to be his missionaries. They keep breaking the deal, and every time they do, God backs up and tries again, first through tribal patriarchs, then through deliverers, kings, prophets, priests, etc.

The different types of literature in the Old Testament either chronicle or reflect on God's redemptive efforts.

Finally, when all else fails, God makes His final move. He enters history in the flesh. The Old Covenant (Testament) of trying to redeem the world through one man (Abraham) and his descendants is finished. It's now back to one man, Jesus the Christ (the anointed one, Messiah).

God risks His own life as a human. He goes all the way to death without giving into the dark forces. Christ dies for all people and God raises Him up. God's redemptive work is finished. There is now a New Covenant (Testament). Whoever accepts Christ and His way is one of God's people and in right relationship with God.

Alex, this is the drama of the first four books of the New Testament, or the Gospels. The remainder of the New Testament is an account of what happened between God and early believers (Church), the believer's interpretation of it, and a mythical symbolic vision of the end of history (Revelation). Just as Genesis 1–11 is "pre-history" and therefore uses myth to convey its truth, so Revelation is "post-history" and must use symbolic imagery as well.

So, Alex, the Bible is of one piece. It is the record of God's redemption of the human race. It contains moral laws and lessons which should be applied to every historical era but it is not a morality manual. It has poetry, allegory, and legends which are invaluable to us. But it is not just "good literature." It is the story of what God has done and will do to finally win all of us to His love.

Okay, that's what the Bible is. Now for your question about its reliability. Is it infallible? Does it have errors? Are we to believe the fanciful parts where axeheads swim and people live to be hundreds of years old?

I think the Bible is totally reliable *in its purpose*, that is, in telling us who God is and who we are and how we are to experience our potential as human beings. In other words, the Bible is infallible in revealing God's redemptive plan. It is not a science book, as we showed earlier. Many parts of it are not interested in being historically accurate. (There are two different dates given for the time of the Exodus, for example.)

The important question is whether the Bible remains an effective tool in reconciling people to God. It certainly does. Therefore, it is reliable.

Concerning the "fanciful tales" and miracles of the Bible, I want to make four brief comments. First, a miracle is anything which changes the hearts of people from self-centeredness to God-centeredness. "Hollywood-special-effects" miracles are not miracles if they don't turn hateful people into loving people, greedy people into generous people, etc.

Second, I wouldn't be surprised if someday we evolve to the place where we can explain in *our naturalistic terms* almost all of the biblical occurrences which we now call "supernatural." In my lifetime I have seen supernatural phenomena become natural phenomena simply because we now understand how they work and how to make them happen.

Third, I believe in the literal bodily resurrection of Jesus. I believe He died and that God gave Him life again. I do not ascribe to the hidden-body/Passover-plot theories. Without the resurrection of Jesus, the Christian faith is a farce not worth our time. If I can believe that God raised Jesus from the dead, I can believe other as-yet-unexplained phenomena in the Bible.

Fourth, I have no doubt that the Bible contains exaggerations and myths as I defined "myth" earlier. Myth does not depend on literalness in order to convey truth. To say that some biblical personage lived 300 years *means* that he was a super-anointed partner with God. He was "unlike" others. I agree with Madeline L'Engle and others who say that the best way to destroy mythical religious truth is to attempt to literalize it.

So, Alex, the Bible is the story of redemption and it is reliable in relating that story. It rests upon the one foundation that God is a God of love who has and does act in history to re-establish ties with His people. He is the "hound of heaven" who will not rest until He gets us all. The Bible is not God. It is a story about the acts of God. To worship the Bible is an idolatry.

This brings me to the subject of inspiration. What do we mean when we say the Bible is inspired? Some mean that God dictated it word for word to the original writers. This position is so obviously impossible to defend that I won't dwell on it beyond asking a simple question: If God dictated it, then why did He dictate four different versions of the life and work of Jesus?

My view is that God acted in history. There were people who witnessed these acts and saw nothing extraordinary about them at all. But there were others who saw them as divine, redemptive interventions. This is inspiration—to see God where others do not.

They told what they had been inspired to see. Some wrote down what they had experienced. Others vocalized their experiences in stories. The stories were retold, passed down orally like many stories of Native American religion. The stories were written down after several years of oral tradition.

Alex, when you look at inspiration this way, you can easily see why there are four different versions of the lifework of Jesus. God did not violate the personal traits of the writers and seers. The Gospels were tailored to the mentality of the recipients as well. Matthew is obviously directed toward Jews, Mark toward Greeks, Luke toward cosmopolitans, and John toward those who would pollute the Gospel with Gnostic philosophy.

Before I give you some practical suggestions on how to "get into" the Bible, Alex, I want to say something about interpreting it. There are several principles which help me.

First, it is important to know what kind of literature you're reading. Is it historical narrative? Is it poetry? Is it allegory? Is it a law code?

For example, the Book of Jonah is an allegory or parable, designed to scold Israel for keeping its religious truth to itself and not having missionary zeal. Jonah (Israel) doesn't want to share God with the heathen of Nineveh for fear they will turn to God. He would rather see them suffer judgment. He can't bear to think of Syrians and Israelites as brothers.

So he runs from God and ends up in the belly of the great fish (Egyptian and Babylonian captivity).

Next it is important to know the historical context of the passages you're reading. Who was talking? What were the circumstances? Who was the audience? What does the writer want the audience to do?

Third, let systematic passages dictate the incidental passages. If you're going to search for what the Bible says about Christian morality, for example, use the Sermon on the Mount (Matt. 5–7). Don't pick one verse which mentions a moral issue in passing. Another example: If you want to know what the Bible says about how people get right with God, read Romans 1–8, or Ephesians. Paul discusses the subject systematically. Do not pluck one verse from a sermon being preached by an Apostle in Acts to build your belief system.

The fourth principle for me as a Christian is the Jesus principle. I read the Old Testament through the New Testament. I spoke earlier of how God had to accommodate His revelation of Himself to the primitive mentality of people so as not to compel them to believe. I believe that Jesus is the clearest revelation of God's will that we have. I read both Testaments through what Jesus said.

The fifth principle which helps me interpret the Bible is what I call the "means-what-it-means" principle. The Bible does not mean what it says, it means what it means. For example, Jesus says, "I am the door." Well, He's not a hole in the wall! He *means* that He is the way to God.

Alex, do not be taken in by those who claim to take the Bible literally. Word for word. They all must and do interpret the words to *mean* something.

Will Campbell tells of a religious meeting where a resolution was passed declaring that every word of the Bible is to be taken literally. A preacher next to him cheered when the vote was taken. Campbell said, "Are you one of those who takes every word of the Bible literally?"

"You're danged tootin'!" said the preacher.

"Good," said Campbell, "can you round up a dozen more brothers who believe that?"

"Sure can."

"Great," said Campbell. "Go get 'em and let's go down to the local prison and open all of the doors and release all of the criminals!"

"You're crazy!" said the preacher.

"I am?" replied Will. "Well Jesus told us that He had come to set all of the captives free and He wants us to do the same thing!"

"That's not what He meant," declared the preacher.

"Well, it's what He said!" Campbell had made his point.

Alex, now for the practical suggestions I promised. First, get yourself a translation of the Bible which you can understand. King James English is hard for me to understand. There are several good translations which express the biblical message in everyday English.

I would start by reading the Gospel of Mark. It's short and it fits the Western mindset best. Then I would read Acts, which tells of the early church and its missionary efforts.

I would then read the Letter to Hebrews. It fits the Christ event into the entire Judeo-Christian history.

From that point I would go outside the Bible and read surveys of the two Testaments. Then I would read Genesis, Exodus, Joshua, I Kings and II Kings. Then Isaiah and Jeremiah.

I would return to the New Testament after this and read Matthew, Romans, and Galatians. With that done I would launch out anywhere I chose.

Personally, I read the Psalms and Proverbs once a month, a little each day.

Alex, I love the Bible, but I don't worship it. It serves as a good barometer and "corrector" of my thoughts and actions. As I grow older, I am amazed at how modern human sciences continue to reconfirm the biblical view of human nature and how it is fulfilled.

The Bible is a living thing, Alex. It throbs with real-life dilemmas and victories and tragedies. It beats with the heart of God. When I call it "God's Word," I mean that it is the sum of what God has to say to all people for all time about His love and intentions toward them.

10

ONE TIMES ONE IS ONE
Understanding the Trinity

Dear Dr. Mann:

I am confused about the Trinity. How could God be one and three at the same time? Also, I hear preachers speak of the Father, the Holy Spirit and Jesus as if they were three different personalities. Does the Bible explain this?

I know it says that Jesus and God were the same, yet Jesus prayed to the Father. How could this be? I've heard that being saved by Jesus is one experience and receiving the Holy Spirit another separate experience.

I am not playing a "curiosity game" in asking you these questions. I accepted Christ as my Savior when I was eleven. I have tried to serve him as best I can. Yet, I am now being told that until I meet all three persons of the Trinity I am not saved.

Dr. Mann, I want to be right with God. If I need something else besides what I already have, I am willing to receive it. Please help me.

Dear Berniece:

I receive many more questions about the Trinity than I expected. At first I chalked them up to those who have nothing more to do than discuss trivia.

However, I have come to see that there is something more serious to these questions, and your letter says it well. The Trinity—that ancient doctrine which says God is Father, Son, and Holy Spirit all at the same time—is being misused. It was once the interest of clergy, professors, and a few laypersons only. But in recent times it is being used as leverage to motivate sincere people to reach for "something more" in their pilgrimage with God. Something more isn't bad unless it's a bait designed to manipulate people.

Let me begin by saying that the Bible never uses the word *Trinity*. The King James version of John 5:7 reads, "There are three that bear record in Heaven, the Father, the Word, and the Holy Ghost: and these three are One." Modern scholarship has proved that this verse was changed years after our earliest manuscripts of John, none of which translates the verse this way.

Paul signs off 2 Corinthians by saying "The grace of our Lord Jesus Christ, the love of God, and the fellowship of the Holy Spirit be with you all."

So Berniece, although the Bible refers to God as Father, Son and Holy Spirit in numerous places, it does not present a formally stated doctrine of the Trinity. In the years immediately following the New Testament era, Christians were busy trying to formulate official belief systems or creeds. They were being attacked by Greek thinkers, especially concerning the biblical references to God as Father, Son, and Holy Spirit.

In the world of Greek logic, which is the ancestor of our Western mentality, the most fundamental principle was that A could not be *A* and *B* at the same time. When this principle was applied to the Trinity, it caused the early Church intellectual misery.

The early Church spent almost three hundred years trying to explain the Trinity in a way that would satisfy Greek logic. Elaborate theories and illustrations were cranked out endlessly. In the end the Trinity was declared a mystery but embraced as true nonetheless.

Berniece, this was and is a useless quest. The writers of the Bible experienced God the same way we do. I ponder the heavens at large and the makeup of an atom "at small," and I marvel at God the Progenitor-Father of all that is.

Then I read the words and works of Jesus and I say along with the soldier at the cross, "Surely this man was the Son of God!"

I listen to Jesus tell His disciples, "I am going back to the Father, but you will not be left alone. God will come back to you in another way, as an indwelling divine presence" (John 14). And that is exactly my experience. When I experience God in "my insides," He is a power-source of spirit.

In short, I experience God sometimes as Father, sometimes as Son, and sometimes as Holy Spirit. The Trinity is not some formal doctrine and was never meant to be. It is an actual way of experiencing God on a daily basis.

There's only one God, and we experience Him in three ways. Can He be two or three places at once in two or three forms? Who cares? I don't. Whenever God comes to me, He is God and I know it's Him.

You asked whether experiencing salvation in Jesus and receiving the Holy Spirit were two separate experiences. The Book of Acts is the main source of this notion. Again, I think much time is wasted on this discussion.

Jesus said God would be present in the world in a new way—the Holy Spirit. Early converts were asked to believe in Jesus and to link up with Him in His current spiritual form.

Berniece, I am not trying to belittle anyone or make light of hundreds of years of labor on the subject of the Trinity. I am simply trying to say that it should have been left in the realm of personal encounter with God and left out of the scholarly wranglings of the clergy.

I'm also saying that using the Holy Spirit as a means of

manufacturing ecstatic trances is a travesty. When people encounter God, they encounter all of Him, not a piece at a time.

My main concern for you, Berniece, is that you not be manipulated into thinking there is some little exotic refinement which will at last allow you to reach the top rung of the spiritual ladder.

It is true that we all can and must grow. Commitment to God is a one-step-at-a-time lifelong trek. But throughout that trek there is one God who is with us all the way. Sometimes we feel Him as Father, sometimes as Son, and sometimes as Holy Spirit.

11

WHY DO THE WICKED PROSPER?
The Issue of Divine Justice

Dear Dr. Mann:

I have a thirty-eight-year-old daughter who put her husband through medical school. They have three children. He is a fine surgeon.

Two years ago when they finally began to prosper after struggling financially for years, he ups and leaves her for a twenty-two-year-old "trophy wife." He sends some child-support but not enough.

My daughter has had to return to work and is trying to raise the kids alone. My former son-in-law is just sailing along like a dream. He has money, a mansion, maids, and a child-bride who worships him.

Dr. Mann, why does God allow people without principles to have it so well, while their victims suffer? It just isn't fair. I watch my daughter trying to raise those kids and refusing to say one negative word about their father to them and my heart breaks.

Dear Joyce:

Your cry, "Why do the wicked prosper?" echoes throughout history. It is also a frequent question in the Bible. The Psalms ask it. Job asks it. The prophet Habakkuk complains to God, "The law is useless and justice is never done. Evil men get the better of the righteous, and so justice is perverted" (Hab. 1:4).

Jeremiah says, "Lord...I question you about matters of justice. Why are the wicked men so prosperous?" (Jer.12:1).

I have about worn out the explanation that God allows people to be wicked because He wants them to have a choice to be good. I won't pursue it further here. But it's worth pursuing still.

Joyce, what's happened to your daughter *is* unfair! There are no two ways about it. Things should not be this way. Your anger is justified.

My first word to you is: Don't let your son-in-law's actions turn you into someone like him. I don't remember who said, "If in order to defeat the beast, I become the beast then bestiality wins." I thank him for it though.

Your anger can curdle into a sourness which will give your three grandchildren one more bad memory of their childhood— a bitter grandma. I know you don't want that to happen.

Also, I cannot believe for a minute that your former son-in-law is all that happy. From your account, he seems to be shallow. Anyone with the brains to become a surgeon could not be insensitive enough to abandon his family without suffering inwardly.

It sounds as if he was never much on relationships. No one "prospers" inwardly unless he can love and be loved. He will buy one toy after another and treat people as toys to be used until he either grows up or becomes one of his things. He can have that kind of "prosperity" for all I care.

Joyce, as harsh as this may sound, I think your daughter's current situation may be better than what she would have had were she still married to the guy. She may have more toys, but she would probably be dying on the inside along with him.

I'm saying, don't be so quick to envy his life-style. It's probably not what it's cracked up to be. But even if it is, you will only become more unhappy by constantly comparing what is to what might have been. As long as you do that, he still rules your life and adds to its misery.

Your grandchildren have also been spared the "rich kid" syndrome. Some of the most purposeless people I've known are those of second-generation wealth. Trust-fund kids have the trophies but never run the race. And believe me, running the race is where the fulfillment is. The chase is more fun than the prize.

Also think of this: You have an opportunity to "mentor" your grandchildren in a way which would otherwise not have been open to you. A *mentor* is an adult, other than the children's parents, who loves them unconditionally and treats them as "apprentices" of life.

Every child needs someone besides the parents to bestow "the gift of delight," to say: "I take great delight in you simply because you *are!*"

Joyce, a little of that goes a long way with children. Without any of it, they die inwardly. But with just a little, they can overcome life's biggest hurts. This is your mission. On the other hand, to add to their burden by cursing their father would be tantamount to joining him.

For you to spend your life reminding the kids of how terribly they have been wronged will only make them grow up thinking the world owes them something. Or worse still, it will give them an easy excuse for not living a decent, fruitful life.

Joyce, I'm not trying to lay a guilt trip on you. I'm just being as candid as I know how to be. The best thing you can ever do for your grandchildren and yourself is to let go of this hatred and resentment.

That's what forgiveness is—letting go of the feelings that result from being hurt. Forgiveness is not forgetting. Whoever thought up the phrase "forgive and forget" did a number on us.

The Bible says God "remembers our sins no more," but we are not God.

You cannot forget what this man did to your daughter. You cannot change what he did. You cannot keep him from prospering. Jesus said, "God causes the rain to fall on the just and the unjust alike."

The only thing you can change, Joyce, is the way you respond to the wrong done to you and yours. Here is where God comes in. Granted, He didn't stop your son-in-law from injuring your family. In fact, it appears that materially speaking, He blessed him.

But God is with you in the "responding business." He will help you find the grace to stop allowing your son-in-law's offense to control you. God doesn't exempt us from being injured, but He's with us in the midst of the fight to overcome our injuries.

How do we connect with God's help? This is the key question. I can only tell you what works for me. First, I take the spotlight of judgment off of the person who has offended me and shine it on myself. I ask myself if I am pure enough to qualify for judging another.

Obviously, the answer is no. Joyce, I believe that the heart of faith is to leave justice in the hands of God and to trust that He will take care of matters. I hear a lot of holy-babble from pulpits (I am one of the babblers) about faith in God.

Real faith is the decision not to play God in righting the wrongs we cannot right. Real faith is entrusting God with the business of vengeance. We are not qualified to avenge the world's wrongs.

The second thing I do when I've been wronged is try to place myself in the offender's shoes . . . to get inside his head and try to think like he thinks. In your case, it would mean trying to feel and think like your son-in-law.

That's abhorrent to you? I know. Maybe you can't get very far but try. Think this way: What must it be like to lack the inward courage to stick with one's commitments? How awful to be a coward! Think of the time you've been a coward. We've all had our moments of failing to live up to the best in ourselves.

You know how it feels when you know you could've done better but lost your nerve. William Glasser says that most human failure is due to the lack of courage. We don't lose excess weight, or stop smoking, or check our tempers because we haven't the courage.

Well, multiply your cowardice several times, Joyce, and you will know how your son-in-law feels. What a desperate grasping "little" man he must be!

I'm trying to share how I prepare my own soul to allow God to take away my resentment. I've said two things so far. First, I look at my own sins. Second, I try to get inside the offender and feel what he's feeling.

Third, I try to talk to him if possible. I simply want to see him up close. As long as he is at a distance he is not a person to me. He is an object—something impersonal which I can hate from afar.

Sometimes, Joyce, when I've done these three things over and over for a long period of time, a miracle happens. The resentment just vanishes...sometimes instantly but most of the time gradually.

It would help you to read the biblical story of Joseph's forgiving his brothers (Genesis 50). He did exactly what I've suggested to you. They had sold him into slavery as a youth. Now, he is the second highest authority in Egypt and has the power to hurt them. Instead he "lets-it-go."

First, he says, "Who am I to judge you? I am not God!" Then he says, "What you did to me was meant to hurt me,

93

that's for sure. But God used it to save His people."

No doubt Joseph placed himself inside his brothers' heads. When they wronged him, they were driven by jealousy. They had been weak. But Joseph had taunted them by reminding them that he was his father's favorite son. He knew he was not guilt-free.

Most of all Joseph decided to let God be God and to use the wrong done to him to build his character.

Joyce, this sounds "high and mighty," I know. But you really only have two choices: to wallow in bitterness or to use the wrong to make something better. It's either bitterness or "betterness."

I do not know why the wicked prosper at the expense of the innocent. I do know that I am not innocent. I do know that there's a day coming when God will sort out the wrongs and rights. We will reap what we sow. And I do know that God is with me most when I am injured most.

You must choose one of two paths. The path of bitterness will simply compound the wrongs done to you. The path of letting-go leads to life. I would like to talk to your grandchildren and daughter twenty years from now.

12

WILL THERE BE ANY MOSLEMS IN HEAVEN?
Comparative Religion

Dear Dr. Mann:

In my secret heart I feel that I am a Christian because I was born in a Christian home in America. Had I been born into a Confucian family in China, I would probably be Confucian.

All of my life I have heard preachers say that the only way to heaven is through Jesus. If I've heard John 14:6 quoted once, I've heard it a thousand times. "I am the way the truth and the life, and no one comes to the Father, except by me."

How could God reject people who sincerely hold to another religious belief? I know that religion is one of the chief causes of strife in the world. Moslems call us infidels and vice versa. I'm beginning to think that we humans just invented gods which suit our particular cultures the best.

I know this makes me sound like an atheist, but I'm really not. I know God exists. I've met him in Jesus. His Spirit lives in me. I just can't see how God could send someone to Hell or deprive them of Heaven because of where they were born. Can you help?

Dear Charles:

I'm going to respond to your questions in two ways. First, I want to personally reassure you that you are not some kind of heretic. Second, I want to speak to the larger subject of relations between the world's great religions. There is not a more important issue facing humankind than how to overcome the enmity caused by religious intolerance.

Charles, you are not an atheist. Anyone with an inquisitive mind should and does ask the questions you're asking. You are correct. Had you been born into a family devoted to another religious faith, you would probably be of that faith as well. Of the many religions in the world, most have a distinctively national character. Only four: Judaism, Christianity, Islam, and Buddhism have an international vision and acceptance.

These four have many things in common. They all believe in the reality of a spiritual realm which is other than the physical. They all believe in a heaven of some kind—or at least certain groups within these faiths do. They all believe in prayer. They all have sacred scriptures which they believe are God-given.

This doesn't mean, Charles, that one religion is as good as another, or that it doesn't matter what you believe, just as long as you're sincere about it.

Personally, I choose to think in terms of which religious belief-system accounts best for all of human experience—scientific, spiritual, intellectual, etc.,—and *most of all*, brings people together. The best religion binds people together. The worst tears them apart. Good religion is inclusive. Bad religion is exclusive. Good religion centers in unifying all people with each other and with God.

Now let me respond to your specific question: Are all non-Christians rejected eternally by God? Of course not! That narrow view simply won't square with the God of the Bible.

But what about scripture passages which claim that Jesus is the "only way." You mentioned the John 14:6 verse where Jesus says "no one comes to the Father except by me." I think it means that people cannot know God as a loving Father unless they relate to Him in Jesus' way of relating. I do not think it means that no one can know God *in any way* without Jesus. Paul says in Romans 1 that all people can discern the existence of a Creator by simply looking at the created order. I also believe that Jesus is the Redeemer of all people whether or not they know it.

Besides if you want to claim Christianity as the only true religion, you have to ask, which kind of Christianity? Catholicism? Mormonism? David Koreshianism? Jim Jonesism?

Charles, no one has the exclusive path to God. I think God has revealed himself to all humans in many ways since they first evolved to a capacity for relationship with Him. Every culture has tailored its experience of God to meet its needs. In so doing, every culture has also corrupted and used these revelations to its own ends.

This was the heart of Jesus' conflict with the Judaism of his day. The religious powers had tried to freeze God in their time-frame and confine Him to their nationalistic agenda. Jesus had a wider vision. Mohammed, the founder of Islam, made a similar break but to the right side of the spectrum. Buddhism is a similar reform-reaction to Hinduism.

God always reveals Himself to people. He does not stay hidden. And people always try to reduce these revelations to their own manageable proportions. They try to capture God within their own tastes and politics and national borders and creeds.

So Charles, there is no use in talking about which religion is the true one. We can only search for the *truest* one—the least corrupted and accommodated one. It is this kind of humility which will allow people of different faiths to embrace each other. I know this is true because I have many friends from different faiths. They are friends because their religion has shown them that we have the same Father and therefore the same lineage.

What about Heaven and Hell and who's going? I covered this earlier (Chapter 5). But I want to simply say here that I'm not in charge of that. I'm only in charge of how I respond to the God of my own experiences and whether I faithfully share that experience throughout my life. There is a kind of sick mentality which appears in all of the major religions. I call it the Leather-and-Whip Syndrome. It seeks punishment. It will not be satisfied unless some flesh is burned and some hair is singed. It anticipates Judgment Day with a sense of glee. It gets "epileptic over the apocalyptic!"

I can only say that on Judgment Day I plan to blend with the crowd. It's perfectly okay with me if God seeks *no* vengeance. For I'll be in the line of fire if He does.

I am a Christian by choice. As I said earlier, I met God as a transcendent reality before I saw Him in the person of Jesus. I studied several faiths before I came to the New Testament.

The Judaeo-Christian worldview fits best with the worldview discovered by science. Take the concept of history as linear, meaning it has a beginning and an ending. We know that the earth is a finite organism. Someday when the sun becomes a dying star, it will suck the earth into its fires. The idea of history as an unending cycle is not viable.

Also the idea of the union of matter and spirit in the Incarnation (the enfleshment of God) gives value to both in a way which no other religion does.

In Chapters 1–7, I spoke of how to reconcile a God who is both sovereign and good with the existence of evil and suffering. My entire philosophy rests upon the notion that God will eventually bring good out of evil beyond this time, and that we as individual persons will survive eternally. The proof is the death and Resurrection of Jesus.

Eastern religion—Buddhism, Hinduism, etc.—has no such promise. The desire for individualism is evil in itself. Hope is centered in escaping the unending world cycle, not in finding meaning in it. Karma is the inexorable law of punishment which leads to ignoring human suffering and insuring social castes.

Charles, these are a few of the reasons I choose to be a Christian. But I am not the only person God loves or intends to redeem. I have met God personally. I keep meeting Him in Jesus Christ who lives. This I know for sure. But I am not prepared to limit God to my own small experience. I have met too many saintly people from other religions to believe that God can be contained by one cultural or religious bias.

In short, I believe in a "way of doing life" where you love the God of your experience as hard as you can and you love your neighbor as you love yourself. This *way* is of God. Religion is what we humans have done with this *way*. The original followers of Jesus were called "Followers of the Way." After years of human doctrinal formation, ritual, and organization the way came to be called "Christianity."

13

DOES THE CHURCH DISPROVE GOD?
The Authenticity of Organized Religion

Dear Dr. Mann:

*I was raised in the church. My parents took me with them
Sunday mornings, Sunday evenings, Wednesday nights, and
any other time the doors were open. Before I was out of high
school I witnessed four church splits, two ministers caught
chasing women (and catching a few), and two elders having a
fistfight on the church steps.*

*Also, I had the daylights scared out of me every Spring and
Fall when professional evangelists came to town to heat up the
fires of Hell for sinners like me. I was baptized three times in
ten years. The evangelists were successful in convincing me
each time that I was not secure in God's favor, and I didn't
want to risk being rejected by Him.*

*My point is that the church is the best evidence I have that
there is no God. If God is who the Bible says He is, and His
people are the church, I want no part of Him.*

*I have tried to take my family to church over the years
because I hoped my bad experiences as a child were the exception. We visited several different churches. My hopes were
dashed. The sermons were boringly redundant. The people
were unfriendly. There was little help for families, which is
why we went in the first place! All we heard were hellfire and
brimstone on the one hand or lectures on equal rights and mil-
itarism on the other.*

And then, of course, there were the unending appeals for

money... money for buildings, money for the poor, money-money-money!

Dr. Mann, when I was very young I would pray with my grandfather. He was a sweet and gentle man and my closest friend. He never missed church and seemed to ignore all of the negatives. When he died I thought the church would be my haven of hope and comfort. I searched for someone like him in the church but couldn't find anyone.

I now believe that my grandfather and all the people like him are the only "gods" who exist. If there were one true God, the church would reflect Him.

I know this letter sounds bitter. I have never said these words to anyone, including my wife and children. They don't know that I don't believe in God. We have become a close, loving, but non-church-going family.

I guess I would like to believe in the God of my childhood, or I would not have taken the time to write this. But if God is active in the world, it can't be through the churches of my experience. Could you comment?

Dear Andy:

Over the years, many people have suggested that the church is corrupt, hypocritical, out of touch, and out of date. But I never realized until I received your letter that questions about "God's Worth" could be tied to the church's flaws.

You have shown me that the sins of organized religion are in the same category as the suffering of the innocent. They cause people to wonder if God is something we humans invented in order to control other humans or to create a false security against the threats which accompany living and dying.

I thank you for your candor. You have opened my eyes to a

new insight: A corrupt church—or to be more kind—a church which does not channel God's love and grace into the hearts of people, is a church which causes them to question God's very existence.

So, I am grateful for your letter. But I am also sad. My first inclination is to be defensive and tell you all of the reasons I think you are misguided. I have the urge to remind you that your experience is limited. I want to tell you that you probably believe in God. You just don't believe in the one you met in the church of your youth. There are many congregations and denominations who help millions of people every day. The very notions of the sacredness of every human being, and the liberation movements of history are church born. I have been all over the world and seen hundreds of schools, hospitals, and orphanages which bear the names of churches. I have never seen one such institution bearing the name of an atheist or anti-church society.

I am tempted to tell you all about my wonderful church which stands as a contradiction to the churches of your experience.

But, Andy, to tell you the truth, these arguments are reactions, not responses. They might give some comfort to church folk who read this, but they won't help you. And that's what I want to do.

How to do this? To begin with I agree with you: Organized religion does not appear to be a very strong proof of God's existence. It is a solid proof that sinners gather to celebrate and learn and energize each other. It proves that humans are religious by nature; but it doesn't prove that the God they worship is real.

Anyone who thinks that the organized church is the "place" to find God is chasing an illusion. And the automatic result of "illusionment" is disillusionment. Andy, you were disillusioned because someone gave you the illusion that the church was God. So, when the church injured you and let you down it took away "your God."

Andy, the church is not God. But it is *God's*. God has chosen to show people who and what He is *through other people*. These people are what we call the church. The biblical word for church is *ecclesia*, meaning "the ones called out" to show God to others.

But here's the problem, Andy: The people need a way to tell others—an organized way, an institution. They need a set of beliefs, a structure, a "bucket" to carry God in. The same thing has always happened. They tend to end up worshipping the bucket God comes in.

This is what you've experienced, Andy. People gather and do the same-old-same-old. The preacher says the same-old. The people fight over the color of the bucket, who gets to hold the handle, etc.

Nevertheless, God continues with His same strategy to reach people with people. If the "Bucket Worshippers" don't tune in, God goes elsewhere. More often He uses the rusty buckets in spite of themselves and reaches people. That's because there are still people like your grandfather, Andy.

You said, "He ignored the negatives." He kept his relationship with God in spite of the flawed church and its misguided people.

Andy, there is always a "church within a church." There are people whose faith is not secondhand. They walk and talk with God, while others tinker with the bucket.

The Bible has a recurring theme about "The Remnant." The Remnant has existed almost from the beginning of God's decision to call certain people to tell other people about Him. The Remnant is made up of a few who don't confuse God with the bucket which He comes in (organized and ritualized religion).

When the majority loses its ties with the driving force within (God) and dies off, the Remnant is always left over to revive and renew.

No doubt your grandfather was part of the Remnant—the "church within the church." He would cringe to hear you call him and all of the people like him *gods*. But he would be pleased to know that the way he lived and related to you has continued to stick with you through all of your years of disillusionment with organized religion. In other words, he would be glad to know that he was God's conduit to you. He was "the church"—not God, but God's. God used him to show a child what God is really like.

And yes, Andy, you would like to believe in the God of your childhood. I would like for you to believe in Him as well. You are right, you don't need the God of secondhand, overgrown institutionalism. You need the God of Grace and help, the God your grandfather knew.

Where to find Him? How to connect with Him? That's a one-to-one experience. God has no grandchildren. You must come to Him ready to change the center of your life. Him at the center, self ready for service.

This is the place to start, Andy. It's the same place your grandfather started. And it was the thing which set him apart from the others. He knew God other than by hearsay. Your grandfather's religion can't be yours by inheritance. You have to meet God on your own. He doesn't live at church either!

Then what? Well, you will find that God wants you to be a conduit too. And what does that mean? Probably it means linking up with others who are on the same track. You need them and they need you. You have the same father, so you must be one family.

And here we go again, Andy. We're back to your dreaded word, *church!* A church is a group of sinners who have joined hands to help each other in the task of showing God to others. It is not a Sacred Society of Secluded Saints! It's a hospital and Good News agency.

Let's say you're correct in your assessment that no such family of faith exists in your community. And let's say that you and a few others of the Remnant start one. Well, how and what are you going to believe? What are you going to do when you gather? Who's going to lead and who's going to follow?

You can see where I'm headed. You'll have to make a bucket to carry your faith in—a *human-made* bucket. Since it's a bucket made by sinners, it won't be long until someone decides the bucket is more important than its contents.

You get the point. The church is not God. It is flawed and filled with sinners. It must constantly be torn down and/or renovated.

But the church is God's, and therefore it will endure. People have been writing the church's epitaph for centuries. They're all dead. Many are buried in church graveyards. Stones with epitaphs mark *their* places of decay.

Andy, I began by saying that organized religion is not a very convincing proof of God's existence. I said this because you have been so bruised by the church. And, I said it because I have been somewhat of an iconoclast all of my life. I feel that we must constantly "grind all of the sacred cows into hamburgers."

The church is forever trying to freeze its beliefs and practices in time, while God is a dynamic God. God continues to reveal Himself and unfold in our understanding. Therefore, the church must change or get left behind.

But having said that, I want to tell you that after all of these years I have come to see that the church is indeed a proof of God's existence. Nothing else could have suffered so much corruption and abuse from people and still have survived! The church is always dying and being reborn.

Why? Not because of human effort. In fact, throughout history, the church has flourished best when people were trying to kill it the most! And the opposite is also true. The church dies every time it cozies up to its culture. The deadest churches in the world today are those that are in bed with their governments.

As I said, the real church, Andy, is the church within the church—the Remnant. They are the people who carry their faith in whatever bucket is necessary. But they always know the difference between the bucket and God.

Andy, no wonder you think the church proves there is no God. You've confused God with the bucket. Whenever people tell me they don't believe in God, I ask them to describe the God they don't believe in. Most of the time I don't believe in that God either. I certainly don't believe in the God shown by those who bruised you, Andy. I do believe in the one shown by your grandpa. Reconnect with that one.

14

WHY DID JESUS HAVE TO DIE?
Understanding the Atonement

Dear Dr. Mann:

All of my life I've been taught that Jesus paid for my sins by dying on the cross. They say if He hadn't died, I couldn't be saved. I understand that the cross is the greatest symbol of God's love. It represents how far God will go to save me. He sent His Son to die for me.

But there are some confusing issues I don't understand. For example, who had to be paid for my sins. The Devil? God? Why would God owe the Devil anything? The Devil's not God's creditor!

And why would God have to pay Himself by killing His son? Is God the kind of God who must have bloodshed in order to be satisfied? If so, doesn't that make Him a slave to His emotions? Couldn't God just forgive because He wants to?

I mentioned bloodshed. When I was growing up in church we sang the "Blood-Songs." The preacher talked about how Jesus' blood washed away our sins. The whole business of blood having to be shed to appease an angry god shows up in every ancient history I've read. Either people or animals are sacrificed to get or keep in the good graces of some god.

Dr. Mann, I find it hard to believe that God could kill someone as good as Jesus in order to satisfy some law higher than Himself.

Yet, when I read of Jesus' willingness to give His life for everyone, including me, I am moved in a way I cannot explain.

There's something about the cross which lets me know I belong to God, and yet at the same time I question why I would want to belong to Him if He's bloodthirsty. Could you help me unravel some of this?

Dear Nancy:

Your questions have sent tremors through the halls of Christian learning for centuries. The answers have caused more strife among the orthodox than any other issue. Volumes have been written, blood has been shed, and bodies burned over the issue of Atonement. (How did Christ's crucifixion atone, or pay for, our sins?)

First, let me give you a brief overview of the history of your question. Let's start with the Bible. As was the case with the Trinity which I dealt with in Chapter 10, the word *atonement* is not used in the New Testament. The King James version of Romans 5:11 uses the word "atonement." However, the Greek word clearly means "reconciliation" or "reunion." The passage means that through Christ's death, God has once again closed the relational gap between people and God. He has reconciled with us.

In fact, this is the meaning of the crucifixion period. Christ's death has cleared away all of the obstacles between us and God. The question, of course, is How?

Nancy, the answer has always been given according to the understanding of people at their particular time. For example, the people in Palestine and the Mediterranean world of Jesus' time had believed for centuries that sin could only be removed by blood sacrifice. As you say in your letter, ancient people were forever sacrificing animals or people to appease an angry god.

The altars of Judaism and other Middle-Eastern faiths reeked of blood. So when the biblical writers called Jesus the Lamb slain for the sins of the world, they were using a symbolism which everyone could understand. There could be no forgiveness without blood-sacrifice.

This image no longer has the meaning that it once had, unless your God is angry and demands someone's blood. It was certainly appropriate in the First Century, and it carries powerful meaning for us today provided we interpret and adapt it to our times.

This adaptation has been going on for centuries. The Early church fathers heard the central message of Christ: "God was in Christ reconciling the world to himself" (2 Cor. 5:19). They also knew that Christ's death was God's central act in bringing about this reconciliation. They also needed to explain the atonement in terms of Greek thought.

So they began to develop theories on how the cross created the reunion. The Ransom Theory emerged. Basically it said that because of human sin, the Devil controlled the human spirit. God gave His son up as a ransom to buy humans back. Then He fooled the Devil and raised Jesus from the dead.

Nancy, you pointed out the fallacy of this theory when you asked why God would owe the Devil anything.

You are not the first one to recognize problems with the Ransom Theory. About a thousand years after Christ, a new theory emerged which was aimed at the Roman mind. According to Roman Law, every sin has to be compensated or punished. A sin against God, however, caused a special problem. No finite human could properly repay an infinite God. Only God's Son would do.

Anselm, a church thinker, came up with a new way to explain Jesus' death. Jesus had to die to repay the righteous side of God's nature. In other words, God gave His son to die in order to satisfy Himself! As Harry Emerson Fosdick said in *Dear Mr. Brown*, "Try fitting (that theory) into Jesus' parable of the Prodigal Son!...These legalistic theories of the Atonement are a disgrace."

In this century two other explanations have emerged which again show how our understanding of the cross changes with our understanding of ourselves, God, and the world. The meaning doesn't change but our application must.

One was called the Substitutionary Theory. Basically it means that Jesus took our place and suffered as our substitute. He went to the gallows, so to speak, in our place.

The other theory is called the Vicarious Theory. It says that in order for any bad thing to get better, someone has to take the evil as his or her responsibility and defeat it. Poverty, crime, racism, tyranny, etc., don't cure themselves. Someone has to be the sacrificial lamb, i.e., the vicarious fighter who takes on evil and defeats it so that the rest of us can be free from it.

Personally, Nancy, both of these theories have meaning for me. Like you, I think of the cross and I know that my forgiveness depends upon what Christ did there. It is a mystery to me, yet it is real.

Jesus did indeed take my place as a substitute. He faced and conquered sin and death in my place. He wasn't compensating the Devil or some part of God's legalistic nature. He was doing *my* dying for me and *my* conquering for me. He blazed the trail through the wilderness on my behalf. Vicariously, He stood on the front line against evil *in my place!*

To me, the cross means that Jesus has done all of the dying that ever has to be done. As Paul says, Jesus has taken "the sting"—the hurt and horror—out of death. I shall die physically but not spiritually. Death, the last enemy, has been defeated.

Nancy, there is another beam of light that helps me understand why Jesus died. If you've read my earlier responses in this collection, you know that I believe God takes the ultimate responsibility for allowing evil and sin to occur in this world. They were the "risks He took for Love." He couldn't know what truly free humans would do before they existed. If He had, then they would not be truly free to love or not to love Him.

The cross was God's taking the responsibility for the way things turned out. God became a human in order to right the ship of creation once and for all. Even though you and I were born into a world with the deck stacked against us, God has already taken responsibility and provided us a way out.

Nancy, the cross cannot be separated from the Resurrection. In the cross/Resurrection, God has opened the way to life. He will not stop until He wins us all to himself. "God was in Christ reconciling the world to Himself." The cross was His ultimate effort. He became one of us, took our place, blazed the trail.

You say that you still have questions? I haven't filled in all of the blanks? I agree. I don't fully understand *how* Jesus' death has made me free. But it has.

PART II

QUESTIONS OF SELF-WORTH

15

THE TRAP

Sexual Temptation in the Workplace

Dear Dr. Mann:

I'm forty-three years old and a happily married father of two teenagers. I'm also the successful founder and CEO of a profitable business, a church elder, and a Little League coach. My wife and I were high school sweethearts, virgins when we married and are still each other's best friends and only lovers. Our sex life is great. We're still learning new things to spice it up. Techniques and fantasies which would bore the veterans of the sexual revolution are novel and exciting to us.

But recently my world has collapsed. The comptroller of my company with whom I work daily told me she was quitting. Her reason was flimsy, so I pressed her. She finally admitted that she was "too tied to me." Then she spilled the beans. She said she was in love with me.

She's a devout Christian and loves my wife and family. She knows I would never leave them. She also knows that at her age (35) and being single, she needs to start making a permanent family relationship.

My first reaction was to beg her to stay. To tell you the truth her confession of affection for me just melted my insides. You see, Doctor, for years I had courted fleeting fantasies of a liaison with her. I never told anyone, never touched her, never even flirted with her. But she is extremely attractive as well as a person of great integrity. I found myself being envious of her various suitors.

Anyway, I don't know what to do. Since she told me, I have been absolutely preoccupied with her. She's hardly ever out of my mind. When we are doing business at the office I smell the soap on her skin and the freshness of her hair. I never did that before! I cannot stay focused on my work.

At church I cannot hold my head up. I'm supposed to be a role model. Yet during worship services I start visualizing. Yes! Drawing mental pictures of secret trysts with my assistant!

There have been times when I've even gone so far as to plot ways to justify leaving my family—those sweet and God-given innocents!

Dr. Mann, can you help me? I have no one with whom to share my problem. I dare not tell my pastor, or fellow church leaders, or closest friends. This is just too private.

Should I let her leave? She's done nothing wrong. Should I close my business and move? Should I resign my office at the church? Should I tell my wife?

I know I've already committed adultery as Jesus defined it. I haven't physically touched, hugged, kissed, or copulated; but God knows I've mentally done it all.

This much I know: I cannot go on like this. I am trapped. How do I get out?

Dear Bob:

I'm both honored and frightened that you asked me for help. I'm honored because you felt you could share such a private and haunting secret with me. You are right, close friends, pastors, and fellow church leaders generally wouldn't handle your dilemma very well. Most likely, they would be quick with preachments and slow with confessions as to how they themselves have confronted similar situations. Many wouldn't even admit that they've had the same experience.

I'm frightened because you have dared to place your fragile and bruised self-image in the hands of my limited wisdom.

First, let's look at what you have going for you. A fierce integrity for one thing. No one could feel as guilty as you and be a good-for-nothing. You and I know plenty of men who would've already bedded the comptroller and figured out how to justify it. They'll be singing hymns come this Sunday.

A man as guilty as you can't be very far from God either. There are two kinds of guilt—false and true, healthy and unhealthy. False or unhealthy guilt is the shame we feel for not measuring up to rules laid upon us by the parents, peers, and preachers of our youth. True, or healthy guilt is what we feel when we fail to measure up to the true self we know we were meant to be.

My guess is that you're feeling both right now. Much of your guilt seems to come from the fear of reprimand you would receive from friends, church folk, and clergy if they found out. You would be labeled an "outcast."

That's not healthy guilt, so let me just say up front that your experience is more the rule than the exception. If you're an outcast because you chased skirts in your fantasies, get in line, my friend! Most men do. I'm not saying it's okay, I'm just saying it's not unusual.

We need to look honestly at what Jesus meant when He said, "Whoever looks upon a woman to lust has committed adultery with her in his heart."

My opinion is that He was simply trying to show His super-righteous audience that they could not keep enough rules to qualify as non-sinners. They had lowered the standards on adultery, murder, truth-telling, and revenge to levels which were easy to reach. Jesus was "painting them into their own corners."

His point was that they were all sinners. Our hope must not rest on being able to keep all of the rules.

So, Bob my friend, you have learned the hard way that you have an adulterous heart, and you are guilty because you think others don't. Well, according to Jesus, we all do. The judgment of others is unwarranted. You can choose not to subject yourself to it.

Your true guilt is real and healthy. You have not fully lived up to what you know you should be. What to do about it?

I'll give you some "inside" and "outside" suggestions... some steps to take in your inward life and some steps for your outward life.

Inwardly you've already taken the biggest step in closing the gap between you and God: *You've confessed!* You've confessed to me, which indicates that you've probably confessed to God. You cannot tell another person what you've told me without having carefully formulated your problem inwardly before God.

So you've confessed to God *and* to another person. That is a huge step, Bob! Many people confess to God and never tell another soul. Perhaps that is best in some cases, but I have found that confessing what you've shared with God to a forgiving human being whom you can trust, has a mysteriously "healing effect."

I think it's because we've come clean in our *total* lives... inside and out. God knows and forgives and another human knows and forgives.

Now that you have taken the first inward step of confession, I have another suggestion about your inward life. Sort out the difference between temptation and sin. You have been tempted, but have you sinned? As I said earlier, there's no doubt that we all have adulterous hearts or inclinations. But that doesn't mean you've committed adultery with the woman at your office.

Only you can tell for sure, but let me give you some food for thought. Scholars of the human psyche tell us that there is a difference between sexual arousal, sexual fantasizing, and sexual action.

We are not responsible for what turns us on sexually. Nor are we responsible for the sexual fantasies which appear in our minds.

We *are* responsible for whether we nurture or suppress those fantasies. Let me summarize: We can't control what arouses us. We can't choose which fantasies crop up. We *can* nurture the fantasies or shut them down. We can also control whether to act out our sexual urges and fantasies.

Bob, you are a normal human being! You were aroused. Not your fault. You fantasized. Not your fault. Did you nurture your fantasies? Are you still nurturing them? (I think this is what Jesus meant by "looking...to lust.") You haven't acted them out. Welcome to the human race, Bob!

Now about the "outside" moves. You and the comptroller need to part company. She was correct in asking to leave. Her staying on after you've begged her to, only reinforces the fact that she should leave. She's tempted and attracted all the more by staying, and so are you. It's not smart to continue to feed the fire.

Should you tell your wife? No one but you can decide, but I would say not now if ever. Not now, because you need to put some distance between you and your associate's leaving. Time will have a way of telling whether this was a normal "temptation crisis" for you, or a real moral crisis.

Also, many women, like your wife, who are reared in a religiously strict world simply cannot fathom their husband's sexual attraction to another woman. They equate attraction with betrayal.

Whatever help you get from all of these words, Bob, I want you to hear loud and clear that you are not "trapped." The opposite is true. You have faced a crisis with courage and common sense. You have not swept your responsibility to God and your family under a rug of convenience. You have not casualized sex in the way that so many would urge us to do.

I think you will make it through this just fine. But what if you don't? What if you cave in, have a fling, get a new wife or go the "singling" route?

Well, there are price tags on those options. Count the costs of your actions and know that God still waits on the other side with bandages for the wounded.

16

PANGS OF A PARIAH
Guilt and Abortion

Dear Dr. Mann:

I've had five abortions. They were all "for the sake of convenience" as they say. I could lie and list all of the reasons I used in order to justify my actions at the time.

The truth is, I turned eighteen in 1967, graduated from a small town high school in the Bible Belt, and "tuned-in, turned-on, and dropped out." In the seventies I rode the tides of so-called "liberation" and went out in search of myself. In the eighties I found the self I originally left to go and look for. It was the same hungry, confused self I left behind in the first place.

Now in mid-life I am a tenured professor living with my cats and wishing I could believe in believing again. I want to believe in commitment to long-term relationships. I want to believe in God. I want to believe that my past has passed. I want to love a man and mother his children.

But all of my thoughts are overshadowed by those five aborted fetuses. The strangest part of it is that both my feminist pro-choice friends and my Fundamentalist religious friends sound remarkably alike when I unload my problem. The feminists are quick to shame me for feeling shame, and the Fundamentalists are quick to shame me with "you reap what you sow." The point is that both groups treat me as a pariah. Neither can stand me for feeling guilty. The pro-choicers hate to see anyone break ranks and admit guilt. The pro-lifers don't

*know what to do with my guilt. They would rather use me as
an example than help me find healing.*

*In my heart, I know they are correct. I am a pariah! For
the sake of sheer self-interest I gave control of my body to others to create "five bodies," and then I terminated them in the
name of "my right to control my body."*

*Dr. Mann, if there is a Hell beyond this life I know I'm
going. If there isn't, I'm in it now. Every day in the midst of
academia my mind is obsessed with the simplest of questions:
Where are those unborn today? What have I done? Can I ever
be free from this torture?*

Dear Jenny:

I receive many questions about abortion, but I seldom
respond to them. It's not because I don't have definite opinions but because most of the debate is futile.

Abortion is usually discussed and argued on two different
levels, the hypothetical and the existential. The hypothetical
arguments are conducted by people who aren't actually facing
the decision in real life. They are "what if" arguments...i.e.,
"What if you were faced with the decision?"

Hypothetically, abortion can be argued endlessly. Is it murder? When is a fetus a person? Is it at conception or when the
umbilical cord is cut? Is it a legal or moral issue or both?

Existential issues are argued by people who actually have to
decide in the midst of their existence—whether to abort. The
decision is not a matter for cocktail-party discussion or talk-
show filler. I counselled with a forty-year-old mother of five
who carried an unplanned fetus. Tests showed the child would
be malformed and unable to function without institutional care.

The decision of whether to abort in situations like this is not the same as it is on the floor of the Legislature or in the hide-bound pulpits. This is a real life, soul-wrenching battle . . . an existential nightmare.

It's one thing to debate abortion and formulate hypotheses and rules, and quite another to face it in real existence. I feel that the abortion issue will never be satisfactorily settled. I don't believe that a national legal policy can be established from the top down. People will choose to abort or not to abort based upon their own value systems clashing with the situations in which they find themselves.

Personally, I have very strong views on abortion, but what I think is of little importance. Your personal decision is between you and God.

I hear from you a cry from the depths of self-hatred, regret, and remorse. You are in fact in a Hell of sorts. Your past choices have come back to haunt you. You wonder if you will ever come to terms with your past and find some sense of peace.

Jenny, let me begin by offering you two lifelines of hope. Your pain is a gift—not a curse—from God. Pain is always a sign that something is broken. In our physical bodies pain is our immune system's rush to burn away and flush away damage. Swelling, for example, is a marshalling of tiny blood vessels to heal a wound.

The same is true for the psyche or soul. You are not beyond the possibility of healing. Jenny, God is not finished with you. If He were you would feel nothing at all. You would have long since rationalized your past or perhaps become a militant advocate in order to justify it or fight it.

Another lifeline is your longing for a relationship of lasting commitment. This means that you know what such a relationship is, even though you've never had one.

So forgiveness and love are not impossibilities for you,

Jenny. Your hurt and your hunger are vital signs. Your soul is not dead.

However, as you say, the real trouble in your soul is the five abortions. You're asking, "Did I take five lives? If so, where are they and what shall I have to pay for them? Did I terminate five little persons whose identities and names were already registered in the Great Roster? Or did I simply remove appendages from my uterus...cells which were only a part of me?"

Let's take the worst and best sides of these questions and then see whether you can connect with enough inward renewal to get on with your life.

Suppose those incipient life forms attached to your uterine wall were indeed persons. They had planned futures and dreams in the mind of God. What can you do now to atone for these tragedies?

Well, let me tell you what *won't* atone for them. The way of militant reversal won't take the guilt away. You can't erase your guilt by taking up the banner and attacking the pro-choicers.

There are many alcoholics who have tried to stay sober by crusading against other alcoholics. They usually get drunker on self-righteousness and manipulation than they ever did on booze.

The same is true for any other guilty person. You can't expel the poison from your soul by injecting it into others.

Nor do I recommend the "monastic commitment" approach. Renouncing your professorship and devoting the rest of your life to "orphans" or the like, may be a wonderful thing to do, but it will not erase the guilt of your past. The saints who bless the world in such endeavors do not serve out of a sense of self-hatred. They do not start out empty, hoping that their service will "fill them up." They start out "full" from a sense of self-worth and pour their love into others.

To make it short, Jenny, there's nothing you can *do* to "work off" your guilt. Only God can relieve the inward torture which you describe.

The route to that cleansing is confession. Careful here! Confession is not the price of forgiveness. It's the route to it. You are not forgiven because you confess. You simply put yourself in the place where God can meet you and give you a new start.

Thus, if we take the worst case and assume that you killed five innocent lives, I am telling you that there is forgiveness. God's love is so radical that He will give you the power to begin again. He may bring to you forgiveness in a mystical epiphany. Most likely, however, He will bring it to you through one or more persons who themselves have been forgiven. Find those who have been wounded as you have, and embrace them.

Believe it or not Jenny there are communities—even in some churches—who exist for the sole purpose of living-out forgiveness to broken and tortured people such as yourself.

Now let's turn to the best-case scenario. Let's suppose those little bright spots on the sonogram were simply tissue...not yet beings at all. I am sure you would feel relieved to know you are not a killer.

But I wonder if you would be free of your inward torment. From what you've said in your letter, I gather that a large part of your hurt is your inability to have established long-term love relationships. In fact I think it's notable that you tied your guilt about the abortions to your lack of significant love, you "tuned-in, turned-on, and dropped-out," as you put it. Many in your generation did, with the same sad results.

Frankly Jenny, I think this "alienation" from significant love is at the heart of your torment and has been from the beginning. The abortions—as terrible as they are—are really symptoms of a deep loneliness. You need to be "touched" by the kind of love which can energize you to love yourself again.

In other words you not only need to feel forgiveness for the sexual promiscuity and irresponsibility which led to five abortions; you also need to be loved in such a way that you can love yourself again.

I must repeat what I said earlier. It's the only thing I know to recommend. You cannot love yourself until you feel loved by God.

You have made a great beginning. You have revealed to one person the awful torment of your secret soul. And you have revealed it to a person who for better or worse represents, in your mind at least, the Source of Love behind all loves. Jenny, that is a significant step. I pray you will find others close to you whom you trust and can bring you love and healing when they know your secret.

One last thing, Jenny. You are haunted by the question of the status and whereabouts of the five fetuses. My answer is a conviction I hold. They are where all innocent life goes eventually—to the womb of God's love from which none can be aborted... and that includes you, Jenny, if you so choose.

17

MY NAME IS LEGION
Facing Sexual Peculiarities

Dear Dr. Mann:

I love God very much and so does my wife. We have a daughter twenty-two. Sir, I am not gay. I am fifty years old and for the past thirty years or so I have had this deep need to occasionally dress in ladies clothing. Actually my problem runs deeper than that. On occasion I feel like a woman trapped in a man's body.

When I'm dressed like a woman, I feel like the real me. I must say that sometimes there is masturbation with this and afterward I feel so dirty.

I don't know what to do. I love the Lord so much and want to please Him. I have never done my "woman thing" in public. No one but you even knows about it. I love my family and would never embarrass them or dishonor God on purpose. I'm not an exhibitionist. If you saw me, you would think I'm a normal, decent, churchgoing, family man. I suppress my desire to be a woman constantly, but I am miserable.

My wife and I haven't much of a sex life. We occupy different bedrooms. As I said, I'm not gay. I have no desire for sex with men. I was born illegitimate and raised by my grandparents who were not affectionate people. They loved me but resented my mom. They reminded me more than once that I was a bastard and a burden to them.

Part of my problem may be related to the fact that my first love dumped me for another guy. I was seventeen and fell

*hopelessly and deliriously in love. She quit me cold turkey.
I've never loved another woman as I loved her.*

*Dr. Mann, what do you make of this? Is it possible I was
born sexually defective in some way? I'm in constant torment.
I feel like a woman, yet I must suppress what seems like my
real self in order to be somebody I'm not. As I said, I love God
and my family, but I feel like that guy whom Jesus met in the
graveyard. My name is "Legion." I have so many identities
that I don't seem to know who and what I am.*

Please help me.

Dear Gordon:

How I hurt for you! Your problem is not only a living
nightmare, it is also compounded by the fact that insensitive
people make jokes about it all the time. Most of us have no
way to relate to your situation. I can only imagine what it
must be like to live with such inner confusion. I wonder how
many others there are out there with similar secrets who cannot
dare to share their hurt.

To make things worse, many from the religious community
simply cannot believe that "people who love the Lord" could
be visited by such sexual peculiarities. In their thinking, loving God and having conventional sexual mores are synonymous.

Gordon, I am not a sexologist nor have I done extensive
research on the subject. No doubt there are experts in the field
of sexual behaviorism who can easily recognize your problem
and explain it. But of course you haven't asked them. You're
too ashamed.

So let's start there... with your deep sense of shame. Where
does it come from? Obviously from your religious and social

affiliations—family, church, friends, and peers. "If they only knew," are the four words that haunt you.

Well, I know! And I am neither repulsed nor surprised nor ready to pronounce judgment on you. How could I scold people for having a condition they have not chosen?

The sexologists I have read and spoken with, tell me that every person has a distinctive "love map," or sexual orientation which results from many factors. You are not responsible for having it. You are only responsible for what you choose to do with it.

So, I do not shame you for your inclination toward transvestitism (dressing like the opposite sex) and you shouldn't shame yourself.

However, you can count on being shamed by almost everyone else if you go public with your inclination. You are really living in fantasyland if you expect those around you to approve. This doesn't mean you are wicked. I want to say this loud and clear.

Each of us is part of a gene pool which is millions of years old. The gene pool is maintained and passed on through procreation, monogamy, and other social conventions which create a protective environment for the survival of the pool.

Anything which threatens the survival of the gene pool will be resisted. You can make all of the rational, religious, and social arguments you want against so-called traditional sex habits and the self-righteous people who uphold them.

It doesn't matter. There is something else going on in our subconscious. Sexual behaviors which threaten to terminate the gene pool from which we came will always be resisted.

I have not mentioned God or biblical ethics in my explanation of why going public with your problem will reap you much scorn. I chose to give you a "naturalistic" explanation. I could have used "preacher words" and said, God has ordained that people should be heterosexual, monogamous, celibate out-side of marriage, etc.

I do indeed believe this. But such talk only pits one group of sinners against another in an argument which creates self-righteousness on one side and shame on the other.

Gordon, to summarize: Your condition is not your fault. I don't condemn you. I don't believe God condemns you. But don't expect most people to approve or accept it. They simply aren't built that way.

Now I want to respond directly to a couple of things you asked in your letter. First, you wonder if you were born sexu-ally defective or if your behavior might be related to having been born illegitimate, raised by unaffectionate grandparents, and dumped by your first love.

My answer is: probably all of the above together and none of the above in particular. For instance, your condition could have been strongly influenced by something that happened during your mother's pregnancy. All fetuses are female until hormonal changes take place and convert them into males. Many researchers now believe that the condition of homosexu-ality especially among males originates in part because of some glitch during this hormonal transformation.

And get this: The glitch is most likely caused by the moth-er's being in an unusually stressful pregnancy. You said your mother was unmarried when you were born. And that was fifty years ago during an era when unwed mothers were out-casts! And your grandparents who raised you reminded you regularly that you were a bastard. I can only imagine what they must have called your mother while she carried you in her womb. Talk about stress! I'm not surprised that she left and never came back.

However, Gordon, there have been millions of other people born under similar circumstances and worse who do not have your condition.

But there's more, isn't there? Your first love jilted you...."cold turkey" as you put it. One moment you were head-over-heels for each other. Your ego boundaries had collapsed. In your mind there was finally "another" who desired and longed for you and you alone. The next moment she had vanished.

The first "first lady" (your mom) in your life abandoned you. Then the second "first lady" (your girlfriend) did likewise. And grandma called you a bastard. She never coddled, held, cooed, or kissed.

I am not surprised, Gordon, that you would fantasize yourself "merging" with the woman (the one you dress up like occasionally) who cannot dump you...the one who responds eagerly to your touch. If she didn't appear in your life now and then, you might not be able to survive!

I'll just come right out and say it. Your transvestite episodes could be the only thing that enables you to be an ordinary productive decent human being most of the time! These episodes could be a plus not a minus!

Let's look at this realistically. You're not molesting children, you're not cruising bars, you're not depriving your wife sexually. (I couldn't recount in detail what you told me about your marital sex life because I must protect your anonymity.) You're involved in helping others. And occasionally—*in utter privacy*—you dress up like a woman and masturbate.

Afterward you feel dirty. Why? I cannot answer for you. I can only speculate. Perhaps it is false guilt. "Parents-preachers-peers" say it's naughty, so it must be.

Or perhaps you know that these episodes could become obsessive habits and wreck your life.

All I'm saying is, don't simply dismiss your guilt because of what I've said. It could be a healthy way of keeping you sane and productive enough to live out your life.

The bottom line, Gordon, is that we shall never know why you have this condition. It is probably due to a number of factors, both biological and psychological, none of which you chose to have.

The important question is what to do about it. Even if you did know why you have it, you would have to decide what to do.

I have only one instruction. Look at the effect of these episodes on others, on God, and on yourself. Are you misusing or abusing any of these three "persons" when you dress up and masturbate? Immoral behavior must always be measured by what it does to persons. If I misuse or abuse other people and myself, I am misusing and abusing God.

I can give you this word of hope. You are not the psychotic man whom Jesus met in the graveyard...the one who said his name was "Legion." You are not two people. You are just one person with the same deep hunger for inward at-one-ness which we all have. We are all separated from the self we know we should be.

The good news is that God loves us in all of our "split-ness." He has known and seen you for all of your life, the public part and the private part. I am not the only person who knows your secret, Gordon. He knows it too. And He loves you anyway.

18

FROM THE DARK
The Handicapped and Faith Healing

Dear Dr. Mann:

Our daughter was born sightless . . . congenitally blind. She is now eighteen months old. The doctors do not know what caused her condition, but I know of three people in my ancestry who were also blind. Because of this, my wife and I have decided not to have any more children.

Until recently we have had a good marriage. We met at church and dated for three years before we wed. Our parents have known each other for years and raised us in the same religious denomination. We have always prayed together and attended Sunday School and worship, and tithed our incomes to the Lord.

About six months ago a woman who works with my wife told her of a new church she was involved in. She said the pastor had the gift of healing and had cured many diseases, even birth defects.

Well, you know what happened. My wife started attending the services with her friend. Then she took me. It wasn't long before she and her friend and several members of the church wanted us to "submit our little girl for healing."

I refused. I'm not a very good talker, so I couldn't express why I was against it. But I just couldn't agree to it. Now, as I think back, I believe it was because I was already about to lose my faith in God for allowing my daughter to be born blind. If we took her to the faith healer and it didn't work, I could not have continued to believe at all.

Anyway, I just refused to discuss the matter with my wife or her friends. I clammed up and wouldn't hear of it.

My wife took our little girl to be healed without telling me. It didn't work. The pastor hinted that it could be because of my stubborn lack of faith. My wife turned bitter toward me.

We are now living in the same house but different bedrooms. I don't know what to do. At first I was angry with the pastor. Now I'm beginning to feel that perhaps he is right. If I had enough faith, God might have given sight to our little girl.

I'm not saying that her healing depends on my faith. I know that God does the healing. I'm just afraid that her blindness might be God's way of punishing me for my failure of faith.

But for some reason I can't give in to the wishes of my wife and the pastor. Something inside me says that God could and would heal my daughter if He chose to, without the faith healer.

As you can tell, Dr. Mann, I'm sort of talking in circles. I'm confused. I'm angry with God for letting all of this happen. Yet I feel like it's my fault too. I suppose I could give in and submit our daughter for healing. My wife would be happy. The pastor would be happy. My daughter's too young to know what's going on.

But what if it didn't work? I'm afraid that would be the end of everything for me. The end of my faith, my marriage, my ability to cope with my child's handicap.

Frankly, I don't believe God is going to reverse her blindness. And I don't believe in faith healers period! This makes it even worse. Because I'm a skeptic, my wife has rejected me and I could be keeping my daughter from a miracle!

If you can make sense of all of this, please help me.

Dear Kevin:

If you read the introduction to this book you know I have no trouble projecting myself into your situation. I know firsthand where you're coming from. You are not "talking in circles." You are going round and round the same treadmill of anger, doubt, hurt, and hope that I've been traveling for over thirty years.

I tried to heal our child's deafness by praying and laying hands on her many times. Every community I've lived in has had well-meaning people who've suggested and even pressured me to go the faith-healer route. I refuse to do it just as you have. And for some of the same reasons.

Fortunately, my wife and I were never at odds about this. I can only imagine how much greater the pain had we been adversaries in our approach to dealing with an exceptional child.

I will speak to that later, but up front I want to reinforce the "gut feelings" which you find difficult to express. For example, you say you resisted the pressure to submit your daughter for healing because you were afraid of what would happen if it didn't work. You're already angry and confused at God. You can barely believe now. If the healing failed that would "do you in" faithwise.

Kevin, this is an altogether legitimate reason for refusing. You have felt in your gut the question countless philosophers and thinkers have expressed cogently. If God is great and God is good, how can He permit birth defects? Either He can't, which means He's not almighty. Or He won't, which means He's not all good.

I tried to deal with this dilemma in Part I. All I want to say here is that your feelings are okay. I have refused the goadings of faith healers to submit my child for the same reason as you.

If it didn't work, how could I believe? My faith was already fragile enough.

Then afterward I've had the same torturous feeling that my refusal was not only selfish and faithless but might have kept God from healing my daughter.

Then one day I had a remarkable experience. I was agonizing over whether my refusal to submit was blasphemous, when a still small voice from deep within said simply, "Why don't you stop playing God?" I needed no translation. I knew what God was saying to me. *Namely, that I could not hinder Him from healing anyone!* If He chose to heal my child, no power on earth could deter Him.

I also realized that if the faith healer's gift were for real, it would be effective with or without my permission. Jesus healed children and adults without consulting them.

Kevin, I was operating under the same illusion that causes many others to become disillusioned...the illusion that there is a magical, as-yet-untried, "something" *we* can do to change harsh realities—those "givens" which cause us pain.

This is the illusion that *we* or some "especially gifted" person can find a way to convince God to change reality to fit us. Healing becomes the gift of Anointed Persuaders who have a key to unlock God's inner sanctum and get Him to perform miracles which are off-limits to ordinary mortals like us.

Whichever way you cut it, that mentality places the responsibility for healing squarely on *human powers of persuasion!* It also says that God is some kind of capricious remote monarch who can be talked into healing by those who have the magic to get His attention.

This kind of thinking is nothing more than witch-doctorism. It demeans God and enthrones the witch doctor. It humanizes Deity and deifies humanity.

God is neither punishing you by giving you a sightless child nor is He continuing to punish you by not restoring her sight.

I find myself in your camp when it comes to your response to the faith-healing issue. I don't mean to say that these practitioners don't effect the healing of some people. There are too many documented cases to deny that some people are indeed healed outside of what we would call understandable medical procedures. I have no problem in giving God the credit, or those whom He uses as His agents.

However, all God-gifted persons should reflect the God who gave them their gifts. I believe that Jesus was the clearest picture of God's spirit and kindness we've had. So obviously my first question to faith healers is whether they reflect the spirit of Jesus.

Frankly, I find no evidence of Jesus using His powers to feather His financial nest or raise His celebrity status. On the contrary, He often told people to "tell no man." He also had a habit of driving the crowds away. And He detested the demand that He prove His spiritual authenticity by performing miracles.

I know that what I've just said is inflammatory. I'm also aware of what Jesus said about our ability to heal as He did. I'm not disputing it. I would like to make it clear that I am not indicting faith healing per se. There is no doubt that miraculous healings occur.

In fact, I think all healing is of God and all healing requires faith! Millions of healing miracles take place daily in hospitals throughout the world. We don't call them miracles anymore because we understand them "scientifically." Regrettably we have separated reality into two realms, the natural and the supernatural. Anything we understand according to our rules for knowledge we relegate to the realm of the natural.

This is a false dichotomy. God has increasingly allowed us to "partner" with Him in the healing process.

Faith is involved in all healing. Karl Menninger, Denton Cooley, and other unquestionably qualified physicians have told me that the patient's *faith* in the doctor and the treatment is integral to the healing process. Bill Moyers' book *Healing and the Mind* reconfirms this.

On July 1, 1993 Cable News Network reported that a medical research team in New York has released its findings after treating sick people with placebos for several months.

The report states that seventy percent of those treated— including those who have untreatable illnesses—got better! Why? Because they *believed* they would get better!

There is no doubt in my mind that we've only scratched the surface when it comes to the role of faith in the healing process.

I want to dispel from your mind the myth which says that God is directly involved in healing only when patients are submitted to religious practitioners in "church healing services." God is directly involved in all healing, and so is the patient's faith.

There are two more things we still need to talk about regarding your present trouble: your estrangement from your wife, and helping your daughter live wholesomely in the years to come.

Your wife is angry at God, but cannot admit it. That's because she's probably not aware of her anger on the conscious level. Yes, it is common to hide our anger at God... to be subconsciously angry.

All anger comes out. It cannot be bottled up, *even if it is subconscious anger.*

Let me point out another factor. Your wife is probably angry at herself for having a sightless child. Sounds crazy, I know, but it's common to think that tragedies are somehow punishments for our "sins."

No doubt you see what I'm leading up to. Her anger at herself cannot be bottled up, so she is redirecting it through a new experiment. She thinks that she can relieve her guilt by trying a new church and a faith healer. Your resistance and the "healing failure" have allowed her to transfer her anger at God and herself to you!

Remember, all of this is going on beneath the surface of her conscious mind. She would honestly deny all of the above. It's more important for you to know it right now than for her to know it.

Be patient. Put yourself in her shoes. She's locked in a world which is ruled by false images of herself, of God, and of religion. She doesn't know that her child's blindness is not a punishment. She doesn't know that it's okay to be angry at God, and to doubt, and to curse the darkness. She doesn't know that God is hurting and weeping with her in the midst of her pain.

Kevin, she needs a counterpart to "the friend" who introduced her to Magic Religion 101. She needs a mentor who can lead her to the place where she accepts the unfairness and mystery of suffering and the will to walk with God in the Valley of the Shadow anyway.

Unfortunately you can't be that mentor now. Many spouses try and most fail. That's why the divorce rate among parents of handicapped children is so great. Each partner's respective load is so heavy that he or she cannot bear the other's as well.

The best you can do at present, Kevin, is learn to talk and listen. Be as candid with your wife as you have been with me. Also, be ready for the temptation to run away from it all. Often, if we can't fix it, we flee from it.

Lois and I are the only couple still married out of the twenty-something couples with deaf children in our daughter's first therapy class. We survived and grew in the process by following some simple rules.

First, we knew we could spill our guts without being counterattacked. One of us could say, "I'm angry at you" without the other reacting with, "Well I'm angry at you!!!"

Second, we agreed never to say, "Don't say that." All feelings could be vented without scolding. It was okay to say, "I don't believe in God today."

Third, we agreed to preserve what Kahlil Gibran called "spaces in our togetherness." We have kept our private spaces for over thirty years. They are inviolate.

Kevin, the best thing I have done for my handicapped child—the very best thing among the many—is love her mother.

There is no use in my giving you advice about the future . . . things like the question of the cruelty of an uneducated society. All of these things will be faced and managed in time. What you need now is to build emergency back-up systems so you'll have the strength and flexibility to respond to problems.

For now the best backup systems are an open growing relationship with your wife and with God. All healthy relationships are built on an open dialogue. Both sides have to be free to express their feelings without fear of scorn.

God welcomes you to that kind of relationship. I pray you and your wife can welcome each other to the same kind.

Now a few words about your daughter. I'm going to give you the benefit of my mistakes. I am not an expert as a result of having succeeded wonderfully in parenting a handicapped child. I am a bruised warrior who's an example of how not to fight the battle.

First, reserve a little sad room in your heart. It's the place where you lock up all of the unfair things, the dreams of what might have been, the downright terrible injustices. I call it the "bitter-bin." Whenever the "if onlies" and "wouldas" and "shouldas" and "couldas" start to take over my feelings, I gather them up and lock them in the bitter-bin.

Here's my point. There are some things you and your daughter will never do or have because of her handicap.

You're not going to change this. You have two choices. Accept it and lock it in the bitter-bin or let it curdle into a full-blown despair. Everybody should reserve a little place in his heart for the sad things.

I did not do this, Kevin. I felt that there was a school, a program, an operation somewhere "out there" that could enable my daughter to overcome her handicap and be like everyone else. I sent her to the best schools and gave her the best of everything. All I succeeded in doing was programming her to fail and to hate herself for it. By the time we all knew that she could not "beat the odds" she was into punishing herself and us for not being what we thought she could be and never was. To dream the impossible dream is great stuff for Broadway. It doesn't always work in real life.

Finally, Kevin, I want to urge you to focus on "life as gift" as you relate to your daughter in years to come. I first heard the phrase from John Claypool when I was depressed over my daughter's problems. Claypool used it in the first sermon he delivered upon returning to his pulpit after losing his daughter to leukemia.

John told his congregation that they could best help him through his grief if they reminded him that his daughter was never his. All of life is a gift on loan from God. And it was better to have had his gift for twelve years and lost her, than never to have had her at all.

This helped me to look at my child in a totally different way. Her verbal abilities are astounding, given her profound hearing loss. Her tenacity is a thing of beauty, her intuitions are incredible. To see her life flourish while locked up inside severe limitations is a proof of God's existence.

So, Kevin, I want to end by assuring you that you can make it. You asked only that I give you some help with your marital squabble over "faith healing." Perhaps I gave you more words than you requested. I hope you will forgive me for that. I did so because I felt deeply that you and your wife are on the edge of a darkness which is far more damaging than the darkness your child inhabits.

I shall pray for your deliverance.

19

DOESN'T NEED A SERMON
Sexual Need and an Incapacitated Spouse

Dear Dr. Mann:

My husband had a severe stroke ten years ago, partially recovered, and then developed Alzheimer's Disease. He is a very large man and I am unable to care for his basic needs. Our children are grown and live far from home.

Our income is very limited. After a long inner struggle, I had to place my husband in a care facility where he has now been for four years. He is only 58 years old but has degenerated to a comatose state except for brief inexplicable moments of limited awareness. He will recognize me or remember something from years past, and then lapse into unconsciousness.

I am only fifty and in good health. I have devoted myself to helping others. In addition to my job (I'm a legal secretary), I lead a caregivers ministry at my church. We visit the sick, provide support for the grieving, and run a soup kitchen to feed the homeless. I coordinate many volunteers.

About a year ago one of our lifelong friends, a widower, started helping me in the soup kitchen. Over the months we became closer and closer. After we cleaned up the soup kitchen we would drink coffee and talk for hours.

Slowly we bonded from friends into something more "serious"... two lonely people... you get the picture. There have been a few times when we left town and spent the night together in a big city where we could be inconspicuous.

Dr. Mann, I feel trapped right now, and so does my "friend-lover," or whatever you call him. I feel like an adulteress. My husband exists but is not completely "alive." I am lonely. I enjoy "John." And he enjoys me. Yet he feels guilty as well. My husband and he were/are great friends.

I need some realistic no-nonsense advice. If I continue this relationship, what will God think? If I don't, am I condemned to loneliness for many years? My husband could live a long time.

Do you think God regards what I'm doing as a sin? What would you advise me to do if I were in your congregation?

I am not some love-struck teenager or "barhopping easy." Until I met John, my husband was the only man I ever slept with.

I feel terrible, yet somehow I don't think what I am doing is all that wicked. Give me your honest reflections on my situation. I don't need a sermon. Just some advice.

Dear Ellen:

You certainly don't need a sermon. What you need is for me to tell you that I checked with God and He said what you're doing is okay.

You say you're asking for realistic no-nonsense advice but you're really asking for my permission.

Ellen, I am not authorized to grant licenses and my permission means little. I *am* called to help people think through their situations, apply the best reason and character they have, and then get on with life, *hopefully.*

This means that only you and John can decide the morality of your life-style. It also means that I do not condemn or condone. I can only consult and comfort.

With that said let me tell you what I think.

First, I think you are a decent person. You've kept your marriage vows, loved your kids, dealt with the "for better" and now the "for worse." You didn't retreat into a shell of self-pity when tragedy struck. You went to work, turned your life outward to help others, and did the best you could with what you had.

I wouldn't be afraid to stand next to you on Judgment Day.

Second, I think we need to talk about what constitutes personhood and marriage. That is, when is a person a person and when is a marriage a marriage?

To be a person you have to be capable of maintaining a relationship...to give and keep vows to care for another's needs, to grow into oneness with the object of your love.

Does this mean that once humans lose this capacity they are no longer of sacred worth? Of course not! Whatever God creates is sacred and requires our respect. Why? Because God relates to everything He's made and He gives us the responsibility to manage and care for it.

So I'm not saying that once humans lose their capacity for relationships they should be discarded. I'm simply saying that people without the capacity to relate cannot grow into oneness with others.

Ellen, this means in your case, that you are relationally alone—single—as a result of your husband's illness. You are not legally single. The state still says you're married. You are not religiously single. The church still says you're married.

But what does God say? Frankly, I do not know. The Bible? I know what *it* says. In the Old Testament there are places which would instruct you to "be cared for" (even sexually) by your husband's relatives (Gen. 38:1–11). I know of nothing in the New Testament that speaks specifically to your situation, although it does lay out an applicable principle.

If you were living in biblical times you would be a widow by now and your dilemma wouldn't exist. Your problem has been created in part by advances in medical science. I believe that all scientific advances which improve the quality of human life are evidence that God is granting us additional responsibilities in sharing ethical decisions with Him. Scientific advancement does not erase God. It reflects God's granting us more responsibility. We now have "more say" in life's affairs.

I don't know what God would say about your behavior. But there is one principle which governs every moral decision. It is the one ethical absolute. It is called the "Law of Love."

In short, the Law of Love says that in every ethical decision we are to ask what comes closest to approximating Jesus' commandment to love God as much as we can and to love our neighbor as we love ourselves (Matt. 22:34–40). All rules of right and wrong are to be governed by this principle.

So, Ellen, I can't tell you what to do. All I can do is ask you to apply the Law of Love. Are you violating your love for your husband by meeting yours and John's needs?

What would your husband want you to do? What would you want him to do if your situations were reversed?

You are in one of those extreme ethical traps where there is no clear line between right and wrong. You must decide between the lesser of wrongs. It is wrong to be married to one and sleeping with another. But it is wrong to leave your honest God-given needs for love unfulfilled because medical science has kept your husband alive longer that he would've been otherwise.

Maybe this will help, Ellen. A few years ago a friend came to me with a similar problem. His wife had been comatose for five years from a cerebral hemorrhage. There was little brain activity although she was able to breathe without a respirator.

My friend visited her every day and saw to her care. As the

years passed, he developed a relationship with another woman. Divorce was out of the question. He felt it would constitute abandonment of his sick wife. He couldn't do it. Yet, he was living with his new love.

He wondered if he would be welcome in our church and I assured him he would. Then he wondered if he was betraying his wife. I said I would pray and think on it. When I did, this thought burned into my brain: "She's sent her valuables on ahead."

Ellen, I definitely feel that some comatose people have sent their "real selves" on ahead into the next life. Perhaps your husband has too. Of course, there's the problem of his brief episodes of lucidity. They cause trouble for my theory. No doubt, you would be more at peace if these episodes didn't occur.

All I can say is what I would want my wife to do, were I in the same place as your husband. I would want her to live and love to the fullest. If she could find a person such as your John and could live out her days happily, I would rejoice.

If that is urging her to sin then I am part of it too. In the end all of us are the same, Ellen. We're sinners, except on different subjects, and all we can rely on is God's mercy and grace to forgive us. (When Martin Luther pondered moral dilemmas like yours, he said, "Love God and do as you please.") That's good advice for you, Ellen. "Love God," means, make sure you're open to His leading. "Do as you please," means, do what is pleasing to the ear that is ruled by God.

To love God and do as you please does not mean that any and all behaviors are acceptable. It means that those who are in union with God are set free to live without the judgment and rules of others.

So, Ellen, I cannot give you "my blessing." Nor can I give you "my prohibition." To do either would be to play God.

Obviously, I do not lean toward the view that you are a blatant adulteress, nor do I take the easy position that you should live out your days deprived of the fulfillment of a loving relationship with John. I simply cannot reduce my religious views to such legalism.

I have no sermon for you. Just some realistic no-nonsense advice—Love God and do as you please.

20

WILL GOD GIVE IT BACK?

When a Loved One Commits Suicide

Dear Dr. Mann:

I came home from work as usual. My son's pie plate and milk glass were empty as usual. His books were spread out on the kitchen table. His stereo was throbbing.

I looked around. No Joe. I turned off the stereo. The house was quiet when I called after him. The door to the cellar was open.

Below hung Joe from a drapery cord. His face was blue. His tongue lolled outside his swollen lips. Dried blood covered his T-shirt.

The note said, "I love you, Mom. This is not your fault. I just can't live in this world anymore."

Dr. Mann, I could go into more detail, but, believe me, none of us saw this coming. Joe was a seemingly ordinary sixteen year old. No drugs, no fights with his girlfriends or his dad. Good grades. Rather shy at school, but not a recluse.

I replayed events and thought about how I could have prevented his suicide. I saw a good counselor who helped me through that phase. I know now that when people decide to take their lives, no one can either stop them or push them over the brink.

But there was one thing the counselor could not tell me. What about Joe's status in the next life? Is there any way I can hope to see him again?

I cannot bear to think that I won't. Every time I picture him in my mind, I see him only as he looked when he was hanging in that cellar. I have photographs of him everywhere, but they do no good.

I know God can forgive any sin if we ask for forgiveness while we are in this *life. But suicidal people don't have that chance.*

Dr. Mann, I am (was) a single mom. Joe was all I had. Whenever I ask counselors, priests, and ministers to answer my question, they give me the runaround. I know they can't speak for God, but I need a shred of hope. Can you give me anything concrete to hold onto?

Dear Joan:

I won't mince words. There is plenty of reason to assure you that you will not only see Joe again, but also laugh and leap for joy with him.

Why am I so emphatic? Is there a Scripture which says that people who commit suicide go to Heaven?

No, there is not a single scripture assuring that. Nor is there one which says suicides are barred from Paradise.

What we have is the total import of what the Bible says about God and people and life and death.

It is true that God is the sole arbiter of life. Life is His and not ours to take. To take your own life is the same as taking any human life. You are taking something which doesn't belong to you. And as you point out, Joan, suicides don't have the opportunity to repent in this life.

But there is one vital difference in killing another and killing oneself. In the case of suicide, one of the selves wants to die. Joan, I build my case for hope on that vital difference.

Obviously we have two selves, don't we? We regularly

acknowledge this when we say things like, "I lost control of myself," or, "I don't know what got into me." We have a shadow self—a "beast in the basement"—where our dark urges and desires dwell. And we have a higher self. I call this the "angel in the attic." It's where our best and highest motives dwell.

When a person commits suicide, he allows his lower self to dominate the attic as well as the basement. In psychological terms, suicide is the ultimate statement against life itself. In other words, you have to see yourself as totally worthless to terminate your life.

Joan, I think suicidal people are already in a Hell of sorts when they take their lives. They are imprisoned in the deepest self-hatred. All outside reality is erased from their consciousness. They are totally isolated. Their hurt consumes all of them. It is as if they and their problem were all that exists. And in this loneliness—this complete alienation from life—they opt for oblivion. For the higher self to lose its self-awareness is a good working definition of Hell.

It is hard for me to believe that such tortured souls would forever be barred from God's compassion. It's hard because of the kind of God God is. The God of the Bible is a God whose sole desire is to reconcile with His creation. I referred to this in Part I. But let me just say here that the God who came to us in Jesus Christ is not the sort to ignore the cries of a sixteen year old who ended his life before he knew what life was about.

Many will think that my reasoning is flimsy at best. How could God give life back to someone who freely chose to reject it? How absurd can you get?

Well, all of us reject our own lives to some degree on a regular basis. We turn against our own God-given life. That's a good working definition of *sin*. To sin is to say *No* to the life God meant for you to have.

When you look at it this way, we are all committing a kind of suicide on a daily basis.

I just ate the deep-fried all-you-can-eat everything for lunch. My cholesterol soars and I've had bypass surgery. I rarely live this dangerously but sometimes *I lose control of my taste buds and say no to life.*

So, Joan, while I am fully aware that I've opened a can of worms by assuring you that there is hope for Joe, I am glad to do it. I do not fear that I will encourage and cause people to take their lives. Suicide is not an act of hope. People don't kill themselves in order to go to Heaven. Suicide is an act of total despair.

Based upon the overwhelming love and compassion of God as shown in Jesus Christ, I have to believe that God will give life back to Joe in the same way He keeps giving it back to us.

21

WIDOWHOOD AMERICAN STYLE
Singles, Faith, and Sex

Dear Dr. Mann:

I'm a thirty-year-old single mom with an eight-year-old daughter. I am active in church and send my little girl to church school. I want to be a good example for her. I don't bring men home to spend the night, nor do I cruise bars or conduct an "ongoing manhunt."

But I do have sexual needs. I would like nothing better than a good loving husband but they are few and far between. Occasionally I do slip up and have sex with a guy I've been dating. Most of my friends would laugh if they knew such things even bothered me.

I asked my pastor for advice and he told me in no uncertain terms that I was to abstain from all sex outside of marriage— even self-stimulation. I asked another minister, and he said to follow my own conscience... Sexual behavior was a private matter and he chose to remain mum on the subject. I felt like he was saying, "Do as you please."

Dr. Mann, I'm not asking for your opinion on whether it's okay or not okay for me to sleep around. I'm asking for advice on how to deal with my desire to be a Christian mom to my child on the one hand, and how to deal with sexual needs and sins on the other. I'm in a constant state of guilt.

Dear Lorene:

How I wish I could simply recite one of the two opposite sexual philosophies which are popular today and be rid of your question. That would be so easy.

I could take the side which says: "No sex outside of marriage, period! This life is hard and temporary at best. The next life is great and forever. Deny yourself and wait for Heaven."

Or I could take the other side, and say: "Ancient biblical prohibitions no longer apply. Thanks to birth control and woman's ability to survive economically outside of marriage, we now live in the age of First Amendment sex. It's your inalienable right to enjoy it whenever and however you please as long as it's with a consenting partner."

Either of these would be easy, but neither would be honest. Besides I'm not going to give you a sexual philosophy which I think you should follow. That is not what you asked for.

What you want from me is a way to cope meaningfully with your situation. You want to honor your commitment to God and your child on one hand, and find sexual and emotional fulfillment with a man on the other. Can you be a "good person" and do both?

Lorene, you don't need preachments, you need help. There are millions like you who ask for bread and only receive stones from the extremists on both sides. I'll try to give you bread.

First, when all is said and done concerning how to satisfy God and your sexual needs at the same time—just about everything's already been said and done. No doubt you've heard of the three most popular substitutes for sex which are usually offered by people like me. I call them the "M. I. S. Approach." M.I.S. stands for *masturbation*, *imagination*, and *sublimation*.

I disagree with the minister who told you masturbation is a sin. There's nothing in the Bible which forbids it. Oh, some interpreters do try to use Genesis 38 as a biblical basis for calling masturbation a sin. It's a "stretch." A man named Onan was supposed to conceive a child with his dead brother's wife in order to carry on the brother's progeny. Onan practiced *coitus interruptus* instead (he withdrew and "spilled his seed on the ground"). God punished him for disobeying the ancient law which required him to sire the child. This passage has nothing to do with masturbation.

Masturbation can be a healthy way to release sexual frustration. It *can* become an obsessive addiction, but so can *any* sexual activity. Very few people become obsessive masturbators, and my guess is that those who do would be sexually obsessive in some other way, if they had a regular sex partner.

Imagination means fantasizing. It often involves props like sexually explicit photographs, videos, etc. The problem with this substitute is that the props always lose their power to arouse after a time. For example, I've known of several married couples who use X-rated films to become sexually aroused. Ultimately, most end up bored and with less fulfillment than when they started.

So I would not recommend pornography as a lasting substitute. But there is more to the human imagination than pornographic stimulants. In the long run, your mind can create more sexual images than Hollywood could ever invent. Single people have confided to me that they have developed fantasy motifs which are quite fulfilling. They dress, play music, create their own private "love nests" and use their minds.

I have contended for years that we have allowed our sexuality to be severely restricted by narrow-sighted pornographers. My main objection to *Playboy* is like that of Father Andrew Greeley in *Sexual Intimacy: Love & Play* (Warner, 1975). It has a limited view of "Play." Play is confined to airbrushed genitalia, oversized breasts, and mannequin-like sirens.

Sublimation means rechannelling your sex drive into other creative endeavors. This has been done with great success throughout history. Many of the Church Fathers who created some of the world's greatest literature and art were celibate. Origen, Jerome, and Augustine, to mention three, all consciously redirected their sexual frustrations into great works.

I know dedicated contemporary humanitarians and Christian ministers—both heterosexual and homosexual—who follow in the footsteps of these giants.

So, Lorene, there is always M.I.S.—masturbation, imagination, and sublimation. Don't discount them as effective means of living your life. In fact, I believe that all people should practice sublimation to some degree, no matter what their marital status.

I have never read what I'm about to tell you. It is simply a hunch. But I believe it will be confirmed by research someday. It may have been already and I don't know it. I believe that society as a whole loses its creative and productive edge whenever it becomes preoccupied with sexual license. In other words, the more "sexually steamed up" a society, the less creative and productive it becomes.

So M.I.S. is not a pie-in-the-sky approach invented by old moralists who were trying to keep us "down on the farm." These methods do allow millions to cope with their inability to gratify their sexual needs because of choice or circumstance. Lorene, I urge you to practice them.

However, you and I know that M.I.S. are not enough to totally gratify someone who has had an intimate, caring, creative sexual relationship. M.I.S. are coping methods and nothing more. They are what we settle for when we cannot have the real thing.

Your problem, Lorene, is that you *can* experience the "real thing" whenever you want it, except for the guilt that comes from being unmarried, devoted to God, and a Christian mother.

You have asked me for help with the guilt. I cannot free you from it. Even if I told you to go ahead and indulge your sexual needs and God would forgive you, you would still have the guilt. It would come from within. You see, Lorene, you have the "higher self" within—the self you were created to be. And this higher self will not let you settle for being less than you can be.

The friends you mentioned in your letter—the ones who sleep around without one twinge of conscience—are faking it. Why are they so lonely? Why are they searching for "Mr. Right" by sleeping with multiple partners they hardly know? It's because what they really want is companionship.

Let me tell you of an actual occurrence. I took my small son to the doctor. We waited thirty minutes in the examining room. The doctor rushed in and apologized. "I've been on the phone with a wealthy, beautiful, high-society, single mom," he said quietly to me. "Her eight-year-old daughter is chronically sick. I'm convinced it's because of her mom's total unhappiness. I sent the mom to a psychiatrist who told her that all she needed was a steamy, no strings affair. What do you think, Dr. Mann?"

"I think what she needs is a companion with whom she also has sex," I said. "But a playmate who isn't a soulmate will only treat the symptoms."

"Well," he said, "that's what I think too, but sometime it's better to treat the symptoms until you can find the cure."

Frankly, I had no response. I do not know which is better...to live out your life with substitutes and suffer, or to treat the symptoms until you can find a cure. You and God will have to sort out that one.

I do know several things. First, your primary need is not sex. It's a "one-flesh" relationship which produces great sex.

Second, the statistical odds of your finding that relationship are not good; but you can improve them by putting yourself in a place where good relationships happen. Where is that? Well, if I could give you the phone number and address, we couldn't print enough of these books.

I have only one thought about finding "Mr. Right": *Go for character before charisma.* Being a divorcee, you know first-hand, Lorene, that people do not fall in love and then get married. They fall into "heat" and after the fire dies down, they may or may not grow into love.

Whether they grow into love depends mostly on the determination of both parties to make the marriage work. Volumes continue to be written on the secret of long-term successful marriages. While they are of value, I contend that the secret of a successful marriage is the decision by both parties that the marriage shall go on. It is commitment. That's why I urge you to look first for character in a potential mate.

But as you said, the pickins are slim. How to live lonely, lovingly, loyally and without guilt, all at the same time?

My answer is: You cannot, Lorene. No one can. Given your situation, you are doing well. Change your situation and you will still do well, but not without guilt. There's no such thing as a guilt-free existence unless you're either thoroughly corrupt or without all of your faculties.

So here is the bread I offer you: Stay in charge of your sexuality. You control it, it does not control you. Use M.I.S. as effectively as you can. Search and pray for at-one-ness with another... a committed-for-life relationship. Choose character over charisma. When, in spite of all of the above, you choose to treat your symptoms of loneliness, know that you can begin again because God is a God of Grace and new beginnings.

Above all, remember that Jesus was kinder and more understanding with the lonely who crashed than with the lofty who criticized. Lorene, you are the biblical equivalent of a "Widow"—alone with a child to support and barred by religious conviction from sexual fulfillment outside of extreme good fortune. You are caught in the trap of "Widowhood American Style."

It perplexes me that Christian communities tend to turn their backs on divorced persons. Pastor friends have confided to me that singles are a "real headache" for their churches, because they demand so much attention and give so little money and service in return. These pastors seem oblivious to the fact that single moms (and dads) are the newest poverty group in America.

No wonder you get the "runaround" when you ask about how to handle your sexual needs. Many who have been fortunate enough to escape divorce don't even think you should remarry, let alone find a way to live with your sexual loneliness without being constantly condemned.

I have every confidence that Jesus would confirm our ability to govern our sexual urges. But I also believe He would have the utmost compassion for those who fall short of the standard. If not, we're all "up a creek."

22

CONDONED OR CONDEMNED?

An Honest Look at Homosexuality

Dear Dr. Mann:

You are the only "straight" minister I listen to or watch on TV. I think it is because you're not threatened by the kind of question I'm about to ask you.

I am a male homosexual both in inclination and in practice. I have not "come out." For thirty years I've had a monogamous relationship with a man my age (52). We live in our own respective houses a few blocks apart, work for the same company, and attend the same church.

I no longer resent our homophobic society. I can't change it, so I've learned to live in it with as little hassle as possible.

Dr. Mann, I accepted Christ at the age of twelve. Shortly thereafter I realized that I wasn't attracted sexually to girls. Throughout high school and college I dated girls and tried to present a heterosexual image. I had sex a couple of times with female prostitutes but that was it.

When I was a senior in college I met my life-mate and we've been together ever since. Both of us went through a period of intense therapy (and celibacy) to try to change our sexual inclination. Nothing worked. We had a "covenant ceremony" where we pledged faithfulness to each other for life.

Obviously I want something from you. Gay people who say they don't want society's blessings are hypocrites. If they don't want the blessing, why are they so combative, angry, and aggressive? Anyone who's rejected or discriminated against for something he didn't choose and can't control feels outrage.

I want two things from you. First, I want to hear you say that you think I'm okay the way I am before God. Second, I want to hear you say that you think what I do with my lover is okay before God.

I listen to the way you respond to homosexuals on talk-TV. These are the two things they want to hear from you. And these are the two things you always "slither out" of answering. Please, no slithering!

Dear Perry:

You're correct, I do indeed "slither." Put yourself in my place (you want me to put myself in yours!). No matter how I answer, I will alienate a segment of people whom I could continue to reach if I continue "to wriggle."

There are some issues worth dying on, Perry. Up to now I haven't chosen to die on the issue of homosexuality. Why erase my influence with a whole group of people I could otherwise address by giving you the two things you so candidly admit you want—my endorsement and God's endorsement of what you do?

Yet, after much prayer and thought I have decided to change my "no-position" position. I will answer your two questions with *what I think*. I'm not doing it because you've put me on the spot. The angry segments of the gay and lesbian community are only succeeding in making their accusations of homophobia come true. Sensible people are always frightened by the radical elements of any group or cause.

Anger, which is a form of fear, always breeds equal "counter-anger." Feminists hopefully learned this in their failed attempt to pass the Equal Rights Amendment. They made the strategic mistake of turning over the microphones to extremists. It prompted an equal reaction from women as well as men.

So, Perry, I will not be forced to take a stand because you've shamed me into it, or because clergymen are supposed to line up on the homosexual issue. I've never been a joiner.

I am responding to your letter for only one reason. I hear you crying for a word of hope. I hear you saying that you want a word of hope from a "straight minister" who communes with the same God you met when you were twelve years old. Can God still love you and accept you in spite of who you are and what you do? Or must you live forever outside of His acceptance and His people's acceptance?

Perry, I'm responding to you as one beggar to another. I'm not issuing my formal treatise on "Homosexuals and the Church." You shouldn't use this letter as Gerald Mann's formal position on anything. This is simply what I think about *you* and *your life-style* in particular.

You've asked the two basic questions which haunt every person who is religious—the questions of Being and Doing. The question of Being goes like this: Is who I am acceptable enough to be acceptable to God? Is it okay to be me, or must I be something different in order to be worthy of His love?

The Question of Doing goes like this: Can what I do disqualify my being acceptable to God? Can my actions cause God to reject me?

If I understand the Good News of God in Jesus Christ, it says that God has decided to love and save us *as we are.* Our being is good enough for God, apart from our doing. Once my being is united with God's being, what I do cannot separate me from God's love. The only thing I can do is decide to give my Being to God's Being.

Perry, that is a radical truth!

It applies to you in this way. You did not choose your homosexual inclination. It is a condition which chose you. It was not a decision of Being—you didn't choose to be homosexual. As I said in Chapter 17, the best wisdom we have attributes your condition to a group of sources—biological, hormonal, and psychological—none of which is your "fault."

God loves and accepts you as you *are* because you have chosen to unite your Being with His Being.

Now comes the question of whether such union with God makes people change their sexual inclination. Does a gay person become heterosexual via Christian conversion? The evidence says no. Sexual orientation is apparently one of those things that does not change when we commit our lives to God. In some cases Christian conversion does change the practice of homosexual behavior, but not the inclination.

I know this will cause objection—even rage—among many. But it is a fact.

So, Perry, you are as acceptable to God as any of us.

What about the biblical passages on homosexuality? Are we to ignore them? Obviously not.

The Old Testament forbids homosexual practices. I'll speak to this when I talk about "Doing" in a moment. For now let me speak to the one passage in the Bible which deals with homosexuality and "Being"—Romans 1:18 ff.

Paul mentions homosexual practices as being one of the several results of humankind's choosing to worship the created order instead of the creator. According to Paul, first there was idolatry—worshiping the things made instead of their Maker. Sexual confusion resulted. Men and women became sexually attracted to their own gender. Then there followed confused thinking or "the corrupted mind" which ushered in greed, vice, jealousy, fighting, deception, murder, gossip, bragging, breaking promises, and disobedience to parents.

My point is that Paul lumps the *condition* of homosexuality—being homosexual—into the *total human condition!* Being gay is not some special class of sinfulness. It is part and parcel of the human situation.

In Romans 2:1 ff, Paul quickly adds that passing judgment on others is also a result of humankind's separation from God.

So, Perry, if you are exiled from God's love for having the condition of homosexuality (Being), the rest of us are unacceptable as well. And if the heterosexual community is going to bar you from the church for being gay, it had best bar everyone else who has the other conditions mentioned by Paul in Romans 1 and 2.

Your first request was to hear me say I think you're okay the way you are before God. How could I think otherwise? You didn't choose to be the way you are.

Now for your second request. You want me to say that I think what you do with your lover is okay before God. Sorry, Perry, I honestly can't say it. I can tell you that God forgives wrong behavior. I can tell you that if a church is going to banish practicing homosexuals then it should also banish heterosexuals who have sex outside of marriage.

If you're asking whether I would accept you into the fellowship of the church, the answer is yes.

I would also add that the Old Testament passages which condemn homosexuals to death (Leviticus 18–20), need to be viewed within their historical context. God was dealing with primitive, violent people who had been twelve loosely connected and autonomous tribes of nomads. They were trying to unite and needed a code of laws which could govern their savage mentality.

The first order of business was to preserve the integrity of the family, meaning the sanctity of monogamy, virginity, and authority. The same passages which command the death penalty for homosexuals, command it for other things like adultery, children's disobedience to parents, and having sex with animals!

It is obvious that with the civilizing of society, many of these laws given to manage savages became obsolete. To be specific, Jesus abrogated capital punishment in cases of adultery, when he saved the adulteress from execution (John 8:1–11), and ministered to the adulteress near the well outside of Samaria (John 4).

I cannot tell you that I think God thinks what you are doing sexually is okay. But it's not because I'm condemning you. It's only because I do not know what God "thinks" in your case. There are some behaviors which are obviously wrong anywhere and at anytime. For example, if you are not "loving your neighbor as yourself," you are doing wrong. You must apply that rule to your situation. I cannot do it for you.

So, Perry, to summarize: God accepts and loves you for who you are—with all of your conditions of being. I cannot say that He condones what you do. Only you can determine that.

If you're asking me whether I think God lets practicing homosexuals into Heaven, I can only say I hope so. Otherwise what will become of the rest of us sinners? Getting to Heaven, Perry, has nothing to do with what we do. It depends on who God is and what He will make of us. It depends on God's Grace, not our works.

Do I think God thinks who you are is okay? Answer: He thinks you're okay enough to give His Son for you . . . in other words: Yes!

Do I think God thinks what you do sexually is okay? Answer: I don't know. But given your description of how you live your life I don't think you're any worse than I am. We both have only one thing to fall back on—God's Grace.

23

CAN'T FIX IT

Institutionalizing Someone You Love

Dear Dr. Mann:

Our son was born bright and beautiful, the joy of our lives. Then at two years of age, he choked on an orange peel. Part of the residue lodged in his lung. He developed an infection, suffered oxygen deprivation and brain damage.

Later we had older children who grew up, married, and moved away. Until our son was thirty-five, we were able to manage him. My husband was a minister. The church people helped a lot and so did the other children.

My husband's health began to fail and I couldn't care for him and our son. We placed our boy in a care facility, intending for him to stay for a short time.

We were hoping that the care facility could help him improve his abilities. We were on the waiting list for three years before we could have him admitted.

My husband's illness turned out to be terminal. After he died, I simply couldn't manage our son. I have arthritis and am not well myself.

My son comes home for holidays and is happier here. When I take him back to the home he gets very upset. I miss him and love him so much. But if I try to bring him home permanently, God only knows when I could get him readmitted. He would lose his place. He is almost 50 years old and I am in my seventies. My other kids can't take him in because it would strain their families too much.

Dr. Mann, I feel so guilty. When people ask me about my son I know they are thinking I should keep him. But they don't understand how hard he is to manage. To be blunt about it, he can't dress himself, shave himself, or hold a conversation. He can walk and holler and he's toilet trained. That's about it. He recognizes me but cannot say my name.

Can you tell me something to ease my mind. I can't sleep. I wake up thinking of him and my husband. I'm a nervous wreck.

What would you do, Dr. Mann, and how do I get rid of this guilt? Please write me. I love to watch you on TV.

Dear Alice:

I've read your letter a dozen times ... and cried. I remember the day when we had to leave our little girl (age 10) in a special school for the deaf, 2,000 miles from home. She hung on for dear life. I thought I would die. For the next six years, it never got easier.

When we tried to share our hurt with others, they simply stared at us quizzically. I know what you mean when you say you can tell what others are thinking. We humans tend to shield ourselves from the hurts of others by choosing not to get inside their situations and feel what they are feeling. Or we tend to blame them for their hurting. Our motto seems to be: "When you can't help the victim, blame him for his plight."

Alice, my first impulse is to tell you that your feelings are ill-founded, i.e., "Don't be guilty!" I truly don't think you should be, but I know that telling you not to *feel* is like telling you not to blink your eyes.

From my own experience I can tell you only this: Feel whatever you need to feel in order to survive. We make a grave error in making people feel guilty for feeling guilty. It just might be that guilt is what keeps you going.

So I'm not going to follow my impulse to tell you to stop feeling guilty. That's not the way to help people get rid of their guilt anyway.

Instead, I want to lead you through a step-by-step analysis of your situation and let your feelings do what they will.

Follow along with me. You had a bright and beautiful child that choked on his food. It was in a time when medical science couldn't do what can be done today. The result was an unfair, totally senseless, and forever painful tragedy.

The tragedy took over and directed your entire life. It forced you to make choices which most people don't have to make. Finally, there came the hardest choice of all: whether to turn your child over to the care of others.

There was no way to know ahead of time whether the choice was right or wrong. Could they care for him better than you? Would they? Were you wrong to leave him there, especially when he would rather be with you?

All of these tormenting unknowns had to be acted upon by someone who didn't have divine foresight.

So you took what you knew and you applied it to the alternatives available and made a decision. Now you're having to live with the decision not knowing whether it was correct.

Alice, my honest feeling is that you are angry at God or fate, or the hand you were dealt to play, or whatever you wish to call it. Also, my hunch is that you've never given yourself permission to be angry at God, and that could be the main source of your guilt. You are guilty for being angry at God.

It may help you to know that I have been angry at God to the point of defiance. I have actually dared God to kill me and then cursed Him when He wouldn't!

At the end of these episodes of venting at God, I have

always been inexplicably surrounded by a sense of His love and support.

In other words, I have discovered that God can handle our anger. He is indeed who Jesus said He was—a loving Father who cries, wrestles, and struggles with us through the worst of it.

All I'm saying, Alice, is that perhaps you should see your guilt as unprocessed pain and that one of the sources of that pain could be your unexpressed anger with God. God is a person. You are a person. Personal relationships are built on honest, open dialogue. Express your feelings toward God. He will not abandon you.

There is another source of your guilt which is not healthy. You could be feeling guilty because you are not God. Don't react to this, and don't feel guilty. Simply hear me out. I bring this up because it happened to me.

I was determined to move heaven and earth to see to it that my daughter overcame her handicap and lived as a "normal hearing person" in a hearing world. I was forever pulling strings to avail her of the newest and best scientific experiments. I even enlisted the help of the President of the United States to have her placed in an institution which had a long waiting list.

At forty-three I had a heart attack. It was caused by many factors. But I'm convinced that one of the major factors was my determination to be God in fixing my child's problem.

Now I look back, Alice, and realize that I did everything I could do. But what if there were something I missed? Something I could've done and didn't? Well, no doubt there was! There always is...especially if you're trying to play God.

Alice, I had to admit that I am not God when it comes to fixing my child; and, dear friend, I say with all compassion, I hope you will also.

Let's summarize what I've said up to now: (1) It's okay to be angry with God and to say so. He won't zap you. (2) You are not God. You cannot change what happened to your son. You made all of the best choices you could make, being an imperfect person in an imperfect world.

Now let's have a look at your current pain. You're alone. Your husband is dead. You miss your boy more than usual since you took him back after the holidays. Most of the days of your life have been lived already and you know it. Your other children are basically gone, living their own lives as they should. You want to care for your son, but if you bring him home, he'll lose his place at the care facility. Then when you die, he will have no place to go.

Alice, I believe your current pain centers in the question of why you're still here. You're thinking, "My best purpose for living is to care for my son, but that is not practical. So what is my purpose in life?"

I wish I had an easy answer. Unfortunately, only you can find the purpose for living out the rest of your days. I do have a practical suggestion, however. I know that the care facility where your son lives is several miles from your residence. But you might think of some ways to be closer to him and more involved with him.

This may be impossible logistically or detrimental to the care of your son. The harsh reality is that he will have to live some years of his life without you. Which means, Alice, that whatever you do from here on must be governed by one principle: What is best for your son, given all of the circumstances?

Life has not been as good to you as it could or should have been. One of my favorite sayings is, "There's a Yes in Every Mess." Keep your mind and memories fixed on the "yeses," Alice. You have loved and been loved. You have endured and overcome tragedy. Your lovely little boy who choked on an orange peel may have sent his valuables on to heaven a half-century ago, and he may be waiting there for you now. If not, then you can wait for him when the time is right.

There *is* coming a day, Alice, when God will make the crooked things straight. I have to believe that or I could not live.

In the meantime, Alice, I urge you to leave your son where he is, enjoy him as he is, use your tear ducts, question God, and keep putting one foot in front of the other.

You've made it this far. You are some kind of strong lady! I'm proud to be part of the human race, knowing that you are too.

24

UNEQUALLY YOKED?
Living with an Irreligious Spouse

Dear Dr. Mann:

I'm an active church-going Christian. My husband is a good provider and an honest businessman. He has a few beers on the weekend and uses some profanity, but otherwise is a great guy. He's involved in our children's sports activities and even attends our girl's dance recitals.

The problem is that he won't go to church with me or say grace at the table. He tells me that whatever I do with my life is fine. He doesn't object to my taking the kids to church, just as long as we leave him out of it.

Our two boys are now old enough to notice that their dad isn't religious. They're beginning to give me trouble about attending church. My husband takes their side. He says that he was forced to go to church as a child and he will not allow his kids to be subjected to the same pressure.

This situation is getting worse, Dr. Mann. At church I am being urged to witness to my family. People wonder why my husband won't participate. I'm feeling that I am "unequally yoked to a pagan" as the Bible puts it.

I don't know what to do. I love my husband and don't want to end the marriage. But I also want to be faithful to God. I can't bear to think that I will have to live this way for the rest of my life. Can you help?

Dear Louise:

I don't have to tell you that your marriage is in danger, but I wonder if you know how much. You say that it's great in every area except the religious. I don't want to alarm you but the problem of unshared values is one of the most prevalent destroyers of relationships.

I chose to use your letter in this book because I feel strongly that your problem is not sufficiently recognized and treated in modern times.

The key question I have, after reading your letter, is whether you and your husband hold differing worldviews and values, or whether he is a believer who has been bruised by negative religious experiences in his youth. In other words, is he anti-faith or is he anti–organized religion?

This question has to be answered before you can decide how to deal with your problem. Many people believe in God but find the church unappealing or downright useless in meeting their needs. They are anti–organized religion.

But if your husband is anti-faith—that is, he believes that there is not a Transcendent Reality called God to whom he can relate—your best course is to try to be a "contact point" between him and God.

This does not mean preaching to him or teaching him your belief system. It means *being* the love of God in the flesh to your husband. He will have to see that your faith makes a difference in the way you live life at home—in the kitchen, bedroom, etc.

Louise, you may be the only reflection of Christ he ever sees. God came to show us what He was like in the flesh, i.e. in Jesus. Jesus left and God now resides as Spirit in His people. Our calling is to reflect Christ in the flesh. God shows Himself to people through people! We are the conduits.

I don't want this to burden you with fear and guilt, Louise. I'm not saying that your husband's eternal estate depends on you. For God's sake, don't buy into that notion! You will run yourself crazy and your husband away, if you think his faith depends upon your perfection. The divorce courts are littered with spouses who believed their mission was to conform their mates to a particular religious mode.

Only God can change your husband. And that will happen only with your husband's permission. When I say you are to be like Christ to your husband, I mean that you are to *reflect* Christ by relating as He did.

Also, Louise, don't take responsibility for the results. Your husband will choose to believe or not to believe on his own volition. You have no control over that. In other words, don't let him use *your* imperfections as *his* excuse for not believing. Remember this: God doesn't not make people believe. He does not reveal so much of Himself that people have no choice but to believe. If they choose to believe, they must do so on the basis of less-than-full disclosure. That's what faith is.

So, Louise, don't try to do what even God refuses to do. You cannot be perfect enough to make your husband believe. Simply be who you are as best you can as a committed Christian.

I'm sorry to inform you that your husband will have to come to you. You cannot lay your beliefs on him. About all you can do is live out your faith before him and wait for him to ask you why you live as you do. Don't force God's timetable.

Louise, I also want to remind you that in some cases our closest family members are the hardest ones for us to reach. It is like a surgeon operating on his own family. You may be the least effective person to lead your husband to faith. I know this contradicts what I said earlier, but it is true under certain circumstances.

The reason is that a family member can feel that embracing our brand of faith is the same as giving power over to us. Jesus' mother and His brothers once came to fetch Him home (Matt. 12:46–50). I think it was because they were reluctant to give into Big Brother's religion.

We also know that Jesus was rejected in His own hometown. The people there had watched Him grow up. It was hard for them to imagine Him as God's Anointed One. And it was harder for them to surrender to someone as familiar to them as He was.

So, Louise, you may have to settle for the fact that your husband may never embrace your faith.

This does not have to spell the end of your marriage, however. No marriage is perfect. There are unresolved conflicts in every one of them. Marriages which work do so in spite of conflict, not because all conflicts are resolved.

Let's turn now to the possibility that your husband is anti–organized religion. He believes in God, but he finds nothing at church which meets his needs. Louise, I think that believers will go to church if their hungers are fed there. Some keep going even if the preacher reads from the Yellow Pages, but they are in the minority.

The main reasons for believers to gather are: (1) to celebrate as a family, (2) to recharge their batteries to love the world from Monday through Saturday, and (3) to find healing for their hurts. If they gather in order to gain brownie points with God, they are wasting their time. He already loves them. God doesn't pass or fail people according to whether they attend classes.

Louise, what I'm suggesting is that you may need to find a church which meets your husband's needs. Ask him to choose one. Keep looking till you find it. Regrettably, there may not be one in your community. If that is the case, you will either have to start one or leave your husband be.

I want to take another direction now. I was a professional clergyman for over twenty years before I asked myself a simple question: What did Jesus teach about changing people? What motivational technique would he recommend?

I re-read the Gospels with this question in mind. I urge you to do the same. It will help you formulate a strategy for living with your husband.

I was interested to realize the one thing Jesus tended to avoid in his motivational techniques was negative criticism. Jesus obviously believed that you *can't change people by pointing out their faults!*

For example, study Jesus' encounters with tax collectors like Zacchaeus (Luke 19). Jesus does not remind Zacchaeus of his decision to sell his soul to the Roman government and betray his own countrymen for money. He begins with a cordial greeting and offers him a new way to live his life.

In Luke 6:37–42, Jesus talks about judging (negatively condemning) others. His point is that there is a law of reciprocal return woven in to the fabric of life. If you send out judgment, He says, it will come back to you in kind. If you send out generous acceptance it will come back to you multiplied.

Louise, this means it is an illusion to think you can lead your husband to faith by pointing out his lack of it. Judgment creates an atmosphere of judgment. He will be prompted to focus on your every flaw and counterattack every time you goad him toward religious commitment.

It took me a long time to realize that there are mainly three responses to negative religious judgment. Two are healthy and one is unhealthy. When we are judged by our peers we either fight, flee, or fold.

The first two are healthy self-defense mechanisms. They are efforts to maintain our sense of self-worth. So, Louise, if you judge your husband and he is psychologically healthy, he will counterattack, as I said earlier, or he will distance himself from you.

The third response to religious judgment is to "fold," that is, to be overcome with guilt and shame and to surrender yourself for correction. I believe strongly that Christian conversion does indeed involve self-capitulation. But the surrender must be to God and *not to the belief system of another human who is shaming me.*

Churches are filled with people who have submitted themselves to dogma and what I call "Jesus jive" as a result of being convinced of their unworthiness. These people find themselves living in a community of criticism driven by the competition to see who can earn the highest self-worth through keeping the most rules.

Louise, this may lie at the heart of your husband's refusal to embrace organized religion. When we are judged negatively we either go for self-preservation or sick capitulation.

Conviction of sin is necessary for coming home to God, but it is a mistake to think we sinners can convict our own kind without convicting ourselves. Only God can convict. It's not our job.

Jesus offered negative criticism and even pronounced divine judgment on some occasions. But read the text and the context. His negativity was always directed at those who used criticism to imprison people in a religion of fear and guilt. In other words, the only people Jesus judged were the "Judgers"! I might add that Jesus was the only person qualified to judge... "Let he who is without sin." That leaves out the rest of us.

So Jesus' strategy for leading people to change began with a non-judgmental approach. In essence, He said, *you cannot change people by pointing out their faults.*

The second part of Jesus' strategy—the positive part—says, *you can help to change people by pointing out your own faults.* In the Luke 6 passage and in other passages in the New Testament, Jesus said, "Tend to the plank in your own eye before your concentrate on the speck of sawdust in your brother's eye" (Matt. 7:1–6, my translation).

Louise, just as there is a Law of Reciprocal Judgment woven into life, there is also a Law of Reciprocal Confession. If we confess our sins to others and testify to God's healing, we prompt others to do the same. Judgment breeds judgment. Confession breeds confession.

One of the reasons why the Twelve-Step Program of Alcoholics Anonymous has been so effective in treating people with obsessive compulsive behaviors is the Law of Reciprocal Confession. No one pretends to be righteous enough to judge another. All are equally sick and they confess it. Confession breeds confession, and a healing community is born.

Louise, this is the kind of community the church was meant to be. All I can do to help change people is confess my faults (expose the sawdust in my own eye) and tell of where and how I found healing. When fellow sinners hear this, they will see me as a fellow struggler instead of an adversary.

Churches, parents, schools, and angry social activists would do well to remember the two fundamental laws of Reciprocal Judgment and Reciprocal Confession. These two principles change the world for the worse or for the better.

And, Louise, they are just as valid for you. You cannot change your husband. You cannot even change yourself. Only God can. Your task is to share in deed and word what God is doing to heal you. Your husband will come around or he won't. If he doesn't, do not blame yourself. You weren't put in this world to save people. You were put here to tell people how God is saving you.

25

DOES GOD HAVE A PRICE?
Your Money and God

Dear Dr. Mann:

I was orphaned at the age of twelve, worked my way through college, and became wealthy by the age of 40. I also had a wonderful family—wife and three kids—along the way.

We have attended church regularly since I was converted at the age of 27 (I'm now forty-eight).

I went broke in the real estate business. We lost our home, our cars, our savings, everything. The IRS auctioned off our personal possessions. We now live in an apartment and I'm trying to start over.

My wife has been a great supporter through all of our trials. All of us are healthy. Our two grown children aren't attending the high-dollar universities we had intended, but they are in school and doing well.

There is one serious problem in our lives, however. It didn't seem like much at first, but it raises its ugly head more and more as the years go by.

When we were well-off, my wife and our pastor kept urging me to give ten percent of our income back to God—meaning the church. I gave $100 a week regularly, but that didn't amount to 1 percent of my income in those days.

My wife now believes that my refusal to tithe is the reason we went bankrupt. She says that God does not allow His people to cheat Him and get away with it. I pointed out that I knew many wealthy people who gave nothing to God and didn't believe in Him and didn't worship Him. But they are still wealthy and prospering.

She answers that these people are pagans and don't know any better. She says we knew better and still refused to give.

Dr. Mann, I am beginning to think maybe she's right. I could have been much more generous. I spent money on junk. I blew thousands of dollars on silly things. I've paid $1,000 for meals and drinks on a single night.

I am now praying for God to forgive me. I even find myself trying to bargain with Him—if He will let me prosper again, I will be faithful in supporting His work in the world.

But everything I touch seems to turn bad. Dr. Mann, do you believe that God punishes us financially when we fail to be generous? (I now give the first 10% of everything I make— small though it may be.)

I guess I'm also asking how I get back on God's good side. This letter may sound silly to you, but I need some encouragement.

Dear Robert:

I don't think your letter is silly because I've been through financial fortune and failure myself. It's a long story, but I made a lot of money in a short period of time and then lost it all. Although I gave at least 10% off the top to my church (and sometimes as much as 50%), I know firsthand what it feels like to go broke.

Robert, we can pretend that money and its rewards aren't vital to our self-image, but in our secret hearts we know we aren't being honest—most of us, that is.

We are children of a materialistic society, heirs of a world-view which measures self-worth in terms of having and accumulating. Try as we may, we cannot shake this reality. Even those who rail against materialism are often tenured professors financed by the endowments of those who lived and died by the philosophy of materialism.

The class warfare of modern American politics is often a study in the battle between greed and envy. The greedy want it all. The envious, who don't have it, don't want others to have it. Both are equally driven by the notion that to have means to be, and not to have means not to be.

So don't apologize for grieving over the loss of your "stuff." It's normal given the way we've been programmed from birth.

It's also normal to feel that our financial losses are evidence of God's punishment. Loss of wealth is a grief experience in the same category as the loss of health. When our financial worth is tied to our self-worth, we lose our inner souls when we lose our money.

It shouldn't be this way, but it is. Let's admit it and proceed.

Did God punish you for not tithing? Nope. Would you still have your loot if you had tithed. Nope. God really doesn't need our money, Robert. The preacher does. The church does. The needy do. God can get money whenever He pleases.

Robert, we *need* to give. Giving is one of the most self-serving exercises I know. It's a proven scientific fact. Generous people live longer, feel better, and enjoy spending what's left, more than stingy people do. Whenever God needs money, He awakens people to this truth.

God did not punish you, Robert. You punished yourself. And, by the way, your current practice of tithing won't bring God's favor back to you. You never lost it!

In fact, your going broke could turn out to be the best thing that ever happened to you . . . *if.*

If you can now see that the *real you*, the Robert whom God created and loves is *not* the *Robert-with-his-things*, then your bankruptcy will become your gold mine.

I don't think this has happened for you yet. Nor for your wife. She is as materialistically imprisoned as you are. She has loved the Robert-with-his-things for years. Before that, she loved the Robert-who-could-get-things. She has also seen herself as the wife-of-Robert-with-his-things. Without "things" life has become a zero to her.

If she can come to love herself and you without the things, she will find the end of the rainbow as well.

I have seen financial reversal wreck relationships many times. I've also seen it become the catalyst for the building of real relationships.

I hope I'm making sense, Robert. What I'm trying to tell you is that you are of great worth to God with *no-thing*. God loves you simply because you *are*, not because you *do* or *have*.

Your task—and your wife's as well—is to love the self which God loves. It will be a great day in your life when you can bury the old Robert-with-things. But how can you do that? As I said, it's nearly impossible given our programming.

To be honest, I trick myself into thinking I've done it and then discover I haven't. I'll be with some wealthy person for five minutes and am driven to tell him of "the good old days" when I was as rich as he is.

It's a bummer, Robert. I don't know that we can ever fully escape the demon of measuring who we are by what we have. I haven't, that's for sure.

But I have made this improvement. I now know that when I chase the bucks (and I still do sometimes) or when I grieve over having lost them, it is not God who creates these feelings of greed and grief. It is the "old whore" of my past . . . the siren who beckons me to buy her cheap grace.

Robert, it is not a sin to be rich. It is a sin to have to be rich.

It is not a sin to be poor. It is a sin to resent being poor.

You and your wife are in the Valley of the Shadow of deciding what is really of value. It can be the Valley of the Shadow of Death for your marriage. Or it can be the valley you pass through to a real life.

Robert, there is a deep gorge in the Judean hills called Wadi Kelt. It is a place of wild animals and crevices. It is a shepherd's nightmare. Many sheep are lost there to this day. Some scholars think that David wrote Psalm 23 as he sat overlooking Wadi Kelt. It is the "Valley of the Shadow of Death" which he talks about.

It leads to a place called Jericho, which is one of the most fertile places on earth. The word *Jericho* derives from a word which means "sweet-smelling," "plentiful," "rich."

You are in the Valley of the Shadow of materialism, Robert. But God is with you there ("Thou art with me"). You and your mate can walk to Jericho from there. You *can* pass through the Valley of the Shadow.

There is only one way to get to Jericho and that's by God's voice leading you from within. God didn't let you go broke in order to punish you but to lead you to Jericho.

26

THE VICTIM
When Your Loved One Is Murdered

Dear Dr. Mann:

My daughter was kidnapped, tortured, and murdered by two parolees with prior murder convictions. They had spent more years of their lives in prison than on the outside.

Today, one has been on death row for several years and the other will soon be freed. He testified for the prosecution against his partner and received a lighter sentence.

Dr. Mann, I am not asking you to explain why God allowed this to happen. I've waded through that swamp many times. My problem is bitterness. I hate the man who killed my child. I hate our judicial system. I am eaten up with hatred. It's all I have to live on.

I watched my husband get sick and die. It was cancer, but I believe the cancer was the result of his bitterness and helplessness to fix the awful wrong we suffered.

I have finally come to the place, Dr. Mann, where I know that for my life to have any good purpose, it must be free of this hatred. I read where others have done it. I've tried their techniques. I've asked God to take away my hatred.

Nothing works. I'm now hopeless. I don't go out. I have no friends. Those monsters took my only child. God has cursed me. I think He's turned His back on me.

You see, Dr. Mann, I eloped with my husband against my parent's wishes. They were Baptists and he was Catholic. I was their only child. We never got back together.

Could it be that I'm paying now for what I did to my parents? I didn't even go to their funerals.

Dr. Mann, to be honest, I can't tell whether my problem is totally due to my hatred toward those who killed my daughter or to my guilt from having abandoned my parents. Can you make any sense of this? I need to hear a wise and friendly voice.

Dear Ruth:

I will be a friendly voice. I'll try to be "wise." I share your anger over the sorry condition of our criminal justice system. I have my own opinion about why it neither prevents crime, nor rehabilitates, nor punishes; but you do not need to hear that. You are a victim of its failure. You need to find a way out.

The brightest ray of hope that I detect from your letter is your awareness that your problem is *inside* you. You can't change what happened. You can't bring your daughter back. You can't ever hurt the perpetrators enough to compensate for your loss.

The only thing you can do, Ruth, is deal with the hatred which is consuming you. As long as it remains, those monsters who killed your daughter are still winning. They are torturing you as they tortured her. Executing them would not remove their control. You would still have to deal with the hatred.

You seem to know this already. In other words, you've come to hate your hatred. This is a sign of hope.

Of course knowing what's wrong with us and doing something about it are two different things. Most people know more than they "do." One of the failures of psychoanalysis stems from the false notion that people will change their behavior once they discover its cause.

How do you deal with this hatred which you recognize to be your archenemy? I agree that it is not a matter of technique. There is no formula or "game" people can play to produce forgiveness. The psychobabble books won't do you much good.

Ruth, I am convinced—after observing acts of forgiveness for years and after being able to forgive a couple of times myself—that forgiving is truly a "miracle." It is a gift which comes from outside ourselves. I'm not much into Hollywood–special-effects miracles, but I do believe strongly in God's regular intervention in people's lives to bring about changes which they cannot achieve by themselves.

Several years ago, someone hurt me deeply. It was one of those rare occasions where I had done no wrong to cause this person's attack. He coldly and wantonly injured me like a predator toys with its prey.

There was no way to "get back at him." I wanted to avenge myself, but I couldn't. I seethed in anger at him and God and "the system."

One day I was reading a story called *Tramp for the Lord* (Jove, 1978) by Corrie ten Boom, the Dutch saint who as a young girl was imprisoned in a Nazi concentration camp because she and her family were aiding Jews.

She and her sister suffered all of the horrors we can imagine. Her sister died after one particularly tortuous episode.

After the war, Corrie, who was a devout Christian, traveled throughout Europe giving testimony of how her faith had seen her through her trials. She also called for wholesale forgiveness as the only way to heal the wounds of the war.

After one such speech, she was leaving a meeting hall. A man's voice said to her, "Ya, Corrie. It is true. We have much to forgive for the past." A hand was thrust out to her. She froze. She knew that voice. She looked up into the face of a former Gestapo guard who had been the cruelest to her and her sister.

She writes that her heart stopped for a second. Her hands couldn't move. The old burning hatred for this man returned. She was prepared to kill him.

"God forgive me," she said, "I cannot forgive this man." At that moment, what seemed like a huge weight was lifted from her soul. The hatred just went away! She was able to take the man's hand.

I thought of her story as it applied to me. My heart raced. My temples pounded. I was like a trapped animal. I couldn't forgive the man who had wronged me. I did not want to.

I came to realize that the man who had victimized me was not my master. It was the hatred within me that ruled. I also realized that I had turned my hatred for him into a hatred toward myself. I had begun to think, "How could you have been so stupid as to allow this to happen? You little wimp, why don't you do something to show you're a man? A real man wouldn't let this monster get away with such evil."

In short, I had come to wallow in my hatred.

Like Corrie ten Boom, in an utter helplessness, I cried out, "God, forgive me, I cannot forgive!" And like Corrie, I experienced a miraculous thing. My hatred disappeared.

I must be honest here, Ruth. My hatred has returned from time to time. I still regard the offender with total disgust. But the hatred no longer controls me.

There was nothing that *I did* to make the bitterness vanish. It was not the result of some mental gymnastic. I can't give you a pamphlet entitled, "Four Ways to Erase Hatred."

What happened to me was a gift. It came on the heels of my admitting that I could do nothing about it, and offering myself up to God, bitterness and all.

Which brings me to the second ray of hope I see in your situation. You acknowledge that you are helpless to defeat your hatred. Ruth, it has been my experience that God helps me only when I am helpless *and* admit it. Why should God get involved in doing something for us, when we don't think we need him?

Ruth, you are not very far from the end of your despair. You know your problem. You know your inability to solve it. You know you will die without some resolution. My suggestion is from my own experience and from the testimonies of others. Say, "God, here I am, hate-filled and all, offering what I am to you."

I want to turn now to your past. You're wondering if your elopement and break with your parents caused your calamity later in life, i.e., you hurt them, so God saw to it that you lost your only child.

Utter nonsense, Ruth! Think back. Why did a young girl have to "divorce" her parents in order to marry the man of her choice? Obviously, because they didn't trust the girl's judgment enough or God's Grace enough to let her go!

Your leaving was not a sign of cruelty but a sign of ego—strength. You knew yourself well enough to become an adult, which is a tribute to your parents as well. They raised a child who was emotionally healthy enough to cut the umbilical cord at the proper time.

You didn't tell me whether you and your parents ever tried to reconcile. But since you didn't attend their funerals, I would guess that no reconciliation occurred. You could blame yourself for that, as you obviously have.

However, you could offer that up to God as well. That's why God remains available to people in this world on an everyday basis—to heal their hurts when they come home to Him.

You can finish your business with your parents, even though

they are dead. Ask for the gift of forgiveness. Forgive them and you will be forgiven. I don't understand how this happens, but believe me, it does.

One more thing, Ruth. What I've suggested to you is a process, not a one-time thing. Don't expect your hatred to vanish in a flash never to return. The same goes for your guilt over the estrangement from your parents.

I'm saying that a *beginning* can occur...a monumental breakthrough which starts a process of healing. The pain will return from time to time, and you will have to do the same thing you did at the beginning—offer it up to God.

Ruth, there are numerous small groups of people who practice this process on a daily and weekly basis. They find that meeting and confessing together is the only way to escape being chronic victims. I suggest that you try one of these. You can find them in churches, Twelve-Step Groups, and other places.

You are weary of being the victim. You don't have to live like this forever. The choice is really yours. One of my favorite sayings is: "It's what happens to what happens to you." You have no control over what has happened to you from the "outside." You can choose what happens to what has happened to you on the inside...but not without God's help.

27

THE ICEMAN COMETH
Hope on Death Row

Dear Dr. Mann:

I have little time left. I'm scheduled to die by lethal injection in a few months. My appeals process is exhausted. The Governor has refused to intervene.

I have issued public statements saying that I have made peace with God and do not fear death. I have also asked forgiveness from the families of the lives I took.

Frankly, Dr. Mann, my statements about peace with God are "whistling in the dark." I have not made peace with God. I am terrified of what lies ahead. I have led an evil and vicious life. I have to admit that I always took the easy way out. When I saw something I wanted, whether it was property or sex, I just took it. I didn't want to go to the trouble of earning anything.

Although I was sodomized by my father and older brother, abandoned by my prostitute mother, and kicked from one foster home to the next, I cannot blame society for my crimes. Society didn't kill those people, I did.

I have used the "society's-to-blame" gimmick as a defense to escape the consequences of my crimes. But inside my soul, I know that I am responsible. Others have endured what I went through and have not become criminals.

I am asking if you think there is any way for me to be forgiven by God. I don't mind suffering in this life. I'm suffering now and I should suffer more. Considering what I did, I deserve a lot more pain than I have had so far.

As far as the execution is concerned, I just want to get it over with. Dying won't hurt as bad as living with what I've done.

Is it selfish of me to ask God for another chance? What do you think?

Dear James:

James, I have never received a letter like yours. I hoped I never would. It forces me to think through an issue I would rather avoid. Namely, can/does God forgive those who do the things you've done?

It would seem unfair for Him to do so. The blood of your victims cries out for justice. To think that God could/would forgive such behavior without punishment is beyond my comprehension. I don't see how He could put a cold-blooded killer (which you admit you were) in the same category of grace with, say, a Mother Teresa.

Of course, if you asked Mother Teresa whether she would like spending eternity with you, she would probably answer with a joyful "yes." Mother Teresas are that way. Those of us who fall somewhere on the scale of virtue between her and you, wouldn't be so enthusiastic.

Which brings me to the very first reaction that came to mind when I was pondering how to respond to your letter. The reason I object to God's forgiving you is because your crimes remind me of the darkest side of my own nature.

Inwardly I thought, *I can't bear to think that I would be capable of doing what he's done. It is simply impossible! I could not do it! There's no way for him and me to be of the same species. He is a different animal—vermin to be extermi-*

nated! Executing him will not be killing a human being. He
gave up his right to humanity when he chose to rape and murder. Ask his victims if they had a second chance! Ask them if
he should be forgiven!*

So, James, I must confess up front to a knee-jerk reaction to
your letter. To grant you forgiveness would be admitting that
you and I share the same need for God's grace and are therefore on the same level of virtue. No one wants to think of himself as being like you.

I would rather place you in the "exception" category. To
admit that God can/will forgive you is to admit that I need the
same forgiveness. I know I need it, but I couldn't possibly be
as bad as you.

So I thought some more. An unexpected image came to
mind—the image of heaven. If Heaven is a dimension of existence in which we are freed to grow without impediments,
there can be no place for resentment and grudges. We don't
know much, but we do know this: Humans cannot grow with
hatred and resentment and revenge in their hearts.

Here's the point: If I'm in Heaven, I won't care whether
you're there too. If I do, I won't be in Heaven!

My initial problem with God forgiving you, James, was the
result of transposing my human feelings onto God. I was trying to make God feel like me. Or worse, I was trying to make
myself God!

James, the truth is that I could not and would not let you off
for free. Neither will any human society, even one as lenient
as ours.

But you and I must not project ourselves onto God. What
He does and what we do are not the same.

From what we know of God through Jesus Christ, His Grace
and love are so radical that He can and does forgive anyone
who wants His forgiveness. Jesus told a story about a farmer

who went out to hire day laborers to harvest his fields (Matt. 20:1–16). Early in the morning, he hired several at an agreed daily wage.

At midday he hired more. Then more at mid-afternoon. Then still more one hour before quitting time.

He paid all of them the same wage. Those who worked the longest began to complain. He answered, "Why are you complaining? Didn't I pay you the agreed wage? Why should you care if the others received the same reward? The reward is just and right for you all."

James, that is good news for you and for me. God pays us all our due. And what is our due? It's up to us. The same rich reward awaits all of us who strike our bargain with God.

The bargain is that, if we confess our sins, we can depend on God. He will always forgive our sins and cleanse us from all of our dirt as well (1 John 1:9).

James, I chose your letter because it was perhaps the most radical example of the same questions asked by so many. "Can God forgive and renew someone like me?" He can and He does. People can in most cases. In some cases, they simply do not have the capacity to do so.

James, remember Jesus' quieting words, "Fear not, I am with thee." I hope to see you on the other side.

28

DAMNED IF YOU DO, DAMNED IF YOU DON'T
Divorce and Remarriage

Dear Dr. Mann:

I married at eighteen, had three children and a bad marriage. I say it was "bad" because my wife and I tried to salvage it for twenty and a half of the twenty-one years we were in it. We went to church, to counselors, to marriage enrichment seminars . . . you name it.

We had a dozen diagnoses and God knows how many sermons. We hung in there till our last child went off to college and then agreed to call it quits.

I never believed that a lasting relationship would be possible for me. But you guessed it, I'm in one now. She is a widow my age. We've dated for two years. We're active in our church singles program and have approached the pastor about marriage.

He asked me if my former wife and I were Christians when we divorced. When I said yes, he refused to marry my fiancee and me. He said that the Bible prohibited divorce and remarriage except in the cases of an unbelieving spouse or adultery.

I know it sounds old-fashioned in this day of multiple marriage and divorce, but Dr. Mann, I don't want to offend God. I want to have a truly Christian marriage and stay in the church where we met.

Do you believe we will be committing adultery before God if we marry? I read Jesus' words in Matthew 19:1–12 like our minister told me to.

It seems that Jesus left no loopholes concerning divorce and remarriage. Yet, I have this wonderful lady I want to spend my life with. I feel damned if I do and damned if I don't.
Do you think God would bless or curse our union?

Dear Fred:

Until I started my television program I would not have dreamed that the question of divorce and remarriage was all that prominent in people's minds. In our age of secularism or enlightenment (whichever you choose to call it), I would have thought it was a non-issue.

Yet, your question comes in the mail and over the phone every day. As I said in the Introduction, I am determined to respond to questions which real people are really asking, not to questions I think they ought to be asking.

Millions are divorcing and remarrying every day still believing in God and obviously under the burden of guilt. Like you, Fred, they were born with the fundamental need for at-one-ness with God and with another human at the same time.

I will not take much time in telling you that I think you should remarry. I will take a little more telling you why I think you should.

It is certainly true that God intends for one person to be married to one person for life. Monogamous unadulterated marriage is the cornerstone of society. In civilized society, four institutions exist: the government, the school, the church, and the family. The family can survive without the other three being strong, but the other three cannot survive without the family being strong. Church, government, and school can neither destroy nor save the family, but the family can save or destroy the other three, depending on its strength.

So, Fred, divorce is always a violation of God's purpose for humans. It should be the last resort. I firmly believe that most divorces are unnecessary. In this country, we teach people how to earn a living, plumb the depths of their psyches, win friends, influence people, and hone their bodies. But we do not adequately teach them to do life's most important task—grow into one-ness with another.

Now with all of that said, let me come to your dilemma. Your first marriage failed, if indeed, it wasn't stillborn to begin with. There's no use preaching to you about God's will for your former marriage. It is "former!"

What about now? Why do I tell you to go ahead and remarry? Haven't I read Matthew 19 as well?

Let's have a look at that passage. First look at the context. Two opposing religious parties of Judaism were trying to entrap Jesus. One party took a liberal view toward divorce and remarriage. Women had no status. They were chattel, bought and sold. The liberal group condoned divorce for the slightest cause.

The conservative group allowed for divorce only under the strictest of circumstances. So they asked Jesus, "Does the law allow a man (note, women aren't even mentioned as having any say) to divorce his wife for any reason?" (Matt. 19:3).

If Jesus answers, "yes," He's in trouble. If He answers "no," He's in trouble. So He calls both parties to a higher level of decision. The issue isn't under what circumstances a *man* can throw away his wife as if she were a *thing*. The issue is whether married men are going to act as persons united with persons as God originally intended.

They immediately cite a loophole from the Mosaic Law which instructs a man to give his ex a divorce document which in effect says she's no longer his property, i.e., his animal.

Jesus throws that one back in their faces. "Moses gave that

law," He says, "because you men were so cruelly calloused (Matt. 19:8)." In other words, it was an accommodation to their cruelty given in order to protect women!

Then Jesus utters the phrase that has formed the basis for your pastor's refusal to remarry you: "If a man divorces his wife for any reason he commits adultery if he remarries." (19:9).

Some interpreters think this verse refers to taking marriage casually, i.e., to divorce for just *any convenient excuse.* In essence, Jesus is saying, "You can't throw your wives away on a whim."

Fred, you certainly didn't treat your marriage casually. You tried to resuscitate it for years.

However, I want to go back to Matthew 19 for another look. I don't know why interpreters don't continue reading past Verse 9. The next three verses have Jesus in a private conversation with His disciples, following His seeming prohibition of divorce and remarriage.

His disciples react to what He said. "If that's the way it is between a man and woman," they say, "then it would be best never to marry!" In other words, "If you can't get out under any circumstance, it's best not ever to get in!"

Jesus' response is crucial. "This teaching," He says. Which teaching? The one He's just given the Jewish partisans! "This teaching does not apply to everyone, but only those to whom God has given it" (19:11). And then, "Let him who can accept this teaching do so" (v. 12).

Fred, I believe that in this passage Jesus is upholding the high and sacred calling of marriage on the one hand, and allowing grace for those who fail to achieve it on the other.

I support this with more than what some might call my "tricky interpretation" of Matthew 19. How could the God of the entire Bible—the God of the second and thousandth chance—create us for relationships and then expect us to live in the prison of loneliness for the rest of our lives because we've botched one of those relationships in the past?

I can't help but think of how Jesus treated the Samaritan woman whom He met at the well (John 4). She had been married five times and was currently living with a man unmarried (John 4:17–18).

Jesus gave her "living water" (God's approving love) and sent her home. Her testimony of Jesus' forgiveness led many to follow Him.

Fred, I am probably too impatient on this issue, but I really don't want to say more than this: God has great ideals for us all. We should never use that fact as an excuse not to reach for them. Divorce is the cancer which eats at the vitals of human society.

But there is grace for those who want to begin again. Learn from your former failure. The place where a broken bone heals is said to be stronger than before. Let it be so in your loving. Let the broken places of your former marriage be the strongest places in your new one.

PART III

QUESTIONS OF LIFE'S WORTH

29

FREE OF THE SHAME
Recovering from Child Abuse

Dear Dr. Mann:

I was sexually abused as a child by my uncle. I was afraid to tell my parents, so the abuse continued from the time I was ten years old until I reached sixteen. My uncle moved away and I never told anyone.

I'm wondering how to get God to forgive me. I have prayed and prayed but the guilt won't go away. The worst part of my guilt is that I like sex so much. As a teenager, I had more experience than others my age. I knew what boys liked and I gave it to them.

I am now married for fifteen years and have never betrayed my husband. We have two sons and we go to church regularly.

But I cannot shake the stain of my sins. I am haunted constantly. When I enjoy sex I feel guilty. I feel like such a hypocrite. It's like there's another me, a dark me nobody knows. I can't feel God's forgiveness and I can't forgive myself.

Should I just keep asking God to forgive me for this sin? If I ask long enough will God finally hear me and heal me?

Dear Rhonda:

Only in the past few years have we learned the magnitude of the problem of sexual abuse of children. As a pastor I heard of this tragedy many years ago. At first I didn't believe it. It was beyond my comprehension.

Now we know that there are millions of women who have carried this dark secret in their souls for years.

Why have they been so quiet? For the same reason you have kept your experience private: Sex was "the unmentionable" for generations. We were also a male-dominated society. Illicit sexual behavior was always connected somehow to the woman. "She was asking for it," was the common attitude. Sex and sin were synonymous. For children, sex was this huge taboo not to be discussed.

Also, in the days before the Pill, sexual activity in marriage was limited because of the fear of pregnancy. Men used this as an excuse for "fulfilling themselves" elsewhere.

We cannot leave the blatant fact of human evil out of the equation either. The harsh fact is that some adults prey upon those who are the most defenseless.

So, Rhonda, you were an easy victim in a conspiracy of silence. The worst part was that you were also made to feel guilty because you had been abused! You felt that it was somehow your fault. Or at least you were made to feel like a willing accomplice.

All of the above made you "afraid to tell your parents," as you put it. How could you bring up a subject which they themselves were ashamed to talk about? How could you give them a graphic description of what your uncle was doing to you, when you didn't have the vocabulary to describe it?

Rhonda, you are a double victim. First, you are the victim of an evil man. Second, you are the victim of a mentality which had so equated sex with sin that it chose to ignore, to sweep under the rug, the reality of the rape of children.

So to begin with, I want to assure you that you need no forgiveness for having been raped by your uncle. And you need no forgiveness for keeping it a secret. You did nothing wrong. How God must weep when he hears you begging for Him to forgive you of something you never did!

What about you behavior later in life? As a result of your sexual experience, you knew what men liked and you liked pleasing them. You like sex now. And, naturally, you feel guilty. You feel like a hypocrite.

You seem to be saying that in order to receive God's forgiveness you would have to stop enjoying sex with your husband. Nonsense!

Rhonda, we all have unprocessed sins, real and imagined, which haunt us. I'll speak to this in a moment. But first let me say that your ability to enjoy sex with your husband now, your ability to be a good mother, and your ability to worship God are all miracles, considering what you've been through.

There are millions of sex-abuse victims who would envy you. Many will never be able to enjoy sex, love any man, or have a functional family.

In my opinion, the clearest evidence of you're being right with God is the way in which you have managed to overcome this horrible crime done to you.

You ask how to *feel* God's forgiveness. I wish I could give you a snap answer or a one-two-three formula. I cannot. However, I can tell you that you are forgiven even if you don't feel it. God's forgiveness is like the sun. Even though it's behind the clouds and you can't feel it, it's still there and it's still giving you life.

Rhonda, God forgave you long ago. The guilt you feel isn't coming from Him. It's coming from what I call the "Shamers of Childhood." We are all born into a society where certain behaviors are considered so shameful that adults only discuss them in whispers and behind closed doors. When children observe the body language which accompanies these subjects, they are awed and shamed by the very thought of them.

The feelings of shame never leave us, even though we grow

up and no longer consciously feel their original curse. Let me give you an example.

I was born just after the Great Depression of the 1930s. My parents had stood in soup lines and worked for fifty cents a day. By the time I was able to perceive things, my parents were doing well financially. However, they were constantly in fear of reliving the hard times of the Depression. They worried over money and things constantly.

When I was about six, my dad made a poor business decision. He and mother went behind closed doors. Their body language told me that something ominous was happening.

I peeked through the keyhole. My father had his head buried in Mom's bosom and he was crying. She was patting him and rocking him back and forth as if he were an infant. I heard him sob, "We are going to lose everything! We won't have a home. Our kids won't have clothes. They will come and take the car and furniture."

For me to see my dad like that was the most horrifying experience of my young life. In a few years, he would be wealthy and we would live on a huge ranch in a huge house.

But as the years passed, I came to realize that something had happened way down inside me on the day I saw my father in his anguish. A Shamer was planted in my soul forever. He is still there. He constantly says to my "feeling box": *Shame on you for not being financially secure! Shame on you, if you don't give your kids the best! Shame on you for not being as rich as so and so!"*

I know in my rational mind that I will probably live my life better off financially than 95 percent of the people who have ever been born. My problem is not having too little, it's having too much.

But the "Shamer of my Childhood" is still there telling me how to feel.

Rhonda, we never completely rid ourselves of the Shamer. All we can do is recognize him for what he is—a false demon, a liar. You cannot change what happened to you. And probably you cannot rid yourself of the Shamer.

But you can know him when you see him. Every time he jumps up you can call him a liar and tell him that God is the only one who can tell you who you are. You are God's own beloved child and nothing can ever change that.

Before I close I want to talk to you about the future. There are some things you may want to consider. First, you have made a beginning by writing to me. You have cracked the door of the closet. You may want to link up with others like yourself. Support groups are a treasure for many. In them you will discover that you are not alone or a freak. You are a child of God who was brutalized by a sick and evil man.

I hesitate to bring this up because you may not be ready for it. If it sounds repulsive just put it in the back of your mind for later consideration. Some sex-abuse victims have found healing by confronting their offenders. Not in a combative way, but in a quiet honest way.

They ask the offender why he committed this act. They also announce to him that his offense will no longer be able to control them. Rhonda, some even find the power to forgive. This is the ultimate release. It opens the door of the closet once and forever. The Shamer sometimes vanishes.

But let me caution you, Rhonda, that this requires the help of a professional coach and a gift from God. First, see a good counselor. Then ask for God's help. Sometimes it is not good to confront the offender. Sometimes it is absolutely the worst thing to do. You must decide this after much prayer and counsel.

If the offender is now dead, you can still "let go" of what he did to you. God can give you this gift. It will set you free from bitterness and shame.

30

THE 500-POUND PRISON
Helpless Isn't Hopeless

Dear Dr. Mann:

I am confined to a wheelchair at the age of thirty-eight. I live in a bungalow at a care complex. Each resident has a separate dwelling with available nursing care and food facilities.

The complex is in a beautiful nature setting ... mountains, animals, trees. Most of the residents are elderly. Almost every week I see someone rolled away in a body bag. They have no family and no friends. They're just hauled off and buried. It is so depressing.

To make things worse, I am not in this wheelchair because I'm crippled or paralyzed. I do have a disease of the joints as well as diabetes, but these problems are complicated by the fact that I weigh almost 500 pounds.

Can you imagine that? I am this mountain of flesh. My problem is self-induced. I could manage my other ailments if I weren't so overweight.

I was once a beautiful girl—the most beautiful in my senior class and the homecoming queen. I was married for a while to a guy who was lazy and adulterous. I couldn't have children. Now I am alone. My parents are dead. I was an only child.

I guess I'm writing to ask you what a person like me should do with her life. I see no reason to go on. Why not commit suicide? I could move to a place where I didn't have to see corpses wheeled by my window. But what then?

How can someone who is trapped in five hundred pounds of

flesh and a wheelchair find anything in life worth living for? I
pray and pray to God for happiness. Nothing happens.

Dear Annette:

I receive many letters like yours asking one of life's most
haunting questions: How do I find meaning in the most miserable of circumstances?

Eventually I answer all of them by saying the same thing:
To find meaning—that energy which gives purpose and fulfillment—is always an inside job. It has nothing to do with our
outward circumstances. It depends on how we choose to
respond to them.

That is a bold statement, Annette. It sounds too absolute,
too demanding. It is easy for me to say because I'm not dia-
betic, overweight, and confined to a wheelchair, right? I can
only tell you two things.

First, many others find meaning in your kind of circumstances. Second, many people who live in circumstances opposite of yours suffer from the same kind of depression.
Meaning is not determined by our circumstances but by how
we choose to respond to them.

Please don't think I'm blaming you for being depressed.
I'm not saying you choose to feel badly. That's a god-awful
opinion preached far and wide these days. We make people
feel guilty and depressed for being depressed! We make them
unhappy for being unhappy. That's like blaming people for
bleeding when they've been cut.

You have not chosen to be depressed. Depression is one of
the ways the soul bleeds. It is psyche's reaction to injury. It is
normal and unavoidable.

You cannot choose to stop being depressed. Every time

someone reads one of the Don't-Worry-Be-Happy books and then announces to me that they have chosen never to be unhappy again, I cringe. They are setting themselves up for a wreck.

When I say we can choose how we respond to our circumstances, I mean, we can choose how to respond to our *depression and all of the other feelings which come with our circumstances.*

Annette, when you look at bodies being wheeled by, you get depressed. That's normal. You are being reminded of your own mortality. You know your time is short. You know that you're confined to a 500 pound "body bag" which has to be wheeled around now.

The question is, what can you choose to do about your depression? Losing 350 pounds is probably not a realistic option. I know that sounds defeatist. But I would guess that you agree. If you don't agree, fine. Get on a weight-reduction program. Plan to take two to three years in the process. It *can* be done.

However, I would suggest a route prior to that one. I know you have a good mind. You write well. You can use the telephone. You can get from your cottage to the cafeteria, so you are ambulatory to some degree.

Here's what I'm suggesting: Take stock of all of the tools you can use, given your situation. Then match those tools with the needs of others around you.

You tell me of lonely, aged people all around you. Their remains pass by your door weekly.

When they get to your door, Annette, they no longer need you. But what about before they get to your door?

The best way I know to handle depression is to "seize it by the throat"—to use it as a way to connect with others around me. Annette, *you* know how these people feel! You can get rid of your depression by helping the depressed. No one can relate to them better than you can.

Or you can try to run from it. You mentioned moving to a place where you wouldn't have to witness death. I don't know where that would be. It is not "their" deaths that is haunting you. It is your own dying! And that fear would move with you wherever you went.

You also mentioned that you pray to God for happiness and nothing happens. There is a great myth about happiness, Annette. Most of us accept it as truth and end up in the fog of unhappiness. The myth is that happiness is some constant pain-free state of being which can be earned with proper effort and proper circumstances. Happiness is a goal, a treasure we can grab onto if we're smart enough, rich enough, spiritual enough, etc.

What a lie! First of all, if we were meant to be pain-free, we wouldn't have been born to die. Death foils the whole notion of happiness as an *achieved state of being*.

Happiness is not something you can go out and get. It's not a possession. It's a by-product. Happiness is something which finds us while we're doing something else.

That's why I am suggesting that you shift your focus from *your* weight, and *your* illness, and *your* circumstances to those of others.

There is a wonderful saying. I don't know where I got it. But it goes like this:

> If you want to be happy for an hour,
>> take a nap.
> If you want to be happy for a day,
>> go fishing.
> If you want to be happy for a year,
>> inherit a fortune.
> If you want to be happy for lifetime,
>> help others.

Annette, I am not surprised to learn that your prayers for happiness aren't working. You're asking God for something He won't give. He will not imbue you with some "Stardust Potion" called Happy. He *will* give you the power to *use what you choose* i.e., to use your tools to turn your life outward. Granted, your tools are limited, but you can choose to use them.

Your prison is not a "500 pound mountain of flesh," as you call it. It is your feeling of hopelessness. Annette, you are not alone, you are not hopeless, and you are not helpless—except in your mind.

31

THE RIGHTEST OF ALL WRONGS
Making Ethical Decisions

Dear Dr. Mann:

I am a sixty-six-year-old widower "living in sin" with a sixty-five-year-old widow. We love each other very much and have a growing relationship. But we haven't legally married.

The reason is that we would lose pension and medical benefits if we were to marry. I know that it is wrong to live together out of wedlock. It is also wrong to choose money over love. The law is the law, after all. However, if we marry legally, our children would probably have to take care of us. This wouldn't be fair to them. Also our medical benefits would decline, which is unthinkable at our age.

I am not asking you to condone or to condemn what we're doing. Knowing you from TV, I don't think you would do either. As you say quite often, God does the judging, not you.

What I want is some advice about how to think through my dilemma to a conclusion. I love God and want to do His will. But I think it is His will for me to love and care for this lady. I think He gave us to each other. Please help me think through this. Don't give me your blessing or your scorn. Give me your helpful thoughts.

Dear George:

I chose to include my response to your letter in this book because it represents the real-life ethical dilemmas which people face every day. Your problem is not some ivory-tower subject for intellectual debate. There is no universal law or religious code which can tell you exactly what to do in your situation.

Absolutes are easy to live by in an abstract world. But you're caught in an imperfect real world. So I will try to help you think through your dilemma, as you have requested. In the end, I won't tell you what I think you should do. You are bright enough and moral enough to make your own decision.

I have already tipped my hand by saying that there are no absolutes which fit your situation. You believe it is wrong to live together without being legally married. You believe it is wrong to choose money over love.

But it is also wrong to marry someone when you know you will not have the adequate financial means to care for her and yourself. It is wrong to shift the responsibility for your financial security to your children who already have commitments to keep.

George, I could shoot some holes in both sides of this thinking. On the one hand I could tell you that there are two kinds of marriage—legal marriage and spiritual marriage. A legal document issued by the State does not make or break a marriage in God's eyes.

There are many who believe that legal marriage and church marriage should be entirely separate. Let a State Magistrate perform a ceremony which gives legal rights to the partners and their heirs, and provides for division of property in the case of divorce. Then let the couple come to the Church and make a covenant of fidelity before God.

Under this scenario, George, your problem would be solved. But I'm not recommending this. For one thing the Bible instructs us to obey the law. There must be order in society and Christians must be supporters of that order. The only time we should break the law is when the State makes us choose between allegiance to itself and allegiance to God. And even then we must be prepared to suffer the penalty for our lawlessness. Jesus did. Paul did. Many others have.

On the other hand, I can shoot holes in the argument that it is wrong to marry someone whom you know you cannot care for financially. You say that if you married legally your medical and retirement benefits would be dramatically reduced.

Well, George, how do you know that God would not honor your integrity and provide for your needs? Also what is love if not a decision to risk everything for another? I could argue that your position exhibits a real lack of faith. No one is *secure* in this world, George. I once saw a man who was worth four hundred million dollars choke to death on one bite of a $50.00 steak!

My point is that I can show you where you're somewhat right and somewhat wrong on either side of the issue. If you continue to live together unmarried for the sake of financial security, you are not completely committing yourself to love and to God. If you marry legally, you are allowing a foolish and unjust law to deprive you of your rightful benefits. You have been faithful, you paid your dues. You and your lady have both suffered the loss of a spouse. It's only right that you should enjoy the years you have left in a relationship of financial *and* spiritual security.

So there it is, George, argued from both sides. There are no laws which can justly cover every situation before it occurs. Whenever I say this, the absolutists howl and the situation-ethicists applaud.

The latter group likes to believe that because there are no absolutes for every situation, there are no absolutes whatsoever. They are forever saying "All things are relative. There are no absolutes."

George, *that* is an absolutist statement if I ever heard one!

It's really saying that each person is his own absolute, his own God, in every situation and that there are no laws or rules higher than what a person wants at any given moment. "Whatever I feel like doing" is the absolute. No individual or society ever survives for very long if it lives by that doctrine.

So, neither the Absolute Legal approach nor the Absolute Feeling approach can meet the needs of choosing between right and wrong in everyday life. Codes of law cover most situations but not all. Your situation, George, is a case in point.

Let me suggest another way of approaching your dilemma. Students of ethics call it the Principle Approach. It says, there are principles which can be applied to situations like yours. In those extreme situations where there's no law to tell us what's right and wrong, we can apply principles which allow us to choose the *rightist of all the wrongs.*

Let's apply your dilemma as an example. It would be wrong to break the law and wrong to choose financial security over love and faith. But it would also be wrong to forfeit your well deserved pension benefits, and wrong to willfully burden your children with the costs of your old age. So it's not a choice between right and wrong. It's a choice between the lesser of wrongs.

Now what principles can we draw from in order to help us decide which is the rightest of all the wrong paths?

As a Christian I would first look to the principles Jesus taught and lived. The chief principle was love. The Greek word for "love" as used in the New Testament was *agape.* It means to pour out yourself for others in such a way that both parties grow. Scott Peck in *The Road Less Travelled* describes it as stretching or expanding oneself in order to expand another self.

Jesus said that all moral laws could be reduced to one principle: Love God as hard as you can, and love your neighbor (the object of your love) as you love yourself (Matt. 22:37–40).

So the governing principle in deciding right from wrong—or in choosing the rightest of the wrongs—is *love* as Jesus defined it.

What would Jesus do if he were in your situation, George? We have some clues. Once He and His disciples were hungry. They stopped by the roadside and picked some grain to eat. It was on the Sabbath (Mark 2). The Law said it was wrong to pick grain on the Sabbath, and Jesus strongly believed in the Law. In fact, He told His disciples that every letter of the Law had to be obeyed (Matt. 5). Whoever disobeyed even the smallest law would be least in the Kingdom of Heaven.

Yet He broke the Law! When He was challenged, He answered, "The Sabbath was established to serve the good of man. Man was not created to serve the Sabbath" (Mark 2:27, my translation).

He was pointing to a principle here, George. It is a principle which is higher than man-made laws. People are to use the Sabbath to help people. Whenever the good of persons clashes with the letter of the Law, persons come first. Love God by loving Neighbor. Love before law.

George, your decision must be governed by this principle. What comes closest to loving your mate as God would have you love her? Would it be better to live out your days together in a relationship of fidelity and commitment without a marriage document, but with financial security? Or would it be best to comply with the law, take the leap of faith and trust that God will see that your needs are met?

There is no law which fits your situation perfectly. But there is a principle . . . the principle of love, Jesus' style.

32

APOCALYPSE NOW?
Facing Discouragement About the World

Dear Dr. Mann:

My wife and I have moved from the city where together we made $150,000 a year. We sold our home, cars, furniture, jewelry, etc., and purchased some acreage in a remote area of the Northwest. We home-school our three children, grow our own food and never go to town unless it's absolutely necessary.

Our only link with the outside world is our satellite TV dish. Occasionally we watch your call-in show and are amazed that you are not discouraged about the future survival of humans on this planet.

We left the so-called "civilized world" because we think it is doomed. We are not willing to subject our children to the continuing deterioration of society. America has obviously passed its Golden Age. To use Spengler's analogy from his book, The Decline of the West, *we are now in the late autumn of our existence. Winter is coming on fast. Although we have the military might to rule the world, we have lost the moral courage to rule ourselves.*

How do you keep from being discouraged? You seem to be a learned man. Why can't you see what the signs of the times are telling us. When America goes down, the entire world will go down with it. The dissolution of the U.S.S.R. is no cause for hope. As America rots within, it will reach a point where it blows up the world in order to save itself.

Our leaders get weaker and weaker. No one with true lead-

*ership capability is permitted by the fourth branch of govern-
ment (the media) to ascend to office.*

*I know I probably sound like a paranoid nut. I am not. I
have no guns and no locks on my doors. We are Christian people. We give away everything but the barest necessities.*

*Also, I am not trying to lure you into an argument. I truly
want to know where and how you find hope for the future in
this decaying world.*

Dear Jack:

I do not think you are a "paranoid nut," as you put it. You
and a growing number of others are seriously embracing the
"Apocalyptic Viewpoint." Observers are quick to point out
that this happens near the turn of every century and especially
near the end of a millennium. They say it is only normal to
expect a "Doom Boom" as the year 2000 approaches.

Time is a human mental construct. The passing of a day or
a year or a millennium has no significance unless we impose
some significance upon it. So, the observers say, we should
simply take attitudes like yours with a grain of salt.

I disagree. Your question is not due to "time-tinkering." It
is based upon an intelligent assessment of world and national
conditions.

At the moment America indeed appears out of control.
Most of the institutions which hold a civilization together are
failing. Federal government has done nothing efficiently or
effectively in recent years except wage war. Arguably its last
real triumph was landing a man on the moon.

Public education no longer works except in limited pockets.
The criminal justice system neither prevents, deters, nor punishes crime.

Organized religion is a dinosaur. The church of my youth no longer exists in a sympathetic culture. It now lives in an indifferent culture. It simply doesn't matter. The only churches which are growing are those who see themselves as missions in a foreign land; or those who peddle narcotic faith to religious addicts. America is truly the greatest mission field in the world today; because most of the people claim they believe in God, but are not seriously involved in a religious movement.

I'm getting ahead of myself, Jack. My point is that I am not naysaying your pessimistic diagnosis of America. We are in a precarious time.

While America was still thirteen British colonies, Alexander Tyler analyzed the fall of Grecian democracy. He said that democracy can last only until the people learn how to vote themselves excessive gratuities from the public treasury. Once they learn how to do this, they elect only those who promise them gratuities if elected. Eventually, says Tyler, the government collapses because of poor fiscal policy.

Frightening thoughts, right? It's enough to make a person liquidate, retreat to the wilderness, live off the land, and insulate his family from a corrupt society. Or maybe start applying the dramatic apocalyptic visions of the Book of Revelation to current events.

But you are correct, Jack. In spite of all of the above, I am not discouraged enough to join you in your retreat. I'm not criticizing your choice. I'm simply not ready to give up; and it's not because I'm a blind optimist.

There are some solid reasons to be hopeful and to give the rest of my life to making my little piece of the world a better place.

Let me give you some things to consider. First, although our social situation is serious, it may not be in as bad a shape as we think. Perception and reality are rarely congruent. I believe our problems have a lot to do with perception. We perceive things as hopeless, therefore they are.

You mentioned the media. News in America is a for-profit enterprise. The Nielsen television ratings drive the content of news, sitcoms, drama, etc. Fear sells. Bad news and disaster sell. Unless the public is jolted out off its couch it switches channels. The finger that pushes the remote button rules the world.

Jack, I think we've had a "snow-job" done on us. We are convinced of doom to the extent that we add to it with a defeatist attitude.

We are also disillusioned because we've believed in an illusion for about thirty-something years now. I agree with historian Paul Johnson in his answer to why Americans feel so bad when they have it so good. He says the Founding Fathers were represented by two kinds of men whose viewpoints served to balance each other.

One group was made up of visionary entrepreneurs. They dreamed of a kind of religious utopia based upon Judaeo-Christian ethics. The poor from Europe could come here and fulfill their dreams of plenty and dignity. The supply of free and cheap land seemed unlimited. These visionaries were like missionary fanatics.

Balancing the religious utopians were pragmatic, hard-nosed businessmen like Thomas Jefferson. They saw the dangers which lay in garnishing power, incurring federal debt, and worshipping material prosperity at the expense of justice.

Throughout America's history, these two factions balanced each other well. Every time the visionaries ran up the federal debt, the pragmatists brought it back down.

Then something crucial happened. The utopian dream was cut loose from its religious moorings. It became a *secular* utopian dream. It was thought that government was able to bring happiness and tranquility to every citizen and cure all human ills. The pragmatists also gave in to the public's desire to vote itself gratuities from the federal treasury.

Johnson feels that we are now in a national state of melancholy because we know we cannot keep on living this way: hocking our children's future, not maintaining order, not giving the educational system back to parents, and not recovering our spiritual center. He believes that we are on the verge of a "reawakening of conscience," which I take to mean a moral and spiritual revival.

I hope he is correct. But I will not be disheartened to the point of resigning from society if he is not. You see, Jack, my hope does not rest on the rise and fall of political, social, or economic structures. In fact, I would expect America to fade as the dominant world power. All other cultures have shined for a while and then faded. Why should it be different for us? We are not God's only pets.

However, I don't think we will collapse or be conquered. I think that globalization is more likely. By this, I mean that I expect the world to grow smaller politically and economically. Democracy is breaking out worldwide. National economies are now so intertwined that no economic power can act without regard for others.

War on a worldwide scale is already obsolete and small regional wars will soon be self-defeating for everyone involved.

America could be on the edge of its finest hour. No one has been able to assimilate people of different cultures like we have. Also, no nation in history has been able to make deep-rooted changes the way we have. When the Great Depression of the 1930s struck, political analysts were singing America's death song. Democracy had failed! The great experiment was a bust!

What did we do? We adjusted, adapted, and recovered! In the 1970s during the Jimmy Carter administration, America's best were telling us that no young couple would ever again be able to afford a home without help from parents or government. As I write this, homes are selling like crazy to people who were born in 1970!

So, Jack, when I say we could be on the edge of our "finest hour," I do not mean we are about to rule the world without peer. I mean we could lead the world toward a new and true unity of nations. We have the power to oversee the unification of the world, technologically, economically, politically, and *yes*, even spiritually.

Earlier I said that I believe America is the world's greatest mission field, spiritually speaking. Over ninety percent of Americans pray every day. Most no longer participate in religious movements, but they are more open to spiritual considerations than at any time in the past half-century.

Herein is my hope, Jack. All of our other would-be saviors have failed us. God has seen to it that we don't settle for idols of our own creation. The time is ripe.

Let's suppose I am wrong and you are right. Then the question becomes: What is the best way to spend one's life in a dying civilization? My answer is: *Spend your life preserving something which will rise out of the ashes when this civilization is gone!*

Malcolm Muggeridge used to talk about the "Stay-Behind Agents." Whenever a war is being lost and the vanquished are preparing to retreat, they choose their most canny, hopeful spies to stay behind and to work in the midst of enemy-occupied territory.

Count me among the "Stay-Behinds," Jack. I do not think the end is near for America. Nor do I think the end is near theologically, i.e., that God is about to wind up everything. But if either be the case, I will be found working right up to the last day, planting the seeds of His grace. And I will stay behind and work in whatever is left if that is my lot.

This is not bravado or religious posturing on my part. My convictions are based upon the belief that God is in the midst of history working His will. That is it, pure and simple. I find no excitement in withdrawing physically and emotionally from the world's corruption. Jesus told us to be yeast in the dough.

One parting question: What are you educating your children to do and to be, after the world goes to Hell and you're dead?

33

MAKING LIFE COUNT
Choosing How to Spend Your Life

Dear Dr. Mann:

I'm a college freshman trying to decide what to do with my life. I want to make it count. I want to do something worthwhile, make a contribution, leave the world a little better off because I was here.

But I am constantly being reminded that today's popular professions are likely to be obsolete by the time I finish my schooling. "Acceleration in the speed of change" is the theme song of all of the seers and experts I read.

I know you can't tell me specifically what and where and how. But could you give me some "hopeful" hints. I could use some helpful ones too, but mostly I need hope. I am haunted by this feeling that I have been born at a time when individuals can no longer make a difference.

Dear Terry:

I hear your "mournful cry" from many young people today. I say "mournful" because many youth are grieving over the perceived loss of possible significance in this chaotic world.

We are all fed a constant diet of propaganda which says that your generation will be the first in American history to be dumber, poorer, and sorrier than the generation before them. Up until the fourth quarter of the twentieth century, supposedly every generation has been better off educationally, financially,

223

and morally than the one preceding it. Your generation, they say, will be the first exception.

No wonder young people are in mourning! You're being led to believe that you've already lost Camelot by virtue of having been born at the wrong time!

Terry, I reject this kind of deterministic pessimism. It is not only self-fulfilling, it is downright incorrect. I was your age in the late 50s, the so-called Golden-Age of America. Morally speaking, things were different but not because people were better. Teenage and unwanted pregnancies ended in marriage. Abortion was unavailable and most women were looking to get married in their late teens and early twenties anyway. It was simply what you *did!*

Many of these "early marriages" contributed to the rising divorce rates of the 60s and 70s.

So you see, Terry, it is easy to misinterpret the lack of options of an earlier generation as a higher moral standard.

Here's another example. We have heard the recurring refrain about the "greedy 70s and 80s." The huge fortunes which were once created by manufacturing and the genius of invention that lay behind it are now being made by the "take-over parasites" who create and manufacture nothing. Disputes once settled with guns and fists now end up in civil courts. Children know the dreaded word "lawsuit" before they get to the second grade.

Well, Terry, again I say this is playing fast and loose with history. The Great Depression of the 1930s was caused by greedy men garnering the nation's wealth. American greed wasn't born in the 1980s!

Urbanization is another example of the fact that times not people have changed. In the rural America of my birth, people had to manufacture quality goods and "make them good" or they went out of business. The producer and the consumer knew each other. Their kids went to the same school. If an appliance failed, the owner could telephone a person not a voice-mail recording.

I once asked my grandfather why the people in our small town of 2,000 were so honest. He said, "Because all of the dishonest ones were either shot or run out of town."

Today, you can be dishonest without the threat of either of those two consequences.

So, Terry, I do not think people are less moral today than before. The definitions of what comprises moral behavior have changed. Behaviors which were once kept in the closet are now the fodder for brainless talk shows which require the most bizarre topics in order to keep their ratings.

In many ways I think today's youth are more morally disciplined than their Boomer parents. Teenagers have earlier exposure to moral decisions. They don't have the luxury of maturation. Also they have more choices. It is simply easier to make bad choices now, than it was twenty-five years ago.

So, Terry, I wouldn't buy the song about your generation being "sorrier" than those preceding it. Nor do I accept the "dumber" label. First, I want to ask, what is a "dumb" person? Does *dumb* mean less informed than one's predecessors? My grandchildren have more information about everything than I did when I was twice their age.

Or does *dumb* mean not as well informed as the children of our economic competitors. Japan is often used as the standard of comparison. Also, a disproportionate number of children of recent immigrants are appearing on dean's lists and honor rolls. This is supposed to mean that we are slipping.

I don't buy it. The academic excellence of immigrants is due more to attitude than aptitude. It is true that America has lost its edge in manufacturing, but so what! The economic future no longer rests upon manufacturing and industrialization.

It rests upon controlling and delivering information. America is without peer in this arena.

Your generation will indeed not do as well in the realms in which your ancestors excelled. But, Terry, *there are always new realms!* And the American pioneer spirit is as strong as ever. We still lead the world in conception of ideas and technologies, even if we don't bring them into reality as efficiently as those who copy us.

The claim that your generation will be poorer is an absolute joke. Again, what is "poorer"? Does it mean you'll have fewer toys? Or you'll travel less? Or you'll have fewer homes? Or less-paying jobs? You certainly won't have fewer toys, if toys mean playthings and objects of amusement. We're on the brink of having a highway of information, pleasure and games, flowing into our living rooms. Television, telephone, and computer technology will merge into a river of "toys."

Now if "toys" means those things we accumulate in order to make us superior to others, your generation may be in for some depression. The only way you and your children will be able to pay off the deficits run up by your so-called "more righteous, smarter and richer" forebears, is via taxation or a complete economic collapse.

The second may not be as disastrous as it seems. Everyone could start over again from zero. People could look to something besides their neighbor's wealth for meaning. Families would not be able to abandon commitments as easily. There would no longer be a Third World, just a First One.

Well, that is a bit idealistic, Terry. I threw it in only to point out that worldwide economic depression would not be the end of the world. It could be the beginning of a better one.

Okay, enough of that. I want to get to your question about how to make your life count. Actually, I have been addressing it already. The first thing I suggest is to rid yourself of the

226

doom and gloom notions of those around you.

In every generation there are those who cry and those who fly. Fly, Terry! Fly above the naysayers! There is some real truth to the corny saying: "It's not your aptitude but your attitude that will determine your altitude in life." Anything which lasts long enough to be called "corny" is both true and nutritious.

The only advice I can give you on choosing how to make your life count is to tell you what has worked for me. Every person has only one story to tell—his own. I couldn't have told you this five years ago. It has only recently come to the surface of my consciousness.

First, I would say, find what you can do *easily* and *joyfully*. Then spend your life trying to do it *perfectly*. Easily... joyfully... perfectly... let's look at them separately.

Easily. Many people spend their lives trying to do something that is extremely difficult or impossible for them to do.

The result is frustration, a sense of failure, and at some point, burnout. They ignore those tasks which "come natural" to them. Choose something which "comes natural." It is your greatest gift.

Joyfully. There are things we can do easily but we do not enjoy doing them. We get no satisfaction from them. Passion must accompany performance. I know a world-class skater who walked away from a multi-million dollar career. Skating was easy. But she was constantly bored. After the initial euphoria of winning and fame, she hated her life.

She is now a coach and a family person and loves her life.

On the other hand, there's Tom Kite, my friend, fellow church member, and of course, one of the greatest golfers who ever picked up a club. He's the all-time leading money winner on the PGA tour and the U.S. Open Champion at 43. Commentators call him the "Grinder," the "Blue-Collar

Golfer," and other names which suggest that he has achieved excellence more through hard work than through talent.

They don't know Tom Kite! He has one of the most repetitive swings in the game. He found at an early age that he could hit the ball "easily" and he loves to hit it joyfully thousands upon thousands of times. His work is his play. Easily, joyfully.

Perfectly. Tom never settles for what he's done. "Every Mountain is a Foothill" is the title of one of my sermons. Tom loves the sermon. It reflects his life.

Once he climbs to the top of the mountain, whether it's the Ryder Cup team or the U.S. Open, he considers it a foothill and starts climbing again.

Terry, that is what I've tried to do with my life as well. Find what I can do easily and joyfully and then try to do it perfectly. The last part of the equation will keep me "climbing" for the rest of my life.

I have left the most important part of my advice to the last. I believe in "the calling." Every person should feel called by God to be a part of something bigger than himself. Now hold on! I'm not saying everyone should become a preacher.

I'm saying that all of us should find a way to use what we're doing to enrich the world spiritually. "Enriching the world spiritually," means bringing people together as one family, relieving misery, bringing joy, erasing hatred, creating generosity and love.

Terry, good work is that which does the above. Unfortunately, people are not always paid for good work which is why calling is so important. Without a sense of calling, we buy into the big lie that unless we're rewarded with fame and fortune our work is not good work.

Terry, I have every confidence that the world is as filled with opportunity as it has ever been. Don't lose your nerve. Don't give in to negative propaganda. Find what you can do easily and joyfully and spend your life trying to do it perfectly. Make sure your work is part of God's plan to better the world or one tiny part of it. And have no regard for whether it brings you fame or fortune.

Joseph Campbell called this "following your bliss." Follow your bliss, Terry.

34

OVER NATURE, UNDER GOD
A Sensible Approach to Humans and Their Environment

Dear Dr. Mann:

I am confused by the mixed signals I receive concerning the environmental crisis on our planet. Some scientists claim that the earth has already suffered irreparable damage because of humankind's destructive practices. Others argue differently.

For example, I was watching a national news program on TV not long ago. When they were going to a commercial break, a question appeared in writing across the screen. It said, "True or False? Most scientists believe that global warming is occurring and is a threat to the survival of life on Earth."

When the program was about to resume, the answer was flashed on the screen. It said: "False. Over eighty percent of scientists do not believe global warming is a proven fact or a threat to the Earth."

I don't believe this! I feel that we are in great danger of killing Mother Earth. Also, Third World countries have no interest in preserving the environment. They are too poor. They welcome corporations who rape the land.

Do you believe that humans will finally destroy themselves by "fouling their own nest"? Could this be God's final judgment? How do we as Christians give a "Christian" response to this problem?

Dear Mary:

It would be easy to get drawn into the debate over the environment. I wouldn't mind this, if the issue weren't so politicized. For a few—and only a few—environmentalism has become the new religion of the old Secular Utopians. And, of course, the media love it because they're always looking for a new threat to publicize.

It is noteworthy that the True or False question you saw on a national news program was "scrawled" across the screen instead of being made a news story in itself. No TV news producer in his right mind would take the scare factor out of the environmental debate.

The public is no longer willing to trust government to use its tax dollars for the failed causes of the Great Society. The utopians need a new cause. Environmentalism fits the bill. It creates fear. It has religious implications. It also allows for the confiscation of private property under the guise of preserving the public good.

Well, I've said too much, haven't I? Mary, you've probably already slammed the book shut.

If you haven't, please remember that my remarks apply to a very small but vocal minority. Most of us know that we humans now have the means—or soon will have—to make our planet uninhabitable. Maybe that's a stretch. Maybe Nature will simply get her fill of us and erase us.

However, I do not think this will be the case. We are different from all other species. We are not helpless pawns of the environment. We are actually co-creators and co-managers of the environment. Just look at what the harnessing and use of electricity has done to "civilize" nature in the past seventy-five years.

Also, when you think of pollution, our environment in

America is healthier than it was a hundred years ago. Streams were filled with deadly microbes. Preservation and production of food was archaic. Society was not nearly as healthy.

But I'm going to alter course here. There are plenty of arguments to dispute everything I'm saying. My goal is to answer your two specific questions: What is the proper Christian response to humans and the environment? And wherein can we find hope in the face of possible environmental calamity?

The Christian position concerning the environment must begin with the biblical notion that humans are *over Nature, but under God.*

We are *over Nature*, in the sense that the Earth is God's gift to us. It is the arena in which we relate to Him. Once, Nature was all we knew. But as we evolved we learned of a reality beyond nature. At that point Earth became our "Eden." It was full of bounty which we could wring from it. We could now "conquer it."

But our problem began when we confused Nature with God. We decided to find meaning by immersing ourselves in "matter," i.e., things, riches. As Paul says in Romans 1, we worshipped the things which *were made* instead of their maker.

Another way to look at this is to point out the difference between ownership and stewardship. God owns the Earth. We are its stewards. Genesis says that God gave Adam and Eve dominion over the Earth and everything in it. But "dominion" means stewardship or management.

The symbol of the forbidden tree represents the reality that while humans are "over Nature" they are still *under God.* The earth is not theirs to do with as they please. It is a sacred trust. We are stewards not owners.

So, Mary, we cannot avoid our responsibility for managing and caring for God's Earth. The question is how shall we best do that? My quarrel with the radical environmentalists is that they seem to regard the Earth as a kind of eternal reality to be worshipped, rather than a finite organism to be used respectfully.

The Earth is not an end in itself. It is a means to an end. It is the arena of relationship between us and God. To deify Nature is as erroneous as wantonly destroying it.

God has arranged Nature so that everything that lives does so at the expense of the life of something else. "Life feeds on life," to use Joseph Campbell's words. He could have stated it in a more "earthy" fashion: Everything lives because something else dies!

So, Mary, the biblical perspective rests on the premise that we are over Nature. We can use it to meet our needs and relate to each other and God. It is not our possession. It is our stewardship, for we are under God.

Your second question is about hope. Is the planet doomed? Are we killing it? Is there any way to stop the slaughter?

Well, Mary, if you've read my earlier comments in this book, you can guess my response.

First, the future of the planet is not as much in our hands as we think. The number-one environmental problem worldwide is overpopulation.

Whenever there are too many "anythings," Nature balances the scales. Disease is usually the method. Or among humans, perhaps war.

Either we control ourselves voluntarily from within or something will control us involuntarily from without. This is a fundamental law. It applies to societies in general and to individuals in particular.

The future of the world is not in our hands. It is in God's hands. He will use Nature's laws or our own concerns to balance existence. Until such time as He decides to consummate history.

Do you realize what would happen to this planet if it were tilted one degree on its axis? Life as we know it would end in an instant.

Those who would like for us to believe that we are more powerful than we are should not discourage us. Our ultimate home is not on Earth. We should use Earth prudently and with respect, but not worship it. It is finite after all, just as we are.

When I think of the implications of what I've just said, I realize that my views are not popular in today's world. For example, what does my position imply about private ownership of property? And hunting? And meat-eating? And animal rights?

Well, those are other topics not suited to your question, Mary. However, I will throw a grenade or two and then run. History has proven that those who conserve nature's bounties best are those who have a vested self-interest in them. Where private ownership is a basic human right, people can afford to be environmentally sensitive. I find it ironic that environmental protection flourishes best where the public owns the least and individuals own the most.

Second grenade. I have hunted all over the world. I never shoot what I or someone else doesn't eat. But I do not hunt in order to eat. I hunt for the same reason that others ride bulls, hit a golf ball, or play chess. It's a sub-rational thing. I can't give you objective sensible reasons why I hunt.

But you can't give me rational, objective reasons why it is a sin for me to hunt! All you can give me are your similar gut-level, emotional, sub-rational objections.

I know this: Wherever hunting is done for sport and money, game abounds. Wherever the factor of human self-interest is removed from hunting, game vanishes. In the 1950s, Kenya had more wild animals per square mile than any area on earth. Then hunting was banned. Today, the game population is com-

paratively small. There are more zebra-striped vans with pho-
tographers than there are animals. Game habitats have been
replaced by people. Just across the border in Tanzania, where
hunting is still done for sport, game abounds.

Third grenade. Every living thing eventually becomes
something else's feces. Whether our remains are eaten by
lions or bacteria, they will be eaten.

We cannot avoid living off the life of something else.
Vegetarians kill plants. They also kill germs. While radical
environmentalists urge us to spend billions preserving bugs
which live in unseen places, they seem to have no objection to
our completely eradicating entire classes of viruses and bacteria. Our own built-in immune systems kill microbes every day.
Are we violating the right to life of those microbes?

Okay, enough grenades. It's time to run away. I only
lobbed them into the fray because I encounter as much despair
on one side of the environmental issue as on the other. Some
see no answer to the problem of using the Earth to gratify and
fulfill themselves without using it up.

My guess is that God will instruct Mother Nature to balance
herself against our abuses, if He cannot persuade us to balance
our use of the Earth.

The most hopeful sign I see is that the typical "American
Problem-Solving Formula" has kicked in concerning the environmental issue. This formula can be seen in the resolution of
almost all great American conflicts.

It begins with extreme abuse. In this case a greedy disre-
gard for the environment. Opposition swells. It starts with
lone voices, usually radical, crying in the wilderness. Then the
people I call "Causes-in-Search-of-an-Issue" move in. They
add the necessary element of fanaticism to the mix. And call
for solutions which overcompensate for the problem.

Then a few timid voices or loudmouth nuts begin an equally

unreasonable countermovement. In the end, the American people as a whole solve the problem by settling somewhere in the middle.

I am glad for the environmental movement. It was and is needed. And I have every hope that after both sides have been sufficiently radicalized (as they should be) we will find a working solution in conducting our stewardship of Earth. But even then, this Earth is not my ultimate home. Nor is it yours.

35

TEENAGERS: PEOPLE GOD DIDN'T CREATE
Guides in Parenting

Dear Dr. Mann:

Our only son is eleven and I am terrified of his teenage years. Many of my friends cannot manage their teenagers. There are so many pitfalls these days. Drugs, sex, brainwashing music, bad influences at school.

Tom has been such a joy to us so far. But lately he is beginning to change. For example, he's always been an early-riser. Now he will sleep 'til noon if I let him. He's been a neat well-organized child. His toys were always stowed to perfection. Now his room is a mess.

I see these as signs of a coming rebellion. His moods are so extreme, too. One moment he's up, the other he's down. He feels that no one at school likes him, yet his teachers tell me he's very popular.

His father says it's just his age. He'll grow out of it. They hardly talk. My husband loses himself in his work and computer programs. My son shuts himself up in his "cave" with the TV and the telephone.

I sense a real earthquake coming. Can you give me some pointers? I don't seem to be able to get through to the two men in my life.

Dear Sally:

I read everything I could find on the subject of adolescence before my first two kids reached puberty. I was certain that I was prepared. I even preached a few grand sermons on how to raise teenagers.

Then they reached puberty and I preached on other subjects until they were grown. In spite of everything, I had trouble with my first two. I really blew it.

Our third child was a belated surprise. His sisters were almost grown when he was born. I was determined not to repeat the mistakes of the past. The more I considered what changes I might make, the more I realized that I had not prepared *myself* to be the parent of a teenager with the first two.

I had learned what all of the experts had to say about teenagers and their inner-workings; but I had not learned what it might be like to be the first-time parent of a teenager.

This time Lois and I worked on ourselves instead of the child. We were older and more mellow. We didn't feel as if we were gods who could, with the proper commitment and smarts, *create* a perfect human being.

We told him "yes" every chance we got and kissed him a lot. We figured we might as well enjoy him before his mutation into monsterhood.

He was and is a delight now in his sophomore year in college. He experimented with and passed through almost everything we feared he would. But this time we spared ourselves the pain of the former times.

There was one key difference. We finally realized that *God didn't create teenagers, we did!*

Think about it. "Teenagerism" is a creation of twentieth century American culture. We see life in six stages: birth, child, teen, adult, elderly, and death. But the Bible sees life in only four stages: birth, child, adult, death. Adolescence is not even mentioned as a stage of life in the Bible!

Here's my point, Sally: *God treats teenagers as adults.* He includes them in his redemptive plan as full-fledged partners. Joseph, David, Daniel, and John were all teenagers when God called them into His service.

Yet we have created this artificial life stage. I don't think we can do much about that. Our culture has the longest period of adolescence in history. I define an adolescent as anyone who is still dependent on parents for economic support.

However, Sally, the point I'm making contains the clue to preparing yourself to parenting a teenager.

God treats him like an adult, so you treat him like an adult! That was my motto as I prepared to raise my third teenager. When he was eleven, we went to the hardware store and bought a lock for his bedroom door. After we installed it, I said, "From now on this is your room. You may keep it as you wish. I'll knock before entering. You do the same for us. There's some neat stuff going on between your mom and me, and it is both sacred and private. If we have guests who want to see your room, we will get your permission first."

I learned about Van Halen, Led Zeppelin, and Cindy Lauper. We discussed the esoteric values of someone repeating "I gotta have your love" one hundred and one times in a single song. In other words, I tried to respect and learn about his interests. I was probably the only forty-seven-year-old dad in town who knew every word Sting had ever sung.

Sally, the only thing that differentiates an adult from a teenager, in God's eyes, is that the latter has two things at home called parents. I am convinced that the root of most teen-parent conflict is our refusal to see teens as young adults and to trust them accordingly. We see them as "tween-agers," neither fish nor fowl, whom we must mollify, control, rear, and hope not to be disgraced by until they (please God!) leave home.

Once we make the commitment to treat teens as young adults, what then? What is our role and what is theirs?

Our role is to *let go and lead*. Theirs is to *grab hold and grow*.

Let's start with our part. To let go means to let go of your teenager as "child." You mentioned that your Tom sleeps late and has huge mood swings. Sally, those are two clear indications that Tom is no longer a child. Early-riser Tom no longer exists. The onset of puberty is always marked by the increased need for sleep. He's not lazy, he's normal.

Pubescents also feel everything more acutely than at any other time of life. That's why they are prone to suicidal thoughts. They fly higher and fall lower emotionally.

The retreat-to-the-cave bit is his way of attempting to be the non-dependent person he is becoming. He has closed the last gate in the fence of his ego boundary that separates him from you. He will open it for another soon...his first love.

The hard fact, Sally, is that Tom has learned about all he can from you as a *dependent* person. If you do not let him go, he will flee. That is another definition of rebellion.

But letting go is not abandonment. It's simply a disconnection. Think of it this way. Since birth, Tom has been tethered to you. You've had him on this emotional leash. If he wanders too far you can pull him to safety.

Now the leash is cut. You must still go ahead of him but without the leash. If he chooses to run ahead of you or away from you, you must let him go. But keep trodding out in front or stop and wait for him. That's called "leading." You must keep leading even when it appears that no one's following.

I made up the five *R*'s of parental leadership so that I could recite them to myself:

Remembering: To lead a teenager you have to remember how it felt to be one. We tend to block out those memories because they were painful. But if we try, we can remember how lonely we were, how sensitive to the slightest criticism, how afraid of being rejected, how scary and sensational our awakening sexuality was, how we liked to poke fun at Dad and hated for him to reciprocate. Remember how he feels and treat him as you would an adult friend who had the same fears.

Rooting: All kids need someone in their corner rooting for them. They need their cheering section. And they need it most when they've blown it most. If Tom ever comes home and tells you he's made Suzy pregnant, remember that your seat is in the cheering section not the press box. I don't mean that he needs applause. He needs support not scorn.

Respecting: I mentioned treating teenagers as friends. How do you treat houseguests? Do you tell them they should do something about their scuffed shoes? Or their hair? Or their clothes? You don't talk to friends that way. That's why they are friends.

Relating: I use it because it starts with *R*. It's an overused word, I know. I could use *talking* or *talking with*. I like the term *meaningful conversation*. There's chatter and banter and prattle, and then there's meaningful talk where we get inside each other's feelings.

I was amazed at how my relationship with my teenager changed the first time I asked him what I could do to be a better friend to him. He was astounded that I treasured his opinion. I was astounded that he had one!

Relaxing: This is my favorite *R* of parental leadership. Here's how I see it. My teenager is not *mine:* He is God's. God has entrusted him to my care or stewardship. I cannot keep him. I can only lead him for a while and send him into life.

About 90 percent of all teenagers eventually turn out okay with or without proper parenting. Some of my British friends have a novel viewpoint which I'll throw into the mix. They feel that all children are natural-born monsters and that whatever good they do in life is directly due to their parenting skills! And all of that together spells, RELAX!

The end result of your letting go and leading, Sally, is beyond your control. For your son will have the ultimate say in the process. His job is to *grab hold and grow*.

To *grab hold* means to pick up and use what's been given to you. Tom will have to choose to take and process what's given. If he doesn't, he is to blame. You can do everything right, Sally, and he may not take hold of your gifts.

To grow is his second task. There is a recorded episode in Jesus' life (Luke 2:41–52) which pulls everything I've been saying together. His parents take Him to Jerusalem when He's twelve, to "present Him to the Temple." It was His bar mitzvah, a ceremony which announced His step from childhood to adulthood.

After the ceremony, the family is enroute back to Nazareth when they discover that Jesus is missing. They rush back to Jerusalem. On the third day of their search, they find Him in the Temple questioning the Elders.

His mother reacts as any mother would. She scolds Him for His insensitivity and smothers Him with kisses of joy at the same time.

Jesus speaks back to her firmly. In essence He says, "You brought me here to signify my becoming an adult, now you're treating me like a child. Don't you know I'm where I'm supposed to be?"

Jesus made Mary let go. He was telling her that the tether had been cut and she had done well. He now had to grab hold of what He'd been given and go forward.

Then, the text says that Jesus returned to Nazareth with His parents. He obeyed them. He *grew* in wisdom, in stature, in favor with God, and in favor with people.

These are the four areas of growth which determine meaning in life. We must grow in wisdom—smarts of all kinds. *Stature* means maturity. *Favor with God* means knowing God as a friend and leader and helper. *Favor with people* means getting on well with others.

Sally, unfortunately you cannot make your son grow in these areas. Don't get me wrong. You can and must set boundaries and rules of acceptable behavior for all family members. A family must have a "Covenant of Caring"—an agreement which governs responsibilities for being part of the family. If a teenager chooses not to keep the covenant all you can do is let go and lead.

36

STAYING TOGETHER BUT COMING APART

Recovering Intimacy

Dear Dr. Mann:

Although we've been married for twelve years, my wife and I do not seem to have the closeness we should have. We don't fight except on rare occasions and it's hard to tell what triggers it. Some silly little thing will burst the dam and we have a knock-down-drag-out!

Our sex life is little more than physical release. We know that someday our kids will be gone and they are the only things we really have in common. We don't want to spend our later years alone or as two grumpy strangers.

One counselor told us that we expect too much of marriage. Maybe she was right. But we're not friends or lovers anymore. We're just parents and house partners.

From this slight bit of information, can you give us some hope? Married life has just got to be better than this.

Dear Wayne:

Although your letter appears to contain scant information, it speaks volumes. I think you are searching for a thing we call *intimacy*. What is that? Well, there are many different definitions because it is difficult to put into words.

Years ago Eric Fromm called it at-one-ness. He used the

analogy of the ancient Greek myth which said that the first human was an Androgyne—a perfect blend of maleness and femaleness. The gods split the Androgyne into two sexes. The result was a never-ending hunger in all humans. We all feel like we're only "halves" and we yearn to be reunited with our "other halves." This explains the human obsession with love.

The Genesis story in our Bible tells of God looking at the first man and seeing that he is incomplete without "another half." In order for humans to be fully human they need to become one with another. It takes male and female to make "human." He joins them together and tells them to become "one flesh."

So, Wayne, I hear you crying out for the most basic of all human desires: intimacy, to become one with another. You are not asking for too much. You are asking for the realization of something you were created to have.

My working definition of intimacy is: "to be fully known and fully safe with another." When a couple can become transparent to each other and that self-revelation is not used by either to abuse the other, then intimacy occurs. It saddens me to read in gossip columns and tabloids that some celebrity has become "intimate" with several different "love interests" on several successive nights. Intimacy has become a trash-word. Nevertheless, it is what we all crave.

Wayne, your letter tells me something else that's significant. You and your wife have not learned to deal with the number one enemy of intimacy—unprocessed anger. You mentioned your occasional "knock-down-drag-outs" which are triggered by "silly little things."

Most great conflicts begin over insignificant things. This is because anger can be bottled up only for so long. It is like inhaled oxygen. It must be exhaled or else it will kill you.

We teach many helpful things about marriage but we do not

teach people how to deal with their anger. Either we act as if it were a sin to become angry or we feel that anger will simply go away provided everything else is okay.

Undissolved anger creates the very kind of old-age grumpiness you fear. By the way, grumpiness is not peculiar to old age. Older people are simply more candid with longstanding unresolved anger. In the earlier years it shows itself in the ways you describe in your letter: A mechanical sex life. A "you-don't-bother-me-and-I-won't-bother-you" way of transacting.

David Mace used to say that long-term unprocessed anger often appears as a kind of "low-level hum" of resentment between spouses.

Many years ago Dr. Mace helped Lois and I in our marriage in pointing out how anger strikes at the heart of intimacy. We were well on our way to the "low-level hum" stage. Over a long period of hard work we have learned that intimacy is possible if two people want it. Let me tell you our story.

First, we had no preparation prior to marriage for achieving intimacy. I equated the term with sex-whenever-I-wanted-it. I was amazed at how quickly sex lost its centrality in holding our relationship together.

Within a few weeks after the wedding, I knew that I didn't know this woman, although we had dated for five years before the marriage. She was experiencing the same discovery.

I would make her angry and vice versa. We'd have a fight, bleed out the poison, and have fun making up. Kids came. My schooling had to be finished. My career forbade divorce, period! So we hung in there.

Our two methods for handling anger were the usual—stuff it or vent it. Neither of these dissolves anger. First, you can't swallow it and keep it down. It will find a way out. It will be transferred onto someone or something else. Or it will make you sick.

Venting anger sounds great, but it is destructive. When we vent anger we get an endorphin rush, not unlike a runner's high or other pleasurable feelings which attend accomplishment and conquest.

Endorphin rushes are addictive. So venting anger creates an addictive pattern of venting. And with venting comes words and actions which cannot be retrieved. Venting becomes nothing more than temper tantrums. Violence must escalate in order to maintain the endorphin flow. Screaming is verbal hitting and every bit as destructive.

Rechanneling anger is another alternative. It's better than stuffing or venting, but it does not heal the breach in relationship or open the way to intimacy. Hitting a golf ball or shooting skeet may keep you from hitting or shooting your spouse, but they will not remove the problem.

Lois and I knew we would have to find a different way. I won't bore you with quotations and research. Here's what we did.

First, we accepted the fact that anger was neither avoidable nor a sin. You can't keep from getting angry, and it's okay. Anger is actually a God-given benefit. It's a defense mechanism against assault.

It is also a sign of love. You cannot be angry at your spouse unless you care about your relationship. As George Bernard Shaw said, "The opposite of love is not hatred but indifference."

So we agreed that we would no longer conceal our anger. It was okay to say, "I'm angry." Then, at Mace's suggestion, we made a pact that whenever one of us said, "I am angry," the other would not counterattack. The other party would not come back with a, "By golly, I'm angry too!"

Instead we would go back over the situation in which the

247

anger occurred. Step by step we would analyze it. Three things resulted. First, the shouting stopped and we had meaningful conversations. Second, we learned how to apologize and forgive in a way we had never experienced before. Third, we learned that "some dogs need to stay in the basement." There are unresolved differences which shall remain so, for the rest of our lives.

Dr. Mace suggests that couples go back to the beginning of their relationship and work through every conflict they can remember. That doesn't work for us. Just as there are boulders in the middle of a stream which have to be circumvented, there are conflicts which can never be removed from a marriage. The marriage must "flow around" them.

People are "broken vessels." No one human can perfectly fulfill all of the love needs of another. To imagine such a case is to invite divorce. Perhaps, Wayne, that was what your counselor meant when she said you expected too much of marriage. Unfortunately, we have been sold the myth that says there is a Mr. or Ms. "Right" out there who can fulfill us *ultimately*. Nonsense!

Wayne, in addition to finding a new way to handle anger, we scheduled some unbreakable commitments on our calendars. That's right, we actually pulled out our calendars and scheduled three unbreakable appointments: (1) a talk a day, (2) a date a week, (3) and a "whoopee" a month.

Every day at a certain time we visit for thirty minutes. Phones are unplugged, no interruptions allowed. We don't schedule the subjects for discussion, we schedule the discussion. The subject is unimportant. Being totally present to each other is the point.

Once a week we have a date. Just the two of us. Parents who feel obligated to take their children on every outing are revealing their inability to relate to each other without the kids being present. Besides, the best thing you can ever do for your kids is love your spouse.

Once a month we spend the night away from home. We've done this since our children were small. Many times our "Whoopee-a-month" has been McDonald's, Motel 6, and a $4 bottle of screw-top wine. As Lois says, money can't take you to a place called "happy." It can only allow you to take "happy" to a lot more places.

All of this may sound contrived, unromantic, and laborious to you, Wayne. Well, it is two of those three. It *is* contrived. We work hard to create all good things in life. Why not work to create the *best thing in life—intimacy?* "The best things in life are free," says the song. Hogwash!

What we do to maintain intimacy is laborious as well. It's hard work. It's easy to replace a talk a day with something "more pressing." It's easy to have a date *at home.* It's easy to give in to the problems of finding baby-sitters, etc., instead of leaving home overnight.

However, we routinely face up to all of these obstacles when our jobs are at stake. Are our jobs more important than our relationships?

Recently there was a national news story about a couple who left their children "home alone" while they took a sailing cruise or something similar. They were criminally charged with child neglect.

They should have been! Obviously anyone who can afford to go on a two-week cruise can afford proper childcare. However, I couldn't help comparing this story to those where parents leave their kids at home alone while they work to afford two cars, more appliances, better draperies, etc. I'm not talking about those parents who have to work for the family to survive. My only point is that the very idea of leaving kids in order to strengthen the marital bond is considered criminal while leaving them in order to buy more "stuff" is not.

Wayne, I hope I have given you some lifelines of hope. I return to what I said earlier. Two people working at it can create intimacy. After thirty-five years of marriage and reading all I can, I am convinced that successful relationships rely on three things: commitment, commitment, and commitment. Don't ever give up, unless she gives up. If you work at being fully known and fully safe, and deal with each issue of irritation one at a time, and accept what you cannot change, and schedule time together—then intimacy will happen to you.

37

TOOLS FOR OLD FOOLS
Divorce Recovery

Dear Dr. Mann:

*You've heard the saying, "There's no fool like an old fool."
Well, I'm the living example of the world's biggest "old fool."*

*My wife of thirty years died when I was fifty-four. We had a
wonderful marriage. I worshipped her. I never dreamed that I
would even consider remarriage.*

*Within eight months of my wife's death, I was in love with a
thirty-year-old woman. We married. To make a long story
short, she stayed long enough to take half of my fortune and
then ran off with one of my top employees.*

*My grown children are saying, "We told you so!" My busi-
ness is in shambles. I am alone again and humiliated. I had a
nightmare one night in which I heard my first wife laughing at
me for being such a fool.*

*I don't know where to go from here. I never thought my life
could get so dismal so quickly. I've heard you say many times,
"Oh, but you can begin again!" How can I?*

Dear Jerry:

I receive many pleas for help in the aftermath of broken
relationships. Our divorce-recovery sessions at church are
packed. I find, in general, that our culture does as poor a job in
helping people reassemble their lives after divorce as it does in
preparing them for marriage.

The churches compound the problem. The divorced are often relegated to second-class membership or even excluded in some cases.

A divorce marks the death of a living thing. A marriage is an "organism." It is not an institution or a contract, although it is symbolized as such. Two people who are in the process of becoming one person are participating in something larger than themselves.

So divorce causes the same grief reaction as death. It is the loss of part of one's own self.

Jerry, you already know all of the above. You've suffered two "deaths in the family," in succession. The only difference is that you feel foolish in the case of the second one. You have not only lost part of yourself, you are guilty for having gotten involved in the first place.

I want to begin, therefore, by telling you that you are not a fool. *Getting married so quickly after your first wife's death is actually a tribute to her and to your first marriage!*

Did you read that right? Yes! Because your first marriage was good, you found that you could not live alone. Widows and widowers who have had great marriages get remarried more quickly than those who have had bad marriages. It is a proven fact.

The reason is that once we've had true intimacy we cannot live without seeking to re-experience it. We were created for it. That's biblical.

Children of widows and widowers should perk up here. Do not interpret your living parent's quick remarriage or re-entry into the dating scene as a sign of disrespect for your deceased parent. On the contrary, it is a sign that your parents had a great thing going. I have often told my children that in the case of my death, I don't care if their mom remarries the day after my funeral.

That's a stretch, but my point is not. I would hope she would repeat or improve what we've had in her remaining life-time.

So, Jerry, you are not a fool for remarrying quickly. Nor should you be too hard on yourself for marrying a woman half your age. There is a truth about fifty-something men which we keep hidden in the closet. The radical feminists scold us for it, as do older women and jealous younger men.

I suppose we deserve it, but nevertheless it is true. At about fifty we men begin to doubt our sexual prowess more severely than before. Our plumbing begins to stop up. We don't urinate as well. And in many cases our erections are not what they use to be, *except* on occasions of extreme passionate arousal.

Mentally speaking 50-plus men are more "feminine" in their lovemaking in that they require more time, creativity, imagination and aggressiveness from their partners. They are not ready in an instant as they were in their earlier years.

But physically speaking they are still stimulated visually. This causes a problem. To be frank (and most of us dare not be) older men are drawn to younger women sexually because: (1) their own sexual certainty is threatened; and (2) they are turned on by visual beauty.

To make things worse, as soon as the "physical charge" wanes, and it always does, two people have to go through the same work of bonding as always, except with the added burden of a generation gap. Usually there are plenty of critics standing on the sidelines cheering the disintegration.

Jerry, your actions are normal. You did what many of us would do. You couldn't bear the loneliness after having had intimacy for so long. And you went for a younger woman. The reasons you're using the "old fool" phrase is because of your failure and your "gloating critics" reminding you of your failure.

Now I want to address your key question. How do you begin again? Financially, you've lost half of your life's work. Your children have lost half of what they expected to inherit. You're on the outs with them. Your respectable standing in the community is shaken. You feel like a real chump.

Well first off, stop letting your *critics* tell you who you are. Second, stop letting your *can'ts* tell you who you are. Third, stop letting your *competitors* tell you who you are. I call these *the 3 C's which spell CCCRAZY.*

The first *C* stands for *critics*. The most important question you must decide now, Jerry, is: Who tells you who *you are?* Who are you going to allow to define you at this critical time in your life? Who will tell you how to feel toward yourself?

If you want to go crazy let your critics define you. They are always more than willing to tell you what a fool you've been.

The second *C* stands for your *can'ts*. What about the cant's? Who/what are they? Your cant's are those things you have no control over. You *can't* turn back the clock. You can't raise your first wife from the dead. It wasn't her you heard laughing in your dreams. It was your own guilt. Buried guilt leaks out in our dreams regularly. That's one of the reasons we dream. Had you heard your wife in the dream, she would have been sorrowful for your pain.

You can't *un*-marry, *un*-divorce, *un*-lose half of your fortune. You can't *un*-fifty-five your age!

These are your *can'ts*. What about the *cans?* What are you able to do? You *can* seek love again and with a lot more wisdom this time. Sounds abhorrent, I know. But you will seek intimacy again, mark my word. You *can* run a business again. You *can* seek a reconciliation with your children, provided they cease pointing fingers.

Focus on your *cans* instead of your *can'ts*. Let the former tell you who you are.

The third *C* of *CCCRAZY* stands for your *competitors*. They are all of those people to whom you compare yourself when you think of who is happy, fulfilled, and successful. Jerry, most unhappiness comes from comparing ourselves to others whom we think are happy.

Years ago, the publisher of *Psychology Today* polled 70,000 subscribers to see if they could determine what made people happy. They couldn't find the specific formula for happiness. But they did determine the number-one cause of unhappiness in America. It was the "comparison game" I'm referring to here. We look at people whom we think are happy, compare our circumstances to theirs and say, "If only I were like them!"

I call this exercise: *letting your competitors tell you who you are.*

Jerry, the three easiest ways to lose your mind are to let critics, can'ts, and competitors tell you who you are. I re-read the Old Testament story of King Saul's mental deterioration not long ago (1 Sam. 9-31).

I was amazed to discover that his "craziness" resulted from the 3 *C*'s. Things started downhill when Saul's mentor, Prophet Samuel, criticized his military strategy in front of his generals. He began letting his critics define him.

Then Saul started focusing on his can'ts. There was no way to completely defeat Israel's archenemy, the Philistines. They had iron weaponry which Israel didn't possess. Saul was a genius in stopping the Philistine advance, but he couldn't possibly pacify and secure the entire country. He let his inabilities define him, instead of his abilities.

Then young David arrived on the scene. He was Samuel's newest protege and a mighty warrior. When he strolled by, the women said, "Saul has killed his thousands, but David his ten-thousands." Saul began his final descent into madness. He let David's success define him.

It was the 3 *C*'s, Jerry. Stop listening to them. That's the first step in beginning again.

Next, surround yourself with people who will love you in your brokenness. We have found in our divorce-recovery ministry that *content* is secondary to *context*. It's not primarily the information we give which helps people to recover, it's the context of mutual caring, acceptance, and hope in which the information is given. Find a new *context*—a setting or group—where you can be you and it's okay.

Most important is a renewal of bonding with a loving God. We can withstand any kind of rejection if we know that God has not and will not reject us.

I once asked the great Karl Menninger whether he thought I might do more good for humankind as a psychiatrist than as a minister. "Oh no," he replied, "You can give people something I could never give them." "What is that?" I asked. "Hope," he said.

He walked away saying nothing more. I know what he meant these many years later. To introduce people to a God who never gives up on them, no matter what, is really the only thing I can do.

Jerry, to connect with this "living hope" requires a fundamental reorientation of life.

The first sermons I heard as a child were from a black preacher in a small country church which had existed since the slave days. It was on an acre of ground which joined our ranch (a former Southern plantation).

In the 1950s there was a car wax called Simonize. It rejuvenated the dullest paint. But it was so difficult to use that you could apply it on only two square feet of the car at a time. Otherwise it would harden and never come off.

The black preacher, whom I loved as a second father, said in one of his memorable sermons that you could make an old jalopy look like new by Simonizing it. But if it had no engine, you had nowhere to go.

Life is like that, he said. We spend too much time "Simonizing" and not enough time replacing our engines or "revolutionizing" as he put it.

Whenever I observe people trying to recover from life's wrecks or trying to move up the ladder, I remember Rev. Digg's picturesque analogy. There are many ways to rejuvenate the visible parts of life. Turn on the TV and they will offer you countless wares.

But, Jerry, you don't need to "Simonize," you need to "revolutionize." There is a loving Friend who sees you and knows all of your follies. You can begin again with Him. Always.

38

GETTING RIGHT WITH GOD
Understanding Religious Experience

Dear Dr. Mann:

I am a baby boomer with all that the term implies. I was a Viet Nam volunteer. I went to serve and conquer for the American way and returned disillusioned. I divorced my teenage bride, made Woodstock and all of the points in between.

Then I went to college, cut my hair (the part that didn't fall out), got a job, married and had kids. I'm forty-five with a thirty-eight-year-old wife and two pre-teens.

It's time for me to get right with God. I believe He exists. I believe Jesus was somehow "God," but I'm not sure how. I have a dislike for organized religion and distrust television ministers. I'm writing you because you at least appear to be different. However, I have my suspicions that you are a fraud, too. But you're the only minister I feel some connection with.

I want you to tell me how to become a Christian and how to find a church where I can practice my faith without pretense. Please do not give me a canned spiel. I've read most of the tracts. I know the "Roman Road" and the "Four Spiritual Laws" by heart.

I need some sensible, real *advice from a real sinner. That's why I chose you.*

Dear Doug:

I am honored that you would ask me about "getting right with God." I will relieve your mind, up front, by telling you that I won't recite some prepared spiel. I share your distaste for them. They ignore the individuality and sanctity of each person and seem to assume that "one size fits all."

I recently saw a video designed to convince pastors of large churches to invite a team of "weight lifters for Jesus" to their parishes. The background music sounded like the kind which accompanies a Wrestlemania commercial. It was a cross between the theme from *Jaws* and a Bruce Lee film.

In successive flashes bulked hulks broke cinder blocks and boards. They bent steel bars and lifted barbells. At intervals the pastor of a large church came on to admonish the viewer that the "Beam Team" (my term) used unorthodox methods to fill their venues with thousands of people. But the results were the most important thing. Thousands at their Crush Mush crusades (also my term) stood up for Jesus.

The message I heard, Doug, was: "Never mind the means. The end always justifies them."

It might surprise you, Doug, to learn that I once conducted such a crusade. We had movie stars, professional athletes, beauty queens, and a gold medal weight lifter on successive nights in a stadium. I preached. We turned out the entire population of the town (12,000) and more each night.

Over a thousand people came forward to profess faith in Jesus. We contacted each one following the crusade. Less than a dozen joined a church or were baptized.

All I'm trying to say, Doug, is that I hear you loud and clear. I'm not writing off mass evangelism. You can't refute the effective life of a Billy Graham or a Dwight Moody, or others.

But I do refute the notion that there is only one way to meet God and that all who fail to use it are heretics.

So let me begin to answer your question by saying there are several ways in which a person can come to know God in Christ personally.

259

There is *radical intervention.* Some people have dramatic conversions in a seeming instant. They are going down the road of life in one direction when they are intercepted miraculously by a personal encounter with a living God.

There are well-known records of these dramatic life experiences in the Bible. Jacob, the deceiver and manipulator, wrestled with God one night and awoke the next morning with a new life and a new name. Paul was swooped up by God while going to Damascus to persecute Christians (Acts 9).

I believe these experiences are for real, Doug, because I had one. I was newly married and wanting out already. I had been injured in sports so my only goal in life—to be a world-class athlete—was gone. Lois was pregnant.

I went to church with her only to avoid an argument. I sat through the service with my mind elsewhere. I have no recollection of what the pastor said. During a hymn I was suddenly overwhelmed. It was a totally unexpected occurrence.

My life flashed before my mind's eye. I was twenty, married, about to be a father, and had no purpose in life. I didn't even want to be married.

The only thing I knew was that God was there and that He loved me. I also knew that He wanted me for something. I was chosen. All I did was give in. I submitted.

My life changed directions. It was a revolution. Doug, some people get right with God by simply offering themselves up to God. I would suggest that you go to a quiet place and in simple words offer your will to God. Don't look for dramatic "corroboration from the other side." There probably will not be any visions and voices. Although there could be. Revolutions do happen.

Some people become Christians by *normal progression.* They are reared in a religious atmosphere. Their parents are devout. Their lives are organized around a regular and friendly relationship with God. Becoming a Christian is a matter of evolving to a place where they declare publicly that they are entering a new level of commitment and responsibility. This kind of evolutionary experience is exemplified in the bar mitzvah and Confirmation services of Judaism and some branches of Christianity. In Acts 8, there is the story of an Ethiopian eunuch who entered the faith by normal progression. He was devout and a Bible reader. When he understood the whole picture, he took a normal final step.

My wife does not know when she became a Christian. She says she has always known God as a friend. Her family practiced Christian devotion from her earliest memory. When she was nine, she stood before her church family and announced that she was being baptized as a testimony of her lifelong faith.

Some become Christians by *experimentation*. They simply decide to start following in the steps of Jesus. They read the Sermon on the Mount (Matt. 5–7) and other teachings of Jesus. Then they begin to ask God to give them the power and grace to live this life-style.

Someone has said it is easier to act yourself into a way of thinking than to think yourself into a way of acting. In psychology this is called modeling. The point is to picture the person you want to be and then start acting as if you were that person.

Doug, I have known several persons over the years who have become Christians precisely this way. At our church we open our doors to experimenters. I know an attorney who came to our church years ago as an agnostic. He is a boomer like yourself. He and his wife were part of the hippie generation. They had kids and grew to the place where they started searching for something spiritual from life.

After several years, the attorney came to see me. "I have practiced myself into believing," he said. "I want to be baptized because Christ is now the center of my life."

William James was correct when he said over a hundred years ago, that there are varieties of religious experience. It is an insult to God and to people to confine becoming a Christian to one patented formula. God is larger than my perception. And you are different from me.

I believe that you have already begun your "conversion" Doug. Becoming a Christian is a lifelong process. We don't get right with God once and for all. There is a time when we begin the process, and it continues for the rest of our lives.

The mere fact that you are seeking to be right with God is a clear sign that you are already in the process. Getting right with God is not a matter of understanding or proclamation. You don't have to know enough doctrines or say enough promises to be right with God.

It is an act of the will. To be right with God is to be *willing* to be right with God. Whenever someone calls me on TV and asks "How can I know I am right with God?" I answer, "Because you want to be."

You can never do enough or believe enough to be right with God. He accepts you as you are. You don't have to go looking for Him. He's waiting for you right where you are.

The second question you asked is about finding a church where you can practice your faith and raise your children.

Doug, you will not find the perfect church. In fact, at the risk of insulting you, I must tell you that with your cynicism toward all institutions, you may not find a church to your liking.

You were disillusioned in Viet Nam with government and every institution in which you had faith. Many in your generation were. Boomers are often accused of being low on commitment. I disagree. They are simply low on tolerance toward institutions which they feel have betrayed them.

There is a tendency to classify baby boomers as "baby bummers" who feel that the world betrayed them in their youth and now owes them something.

In my experience, this is not an attitude which is peculiar to any age group. The reason it shows up more in your group is because your group is larger.

Anyway, Doug, I feel that you must look for a church which is not strangled by or anchored to traditions which you already hold as highly suspect. There are some churches these days which are "consumer-driven," as against "product-driven."

Product-driven churches are like the General Motors of a few years ago. They say "Here's our product! You use it and like it or you're a traitor!" Consumer-driven churches, however, begin by asking as Toyota did, "What are your needs? We want to match the *Good News* with *your needs!*"

Doug, you need a church which matches "The News with the needs." This church does not water down the Gospel, as its critics love to claim. It brings the Gospel to people where they hurt.

Here are some telltale signs of News-and-Needs, or NAN, churches:

(1) NAN churches have fun at worship services. Sermons are 20 minutes or less. You can sing the songs. They have tunes you know.

(2) NAN churches are places which kids like. Kids can spot a NAN church as quickly as they spot a friendly dog.

(3) NAN churches are inclusive. They dredge the pond and keep everything—turtles, fish, crawfish, snakes, snails, and clams. Then they try to help all of them experience transformation.

(4) NAN churches give you concrete ways to help real

people. They're not big on asking you to support impersonal budgets or societies.

(5)   NAN churches thrive on chaos. A long-range plan is ninety days. They are always out of money. They do more for less. Change is the only constant.

(6)   NAN churches are full of the bruised, the battered, the broken, and the bored from traditional churches.

(7)   NAN churches are long on grace. When you go there, they have to take you in. From the pastor to the pew, people are glad to see you.

(8)   Finally, NAN churches are criticized. If it isn't being called names and pronounced dead by traditional churches, it isn't a NAN church.

Doug, I feel that you are already closer to God than you think, or you would not have asked me how to connect with Him. I have every confidence that you will develop a living and powerful faith. You will need to link up with others who are on your same pilgrimage. Find a group of pilgrims whose passion is to match the Good News of God's inclusive love with the real needs of hurting people. If such a group doesn't exist in your town, start one.

39

WHEN YOU'RE CAUGHT RED-HANDED
Recovering from Disgrace

Dear Dr. Mann:

I spent twenty years building a prosperous business, a good moral reputation, and strong family. I live in a small town where everybody knows everybody's business.

At forty-four I just "lost it." I started philandering, spending money, drinking, lying, gambling. I've lost and wasted half of my life savings. My wife and I are separated. My children are ashamed of me. Kids at school make fun of them. I've been kicked out of my church.

I now live in a small apartment. People in town make jokes about me. I drink myself to sleep every night.

Dr. Mann, I want my family and my life back. I am as guilty as sin itself, and I don't know where to start. I could make a lot of excuses but that's all they are. The truth is that I let my bad self get out of control. There's no one but yours truly to blame.

No pastor in town will talk to me. My wife says she would like for me to come back home, but she doesn't know if she can ever trust me again.

What does a person do when they've been caught red-handed?

Dear Ed:

I have given considerable thought and prayer to your cry for help. There is much hope in it. For one thing you have passed the self-defense stage. You don't need an analysis of what went wrong.

You need to see a light in the darkness—a beacon which tells you how to come home to yourself, your family, your God.

I have decided to point you toward a biblical character who after great success in life collapsed morally and disgraced everything he had ever stood for. His name was David.

Ease up! I'm not going to give you a Bible lecture. You know the story of David's affair with Bathsheba. He committed adultery with her, got her pregnant, had her husband killed, and tried to cover it all up. No such luck!

But I want to get past the tabloid part of the story and look at what David did when he was caught red-handed. You can read two accounts from the Bible: 2 Samuel 11–12, and Psalm 51.

David's recovery is a timeless model for all of us who have allowed the best in us to be dominated by the worst in us. Ed, after studying the recovery techniques of many psychological and Twelve-Step programs, I cannot find one which is superior to the path David chose. In fact, the Twelve-Step program is very similar.

In the 2 Samuel passage, it says simply that David's first reaction to the public exposure of his sin was: "I have sinned against the Lord" (2 Sam. 12:13). In other words, he confessed his error openly and pointed all ten of his fingers at himself. Psalm 51 is a hymn of confession in which David expresses his inner feelings and decisions in greater detail. It contains great insights for recovery.

Ed, you have already made the first big step toward recovering from your shame. You have confessed without excuses. You know that your collapse can't be completely excused by some emotional or childish quirk in your psyche. You are not saying, "My legs were too short and my mother never loved me."

But, even though this is a big and necessary step, it will not lead you to recovery unless you take further steps. There is a fallacy about confession, which says that all one needs for recovery is to acknowledge his or her errors, i.e., Confession = Recovery. This is simply not true.

Readily acknowledging we're wrong can be a convenient dodge for never correcting it. There is as much dishonesty in "bragging" about our sins as there is in denying them.

So, Ed, there is a fake kind of confession which is designed to elicit sympathy, but not to change the heart. The reason I point you to Psalm 51 is because it is a prime example of the kind of authentic confession which will lead you to recovery.

Unless your confession leads you to a new life, it will become an excuse for you to wallow in your guilt forever. You will go down in history as "Edward the Confessor." You will be remembered as the guy who sinned and admitted it. Big deal!

Let's begin with a simple definition of authentic confession. To confess is to "own up." To take sole responsibility for certain realities. You have done this somewhat in your letter. That is why I see hope in your situation. You have owned up to giving into your "bad self," as you put it. You have owned up to disgracing yourself and your family.

I want to be gentle here. You do not need any more shame from me. You need a line with which to pull yourself up. So please don't react too quickly when I tell you that David did not begin his confession where you did. He didn't first focus on what he had done to himself and others. He focused first on what he had done to God.

"I know my real problem," he says. "I have sinned against you, O God, and you only" (v. 3-4). To sin against others and oneself is first to sin against God.

David realized something crucial, Ed. His troubles began

when he started excluding God from the equations of his life... from his relationships, from his military strategies, from his politics, and from his mind. There was a deeper reason for his moral collapse than merely giving in to his "bad self." He gave in to his "bad self" because He had neglected his friendship with the God who strengthened his "good self."

So the first step to David's recovery was to own up to what really went wrong. That is why David says "Against thee and thee only."

Of the many scandals involving public figures over the years, the one which had real redemption in it—in my opinion—involved the great baseball player Wade Boggs. He was a "David" of sorts. A hero among heroes. At the height of his career he acquired a traveling mistress and tried to live a double life as family man and playboy.

When the news of the scandal broke, Mrs. Boggs had already heard the story from her husband. The affair was already ended. She had forgiven her husband. It became "Barbara Walters" material.

I'll never forget Barbara asking Boggs what went wrong. Was it the glitz and glitter of fame and fortune? Was it the wicked "other woman," etc.?

Boggs sitting quietly before the camera, holding his wife's hand, said "No" to all of the above. "I simply lost my connection with my spiritual and moral center. I have a dark place in my heart and when I lost the moral power within, it took over. I did it because I was a sinner!" (These were not his exact words, but the meaning is accurate.)

The expression on Walter's face read, "No one at home." It was obvious that she hadn't expected the answer she received. She turned quickly to Mrs. Boggs, "And you actually forgive him?!?" "Yes," came the quiet answer. Again, "No one at home," on Walters' face.

Ed, I know of no other route to recovery from moral collapse than to own up to what really went wrong. God was left out of the equation. It all began with the loss of a spiritual-moral center.

Continue reading David's confession. After he confesses to what *really* went wrong, he owns up to what he *really* needs. In verses 6-15, he asks God for seven different ingredients which make up the inward courage to go forward after moral collapse. He does not ask for people's approval or a light sentence from society. He knows what he *really* needs is a restoration of his inward self.

Listen to his list of real needs: (1) God's cleansing and forgiveness, (2) sounds of joy and gladness, the power to sing and dance again, (3) God's forgetfulness of his sins, no more reminders, (4) a new heart, which in Hebrew thought means willpower, (5) a new spirit of loyalty, or the courage to be faithful, (6) God's presence once again, and (7) the power to use his past as a way of helping others.

Ed, what we all really need when we've been caught red-handed is a new set of insides which only God can give us. Do not expect the people in your small town to ever treat you the same again. You are too convenient as a whipping boy.

They need someone to be *better than* in order to count themselves among the righteous. If you're going to remain in the community, you will have to get your strength from the God within you. Approval from peers will be in short supply. Support from your family and a handful of friends would be somewhat of a miracle. (Which is actually true for all of us.)

David finishes his hymn of recovery by owning up to the only thing he can *really* do (verses 16-17). Ed, this may be the most meaningful help I can give you in your effort to rebuild your life. It is the main reason I decided to use the biblical model of David's recovery from moral disaster in my response to your letter.

He says to God, "I cannot offer sacrifices to you as compensation for my sins. You don't want my burnt offerings." In other words, there is *no thing* David can do to pay for what he has done. No action on his part will revive the man he killed or undo his sins.

There is only one course he can take: "My sacrifice is a humble, repentant heart, Oh God. You will not reject this kind of spirit" (v. 17). David cut through all of the fluff to the only thing he could rely on—God's faithfulness to forgive and welcome sinners home. Later in the New Testament times, this would be referred to as the "Grace of God."

A clergyman who had an affair and confessed it "David-style" says, "Grace is believing that God is the only thing left that will provide you with a tomorrow."

Ed, God is truly the only thing left that will provide you with a tomorrow. The good news is that He will. You have confessed to having blown it. Now own up to what *really* went wrong: God was left out of the equation. Own up to what you *really* need: a new inwardness which only God can give. And own up to the only thing you can *really* do: Depend upon God's Grace.

You can leave town and go elsewhere to "make a new start." But the real problem, the real need, and the real solution cannot be left behind in your hometown. You can begin again, Ed. But start from the inside.

40

KIDS WHO WEATHER THE STORM
Equipping Children to Face Life

Dear Dr. Mann:

We have three young boys, six, four, and three. And we are worried. The schools in our upper middle class suburb are getting worse each year. Drugs are sold on elementary school campuses. We don't know where to send our kids to camp for fear they will be molested.

I know we cannot shelter them from the storms of life, but we want to prepare them to weather the storms. We read everything on child rearing. We go to church. We try to maintain consistent discipline.

But how can two well-meaning parents protect three boys from a huge world full of bad influences? Sometimes, I want to flee to the desert. Could you give us some concrete hints for giving our kids what they need to make it through life?

Dear Kim:

I saw a news report not long ago which showed an aerial view of damage done by a tornado. Many buildings were leveled. Yet, several seemed to have sustained only minimal damage. The reporter noted that the buildings which weathered the storm had two things in common: a solid foundation and a flexible superstructure.

We preachers are always looking for sermon material. I immediately exclaimed, "That'll preach!" Children who weather the storm have solid foundations and flexible super-structures. They stand on unshakable ground and they are not broken by change.

Of course the question is, How do we give them these two indispensable gifts? First, by being confident that we can! Parents who are terrified, uptight, and driven by the anxiety of possible failure, usually succeed in fulfilling their worst night-mares. Kids don't need helicopter moms hovering over their every hangnail or drill-sergeant dads barking over every scuff mark on their shoes.

Parents are too frightened these days. They don't realize their power. Surveys still show that children derive about 60 percent of their moral values from mom and dad. About 30 percent comes from peers. The rest comes from schoolteach-ers, ministers, etc.

Kim, you are not a tiny impotent force against a huge indomitable foe. You have the power, unless you allow fear to diminish it. And, while we're on the subject, I want to add that children have a radar detector for their parent's fears. As they grow older they naturally look for ways to "Jerk Your Chain."

Kids live in a world of big people in which they feel power-less. Anything which gives them power over adults is like a narcotic. Once they learn how to use it to manipulate mom or dad, they simply cannot cease doing it.

This means that once they learn your terror-buttons (the things you fear them doing the most) they will be prone to push them.

A common example of this is what I call the "I'll-live-up-to-your-label" phenomenon. It goes like this. Your boy hears you tell a friend that he's a rowdy "ring-tailed-tooter," hard-headed and unmanageable. You sigh and lament the conflicts which probably lie ahead. Maybe you even give him a nick-name to fit your opinion. Something like "Buster" or "Biff" or

"Rowdy." He will live up to your label. It's his leverage as a little person in a big world.

So my first word of hope to you, Kim, is don't throw in the towel. The hand that rocks the cradle still rocks the world.

My second word of hope to you is that three parties are involved in building the foundations and superstructures of children's lives, and you are only one of them. It takes the parents, the children, and God to build lives that weather the storms. You can only do so much. Do not appoint yourself as all three. You are not God, which means your child's destiny is not in your power. Try to play God, and you will learn the hard way that you are not.

And you are not your child, you cannot dictate, decide, or determine his future. As Kahlil Gibran says, "You are the bow from which your children as arrows are sent forth." You cannot go with them. You cannot be the bow and the arrow at the same time. Nor can you be the Archer. The Archer is God.

Why is this a word of hope? Well it should remove your feeling that you and you alone are responsible for how your boys turn out. You don't have to "save" your kids from some awful fate. I have news for you. Not only do you not have to save them, you can't!

What can you do? What is the part of the foundation and superstructure which you can build?

There are many people ready to answer your question. Bookshelves are filled with their advice. Most of it is good and helpful. But you didn't ask them. You asked me.

So I will give you my advice. What your boys need most from you and your husband is K.I.S.S.

K is for *kindness*. Kindness is a word which includes non-verbal gestures or ways of relating to children. About two-thirds of everything you say to a child is non-verbal. Looks, gestures, body language, say more than words. The first ingredient of kindness is what I call "delight." A child needs to know how he is received into the world. "Are you delighted that I am here? Or am I the cause of stress to you? Are you glad to see me? How am I received here?"

These questions are the felt-questions of an infant from birth. Before he can articulate them with words, he *feels* them. Without the gift of delight, he will never love himself.

Kindness also includes what Carl Rogers called *genuineness*. A child needs honest parents, not fake ones. To be genuine means to walk what you talk, to apologize when you don't, to confess when you've blown it.

I is for *intimacy*. To be fully known and fully safe is the oxygen of the soul. If a child has to hide his feelings and pretend in order to be loved, he will become an adept deceiver. Rogers used to say that another absolute requirement for children is *valuing*. A child must be valued *intrinsically*, for who and what he is, apart from what he achieves.

We tend to forget the difference between intrinsic and extrinsic value. A $100 bill, for instance, has extrinsic value. The paper and ink are worthless. What makes the bill worth something is that it represents a value. It is only valuable because of what it stands for.

Unfortunately many children grow up believing that they are worth only what they represent. They have no intrinsic value in and of themselves. They feel that in order to have value they must do, have achieve, and stand for something valuable.

S is for *stability*. The real world is a cause and effect world. Certain behaviors produce certain consequences. While every child needs kindness or affirmation, he also needs expectation. Rogers and others call this *responsibility*. "Respond-ability" might be more accurate. A child cannot respond to change unless he has something stable to rely upon. He needs a predictable world to some extent.

Among the staples of stability are: definite boundaries, undoubted love, constant forgiveness, and a refusal to allow deceit to go unchallenged.

The final *S* stands for *sayonara*. Every child must be set free. Kim, as much as you fear losing your boys into "the world of predators," that is where they must go. "A man shall leave his father and mother," the Bible says. The day will come when they will try to cut the cord if you don't. If they are unsuccessful, the day will come when you will have to cut it.

If neither occurs, they will still hear your commanding voice within their subconscious long after you are gone. Millions of adults live their daily lives according to inward feelings of a scolded and dependent child. They have never finished their business with their parents. The cord is still intact. They are tethered.

This sounds too dismal for what I am trying to say to you, Kim. You are at the helm when it comes to what you can do— give each of your boys K.I.S.S. They and God are at the helm when it comes to what is done with your gifts.

It may help you to know that mothers have been sharing your same fears since the dawn of time, but they still remain the world's most powerful people.

You may think that I have sounded more psychological than religious in answering your questions about how to give your boys a solid foundation and a flexible superstructure.

Not so. The best way to give children a sense of God is to give them K.I.S.S. For that is exactly what God has given us. God is Kind. He takes great delight in us. He is glad to have us. He is genuine. He tells us the unvarnished truth about Himself and us.

We learn true intimacy from God. He sees us as we are and loves us still. He values us intrinsically, for who and what we are. Stability is one of God's characteristics He has placed us in a world of boundaries and cause and effect. He is dependable to love and forgive us. We are never alone.

And God has allowed us to choose for ourselves. He cuts the cord and lets us go. And He stands at the door with the band aids and salve when we return wounded.

Kim, this model for parenting is definitely religious in the sense that it is based upon the way God parents us. When Jesus described God, he used the Aramaic, *Abba*. It is a term which indicates great respect, great intimacy, great dependence, and great freedom.

The Bible translates it *Father.* Some translate it, *Dada,* the words of a toddler. Some scholars say *Abba* represented the sum total of a child's feelings toward both his mother and his father. *Abba* is a toddler's word for Mom and Dad. Of such is the Kingdom of Heaven.

41

BURNING BUSHES FOR THE BURNED OUT AND BUSHED
Recovering from Burnout

Dear Dr. Mann:

At thirty-nine I have come to the sad realization that I am in the wrong profession. I am a dentist. My wife put me through school and is my best friend. I have two kids, two mortgages, and several employees.

I get no satisfaction from my work. A counselor told me that I suffer from classic burnout. I hate labels but I think maybe he is right. I am sick of looking at teeth, tongues, and tonsils. In order to stay afloat financially, I must work long hours, six days a week. I've never minded hard work as long as it is meaningful work.

Lately, I have awakened to the fact that my work is nothing but a means of supporting myself and my family financially. I went to dental school because I had a dream of helping people. Now I get no charge out of grinding, polishing, gouging, and lecturing against poor dental hygiene.

What does a person do when he's burned out and trapped as I am?

Dear Randall:

Burnout is one of the buzzwords of modern overly stressed America. Some say that the phrase itself is overly stressed.

Humans have had difficulty finding meaning in their work since the beginning of time.

One of the purposes of the early chapters in Genesis is to answer several universal and primal questions like: "Why do we abhor snakes?" And, "Why is there pain in childbirth?" Also one of the primal questions is, "Why is our work so laborious and meaningless?"

Of course, the answer in that ancient story is that meaningless work is a result of Adam's original sin. If you read the earlier chapters of this book, you know that I view the first few chapters of Genesis as a symbolic way of telling us timeless and universal truths about ourselves.

In my view, the point of Genesis regarding work is that it always becomes a burden, or even a curse, when its purpose is separated from the purposes of God. If the primary purpose of our work is material prosperity (worshiping the creation instead of the Creator) then our work will never satisfy our search for meaning.

My point, Randall, is that no job will ever be totally fulfilling because every job is partially motivated by material prosperity. Not many Americans work merely for food, shelter, and clothing. They work for more and more "stuff." As long as this is the case, burnout is not totally avoidable. All people go through "dry spells" in their work, and no job is a hundred-percent fulfilling.

One of the fallacies we Americans have allowed ourselves to believe is that work can be ultimately fulfilling. It leads us to the illusion that somewhere out there is the perfect occupation and career. I heard a definition of burnout which fits here: "Burnout is the result of an over-estimation of the amount of the world I can change."

So, Randall, don't be surprised that your dream of helping people has turned into a tedious treadmill of tinkering with teeth, tongues, and tonsils. Thirty-nine is about the right time for these feelings to begin. It is a sign of your maturation. You are preparing yourself for the passage from *success to significance*.

I am not discouraged by your depression. I think you are on the verge of taking charge of your life in a new way.

Randall, I was in middle age before I began to look to the Bible for ancient answers to modern human predicaments. The first time I experienced burnout was at about your age. I asked myself, "Is there a place in the Bible where someone experienced burnout and lived through it?"

There were several. Elijah fled to a cave of despair after his dream failed. David got bored and lost his drive. But Moses is probably the best example. His experience of burnout and recovery reads like a modern case study from a psychology manual (Read Exodus 1–4).

Young Moses had a dream and the tools to make it come true. He was a Hebrew raised in the king's court as a prince. He saw the oppression of his native people and he was determined to set them free.

In the heat of youthful idealism, he tried to start a revolution. He took up arms and killed an Egyptian slavemaster. To his astonishment, his Hebrew brothers and sisters didn't rally to the cause.

At forty years of age, Moses fled in despair to the "backside of the desert." He became a reclusive shepherd. Then he had the burning-bush experience and received a call from God to reclaim his lost dream. The rest is history, as they say.

I want you to look at the "Moses Model" for dealing with burnout. It has been helpful to me over the years. Moses did four things which are essential to restarting the engines of our lost enthusiasm.

First, he went where the action wasn't. Instead of looking for new excitement or, "action," he went to a place where he wouldn't be distracted by the "Sirens." The backside of the desert was a lonely place. Herding sheep was a solitary exercise. There a man had time to reflect and rest and restore sensible rhythms to his life.

Lyle Schaller, the church-growth guru and wise counselor to ministers said to me once, "Life's most significant changes for the better almost always occur in a setting where life's regular routines are altered."

I stopped at a small-town one-room restaurant which had a big sign out front. It said, "World's Greatest Hamburgers!"

A man stood behind an open grill flipping hamburgers over a mesquite fire. His wife waited tables. His teenagers handled the dishes and the cash register. They were a close-knit team, and the sign didn't lie about the hamburgers.

I asked him about his life and work. He said, "I'm a millionaire several times over. I used to work seven days a week and fly around in a Falcon jet. I never saw my kids. I've been 'where it's at' but it ain't there! I always liked to cook and I was tired of eating hamburgers which consisted of the three basic food groups—fat, salt, and preservatives."

He continued, "I talk to real people now, instead of things which look like people. I'm friends with my family, and I can hear God."

I suggest that you go where the action isn't for a while. First, go alone. Then bring your family into it. A lot of burnout can be cured by two days alone each week and additional hours of sleep each day.

The second thing Moses did to recover his dream was *wander but with wonder*. That is, he ventured into new territory (wandered) but he never lost his sense of curiosity and expectancy (wonder). He was open to whatever God and life offered him.

Randall, many of us have a great urge to wander off when we experience burnout; but without an open mind we tend to get jaded. We think we've seen it all and heard it all.

The story of Moses' receiving his new mission in life via the burning-bush episode is an illustration of wandering with wonder. Burning bushes were not rare in the desert. Heat and the sun's reflection off rock caused fires.

The text says that God did not speak to Moses until *after* Moses turned aside to inspect and ponder the burning bush (Exodus 3:4). Moses never lost his sense of wonder. He believed that God could still speak to him. He never saw his life as being "finished" or "over the hill."

Let this tell you something. My worst fear for you is that in your depression you will lose your sensitivity to the new. By all means wander. Go exploring. But not aimlessly. Wander with a sense of wonder. You will either find a different calling or a new calling within your current profession.

I'm thinking of a plastic surgeon in my congregation. He wasn't bored with doing cosmetic surgery. He liked to make people feel better about their looks and he was and is a wizard at it. Then he heard of the many children in Central and South America who had cleft palates and other facial deformities.

He's now involved in a network of surgeons which gives hundreds of hours a year to restoring the smiles of thousands of children.

Not long ago he said to me, "I have a wonderful practice in helping people feel good about themselves. But I now have a calling as well." Finding a way to make your work into a calling is a cure for burnout.

The third thing Moses did to recover from burnout was adopt a "can't do" spirit. He accepted the limits of his abilities. As a young man he saw himself as a one-man-world-beater. Now he says to God, "I am not able to lead anyone out of anything. I tried and I ran full-bore into the wall of my limitations."

This may sound defeatist, Randall. I know that the seminars on burnout try to charge up people with a "can-do" spirit. I'm all for positive thinking and positive mental attitude, etc. But knowing what you can't do, and working within those limits is the key to life.

Someone has said that in America:

> We worship our work.
> We play at our worship.
> We work at our play.

What a diagnosis of the causes of burnout! We overestimate the amount of the world we are able to change.

The first step of the Twelve Step Recovery Program of AA says: "We admitted we were powerless over alcohol and that our lives had become unmanageable." I call this developing a "can't do" spirit. To draw a line between what we can't do and what only God can do is the first step of *any kind of recovery*.

There is no way that you, in and of yourself, can restore the zest for life which you seek. Changing jobs, locations, and circumstances may help some, but recovering from burnout means learning to play well within the boundaries of the field that God has given you.

The most important step to Moses' recovery was that he acquired a new partner. He was no longer the leader of a secular utopian civil rights movement. This time he was part of a God-given dream. He no longer had a job, he had a "calling."

In an earlier chapter I talked about the loss of the concept of "calling" in American life. The key to the Protestant work ethic of earlier times was that every person saw work as a contribution to God's purpose. There was no such thing as a *menial* or *meaningless* job. To work diligently and honestly was a duty to God, not just a way to put beans on the table.

The main reason that burnout is a 20th Century American disease is that work has been separated from "calling." Moses took a stick—a shepherd's staff—and a calling from God, back to Egypt and accomplished what no prince with a sword could. The difference was not in his strength and enthusiasm. It was his Partner. He was part of something larger than himself. In the civil rights movement of the sixties, this is precisely what set Martin Luther King apart from the other leaders.

How to find a burning bush when you're burned out and bushed? Go where the action isn't. Wander with wonder. Have a "can't-do" spirit. Get a new partner.

A preacher once shouted a question at his congregation: "What's the first thing you must do to be saved!?!?" Some clown in the back of the room said, "Sin!!"

What's the first thing you must do to recover from burnout? The answer is *experience burnout!* Until you've faced this pain, you cannot take the necessary steps to find a sense of purpose.

42

BACKUP SYSTEMS
Handling Temptation

Dear Dr. Mann:

How do you handle temptation? I sometimes feel that I am truly sick. I am not only a Christian, I am a minister! I serve a growing church. I have a wife and a child. Yet, I lust and I lie and I am jealous of the success of colleagues.

People tell me that I am destined for a leadership position in our denomination. When I stand in the pulpit on Sundays I think, "Boy, if they only knew what goes through my mind they would crucify me."

Dr. Mann, I don't want to end up in the wrecking yard of fallen ministers. Can you tell me how you handle temptation?

Dear Todd:

I chose your letter to deal with the subject of temptation because of its raw honesty. I could've used others which deal with specific temptations.

I feel a connection with you not only because you are a minister, but also because you represent a host of Christians who fear that they cannot reveal their innermost temptations without being condemned.

You should feel no shame for being tempted. The Bible says that Jesus was tempted in every way that we are. That should be cause for comfort to us all. It is no sin to be tempted. It is a sin to deny that we are. The shame is that people like us, Todd, are pronounced guilty for being tempted!

I always answer questions on how to handle temptation by using Jesus as the model. Matthew 4:1–11, portrays His struggle with His own calling from God. He had just gone public with His ministry. The time for Him to do what God had called Him to do had come.

He went to the wilderness for forty days to fast and to plot His strategy for fulfilling His mission as God's chosen Messiah. The temptation was to do it His way instead of God's way. This is what every temptation is about, Todd. Shall I do it God's way or my way?

The secret to Jesus' victory lay in what I call His backup systems. Let me use an illustration given several years ago by John Paul Carter.

In 1912, the passenger ship *Titanic* was lost at sea. Hundreds perished unnecessarily. The ship was thought to be unsinkable because of its compartmentalized hull. It struck an iceberg which ripped a huge gash the length of its underside. Ice clogged the chains which could have lowered enough lifeboats for all of the passengers to survive. The ship sunk with the lifeboats still attached.

Fifty-eight years later, the crew of *Apollo 13* reached moon's orbit in their *Apollo* capsule with the Lunar Excursion Module (LEM) attached. The fuel tank of *Apollo* exploded. The crew retreated into the LEM. They used its fuel and booster, which had been designed to lift them off of the moon and rendezvous with *Apollo,* to boost them back to Earth.

As they approached Earth, they re-entered *Apollo,* jettisoned the LEM and used the scant remaining fuel to retro-fire and land within sight of the recovery ship. It was truly one of the most heroic episodes of adaptation and survival in history.

The difference between the *Titanic's* tragedy and *Apollo's* heroic salvation was backup systems. The *Apollo* crew had practiced simulated disasters of every kind. The crew of the *Titanic* had not.

Todd, the secret in Jesus' victory over temptation was also His backup systems. If you read of His temptation in the wilderness (also in Luke 4), or throughout His entire life, He came to each crucial test equipped with three basic backup systems.

First, was an ongoing relationship with the Father. Immediately preceding His journey into the wilderness He heard a voice from heaven saying, "This is my beloved son, in whom I am well pleased" (Matt. 3:19).

This was to be the pattern throughout His life. He always came armed with the inward voice of the Father.

Todd, the first line of defense against temptation is to know who you *really* are. *Jesus never wanted to be anyone but himself!* Match that stupendous truth with our experience. Most of us spend our entire lives wanting to be someone or somewhere else! Our superstar culture breeds this dissatisfaction. There's a TV commercial featuring the great basketball star Michael Jordan. The jingle says, "I want to be like Mike." Jesus' jingle said, "I want to be like me." You're jealous of your colleagues' success because you don't want to be you.

There's no substitute for an ongoing relationship with the Father which results in our hearing from Him the affirmation, "This is my beloved child in whom I am well pleased."

Jesus' second backup system was an ongoing relationship with Scripture. Everytime the Devil tempts Him, Jesus answers with Scripture. "Make stones into bread," says Satan. "The Scripture says..." answers Jesus. And when Satan tempts Him with a Scripture, Jesus answers back with another Scripture!

Scripture is our reality check. There's no value in studying the Bible merely to study the Bible. Bible study is not an end in itself. It's a means. We use it to check our standards against the standards which God set for those who went before us.

I love the story about the great British Admiral Lord Nelson. Before each battle, he would lock himself in his cabin, open the drawer of his desk, pull out the same yellowed piece of paper and study it intently for a few seconds. Then he would proceed to lead his fleet to war.

One day he left his cabin unlocked. His orderly couldn't resist the temptation. He crept in, opened the drawer, and read the paper. It said: "Remember, starboard is right! Port is left! Starboard is right! Port is left!..."

There's no way to win the war if you don't arm yourself with the basics.

An ongoing relationship with the Father and with Scripture—these were two of Jesus' weapons as He met temptation.

His third backup system was an ongoing relationship with the "Angels." The text says that after the Devil left Jesus, the Angels came and helped him (Matt. 4:11).

I have an unorthodox view of angels, Todd. To me they are anyone and anything God sends to strengthen us when we do the right thing or need help in doing the right thing. Angels are God's "Attaboys!": people, events, and the inside glow we feel when we've catered to the best in ourselves.

I don't know about those critters with wings. I've never seen one. But I have seen many people who were God's angels to me. I have felt the tug of the "angels in my attic" when I'm tempted to surrender to the "beasts in my basement."

Todd, I'm going to tell you a secret. Several years ago I made a decision which changed my ministry. I had been serving churches for over twenty years. In every church there were the usual critics who prayed daily for God to change me to fit their expectations.

I call them "basement dwellers." They have hidden agendas. They are unhappy and judgmental. You cannot please them.

I woke up one day and realized that I had spent most of my ministry trying to please and appease the basement dwellers. Every day was a chess game of outwitting them and dodging their criticism.

I simply decided to stop living that way. Every church also has "attic dwellers." These are the ones who let me be me. They let me sweat and stink and stumble. They have no agenda but a mutual hope that together we can find grace.

I decided to spend the rest of my life pleasing the attic dwellers. Those who love to wallow in the basement can either leave or climb the stairs to the attic!

To my great surprise, I didn't get fired. To my greater surprise I discovered that there are more angels in the attic than I ever imagined. It is they who help me most when I'm tempted to stray.

As a result, our church has become a hospital. It is now organized around treating health instead of sickness. There is a big difference you know. Treating health means making people well. Treating sickness means keeping them in the hospital. Instead of building on islands of weakness, we now build on islands of strength.

Todd, I hope you stay in the ministry if that's where you belong. Build some backup systems: An ongoing friendship with the Father; an ongoing familiarity with Scripture; an ongoing relationship with the Angels...the attic dwellers.

But even after all of the above, you will still cave in to temptation now and then. I have found that confessing it openly is the best route, unless you are one of those preachers who scolds people from the pulpit. Scolders don't get forgiven when they stumble. The people they have been whipping always want their turn.

CONCLUSION:

THE SEEPING POWER OF GRACE

How to wrap up a book like this? I struggled with this question in the beginning when I decided the direction I would take. I've never written anything like this. In many ways it is a grab bag of unrelated subjects.

The thread which holds it together is hope. I have tried to offer lifelines for the hopeless.

Through it all I have been asking myself *wherein lies my real hope?* Am I hopeful because I'm supposed to be? Am I afraid to be pessimistic? It is easy to be hopeful simply because you can't stand to be hopeless.

I remember seeing an interview on TV during the 1993 floods which devastated the Midwest. There were scenes of massive destruction. A news reporter was interviewing a civil engineer on the subject of why levees were failing along the swollen Mississippi River. The engineer said that there is no way to keep water from eventually seeping through a levee. It must go over, under, or through. "No levee can withstand the seeping power of water," he said.

This is a powerful image for me. It symbolizes the basis of my hope.

The seeping power of the message of God's Grace is my hope. Grace means that the Reality which is in, under, and above all things is gracious. He is a God who welcomes sinners, even goes in search of them and will not stop until He has won all of His children back to Himself.

There's no stopping this message. It will seep through all of the walls we devise. No other message of religion has this much power.

Only the message of Grace can seep through the walls which separate us religiously. I have developed a solid friendship with Rabbi Elliot Gertel of Chicago. We quote each other frequently.

He and I will never agree theologically, but we have something higher which creates a bond. We know that we have the same Father, the same need for redemption, and the same remedy for that need—a gracious God.

Arguing laws and rituals and doctrines will never remove the walls which separate people religiously. Only the common experience of grace can do that. This is the foundation of my hopefulness.

Only a message of grace can seep through the walls of secularism. There is so much trash heaped on top of the word "secularism" today that I must define what I mean by it. Secularism is simply the organization of everyday life without reference to God or formal religion. To be secular does not mean you are anti-God. It means that you no longer see anything on the religious scene which helps you conduct your daily life. God is a functional absentee.

Secular America is not atheistic. It is simply uninterested in what formal religion has to say. This was evident in the aftermath of the Koresh tragedy in Waco, Texas, in 1993. Psychologists, sociologists, and journalists were sought out for their lengthy analysis on national television. Not one clergyman, professor of theology, or religious writer was consulted. We had plenty to say, but no one really cared to hear it.

I believe we are ignored because the God we talk about is rather unfriendly and outdated, i.e., He is not *gracious*.

Secular America does not give a hoot about what David did

to the Amalekites. Nor does it care to hear debates about whether there were one or two Isaiahs. They think there is only one and he plays basketball.

But the message of a God who welcomes sinners and puts lives back together and gives hope to the hopeless, can sweep away the walls of secular indifference. This is my hope.

And only the message of Grace can seep through the walls of the deepest human addictions. I agree with my friend Keith Miller and others that we are all addicted to something, and that the ultimate deadly addiction is to control our own lives apart from God. I have talked to hundreds of recovering people who have been reclaimed by practicing the Twelve Steps of Alcoholics Anonymous. The recurring refrain is that they have found in AA the one thing which they could not find at church—Grace.

AA is all about Grace. That is its secret. Whoever wants to get well, can! Whoever falls off the wagon can climb back on and find others in the wagon who will cling to you for dear life.

The fact that God is Grace is my hope. That message is the most powerful force in the world today. It will seep through when nothing else can.

The movie classic, *A River Runs Through It,* echoes this theme. It is the story of the family of a Presbyterian minister, his wife, and two sons in Missoula, Montana at the opening of the Twentieth Century. The storyline is supported by the voice-over of director Robert Redford who reads the lines from Norman Maclean's book on which the movie is based.

At the beginning Maclean (Redford) says, "In our family there was no clear line between religion and fly-fishing." A scene shows the minister in the front yard coaching his two young sons in flycasting.

Another scene has the three of them squatting beside the waters of the Big Blackfoot River where they would spend much of their lives bonding as they fished together.

The father fetches a rock from the waters and says, "Long ago, rain fell on mud and became rock...half a billion years ago. But even before that beneath the rocks...are the words of God. Listen." Maclean reflects, "And if Paul and I listened very carefully all of our lives we might hear those words."

The scene switches back to the father with his sons in the yard of their home. The boys are practicing their casting to the four-count rhythm of a metronome as the father claps his hands to the beat.

"As a Presbyterian, my father believed that man by nature was a damned mess, and that only by picking up God's rhythms were we able to regain power and beauty," continues the narration. "To him, all good things—trout as well as eternal salvation—come by Grace. And Grace comes by art. And art does not come easy."

At the end of the movie an elderly Norman Maclean is standing beside his beloved river. He's tying a fly to his line with trembling fingers. All of those he loved are now dead, including his wild young brother who had been beaten to death years before in some back alley. As he casts his line to the rhythm learned long ago from his father, and remembers all of those he loved and did not understand in his youth, his thoughts are echoed by Redford's golden voice: "Eventually, all things merge into one. And a river runs through it. The river was cut by the World's Great Flood and runs over rocks from the basement of time. On some of the rocks are timeless raindrops. Under the rocks are the words. And some of the words are theirs."

The River of time wipes away everything. You, and I, and all we love shall be no more. Nothing really matters to the River. It eventually pulls everything to itself and washes it away. Nothing lasts...Except!...Except what? Except that which lies beneath the River... even beneath the River's rocky basement.

The only thing which is permanent is that which undergirds the River of Time, namely "The Words of God."

And what are these "words"? They are the words of Grace. The Reality beneath all things is gracious. He speaks His words to us and if we receive them we become part of that Reality. And when we pass on those words of Grace, then some of the words which last forever are ours.

This is the foundation of my hope. Ultimate Reality (God) is gracious. He delights in us. And He speaks a language which we can hear above the noises of the waters of our impermanent existence.

The words I hear from a welcoming and happy God give me hope. The words of all self-righteous religions, ideologies, and utopianisms cannot seep through the walls which separate us from ourselves and each other and God. Only the words of Grace can do that.

> Through many dangers, toils, and snares
> I have already come.
> T'was Grace that brought me safe thus far,
> And Grace shall lead me home.

Notes

INTRODUCTION

Page 6: The article about "Why do we feel so bad, when we have it so good?" appeared in *Forbes*, Vol. 150, No. 6 (New York: Forbes, Inc., Sept. 14, 1992), pp. 47–193 as "An Awakened Conscience."

PART I: QUESTIONS OF GOD'S WORTH

Chapter 2: Why Does God Let Big People Kill Kids

Page 28: "Goodness is a far greater problem for the atheist than evil is for the believer." Harry Emerson Fosdick, *Dear Mr. Brown* (New York: Harper & Row, 1961), p. 65 ff.

Chapter 3: Is Genesis a Dinosaur?

Page 34: For a detailed explanation of the forbidden fruit viewed as the first scientific experiment, see John Hick, *Evil and the Love of God* (New York: Harper & Row, 1966), p. 320 ff.

Chapter 7: How Do You Picture God?

Page 61: "Unconditional acceptance" is from Lewis Smedes, *Shame and Grace* (San Francisco: Zondervan, 1993), p. 102.

Page 62: Human tenacity as a sign of God's grace is found in M. Scott Peck's *The Road Less Travelled* (New York: Simon and Schuster, 1978), p. 260 ff.

Page 63: The story of the girl's reaction to the killing of innocents is in Fosdick, *Dear Mr. Brown,* op. cit., p. 41.

Chapter 8: The Puzzlements of Prayer

Page 69: Henri Nouwen, *With Open Hands* (New York: Ballantine), p. 3 ff.

Chapter 11: Why Do the Wicked Prosper?

Page 93: Human failure due to lack of courage is discussed in William Glasser, *Positive Addiction* (New York: Harper & Row, 1076), p. 4 ff.

PART II: QUESTIONS OF SELF-WORTH

Chapter 17: My Name is Legion

Page 130: Scientific information about homosexuality is found in Alan Bell, Martin Weinberg, Sue Hammersmith, *Sexual Preference: Its Development in Men and Women* (Bloomington, IN: Indiana University Press, 1981).

Chapter 18: From the Dark

Page 138: The importance of faith to the healing process is well covered in Bill Moyers, *Healing and the Mind* (New York: Doubleday, 1993).

Page 141: See John Claypool, *Tracks of a Fellow Struggler* (Waco, TX: Word, 1974), p. 63 ff.

Chapter 25: Does God Have a Price?

Page 181: The fact that giving is self-serving is proven in Douglas M. Lawson, *Give to Live* (La Jolla, CA, ALTI Publishing, 1991), p. 19 ff.

PART III: QUESTIONS OF LIFE'S WORTH

Chapter 32: Apocalypse Now?

Page 219: For more information on why Americans feel so bad see Paul Johnson, "An Awakened Conscience," *Forbes* (New York: Forbes, Inc., Sept. 14, 1992), p. 176 ff.

Chapter 35: Teenagers: People God Didn't Create

Page 239: I am indebted to Charles Mueller for introducing me to the differing views of the stages of life. See Charles S. Mueller, *Thank God I Have a Teenager* (Minneapolis: Augsburg Press, 1985).

Chapter 36: Staying Together But Coming Apart

Page 244: Eric Fromm, *The Art of Loving* (New York: Harper & Row, 1956), p. 8.

Chapter 37: Tools for Old Fools

Page 255: For more information on what makes people happy read "Happiness in America," *Psychology Today,* June 1977, pp. 38–44.

Chapter 39: When You're Caught Red-Handed

Page 270: Gordon MacDonald, *Rebuilding Your Broken Word* (Nashville: Nelson, 1988), p. 184.

Chapter 40: Kids Who Weather the Storm

Page 274: I am indebted to John Claypool for introducing me to the notion of "Gift of Delight." See John Claypool, *Stages* (Waco, TX: Word, 1977), p. 22 ff.

Chapter 42: Backup Systems

Page 285: cf. John Paul Carter, Sermon delivered July 20, 1975, Ft. Worth, TX.

ABOUT THE AUTHOR

DR. GERALD MANN is a minister, writer, humorist, businessman, and a well-known voice for common sense Christianity. A native of West Columbia, Texas, Dr. Mann graduated from the University of Corpus Christi and earned a Master of Divinity (M.Div.) and a Doctor of Theology (Th.D.) from Southwestern Baptist Theological Seminary.

Dr. Mann has been featured in *TV Guide, USA Today, Advertising Age* and *Texas Monthly*. He has been quoted by "NBC Nightly News," Paul Harvey, and nearly every major newspaper in America, including *US News and World Report,* and *The Wall Street Journal*.

Currently, his national television program, "Real Life...with Dr. Gerald Mann!," is available every Sunday in seventy to eighty million homes across America. He is chaplain of the Texas legislature and the pastor of Riverbend Church in Austin, Texas. Dr. Mann founded this church in 1979 with 60 adult family members. Today over 8,000 people regularly attend.

Author of five books, Dr. Mann married his high school sweetheart, Lois. They have three children.

For information regarding other books and tapes by Dr. Mann, call (512) 347-8608.